THE CHOSEN PEOPLE IN AMERICA

The Modern Jewish Experience
Paula Hyman and Deborah Dash Moore, editors

THE CHOSEN PEOPLE IN AMERICA

A Study in Jewish Religious Ideology

Arnold M. Eisen

INDIANA UNIVERSITY PRESS
Bloomington and Indianapolis

Acknowledgment is made to The Johns Hopkins University Press for kind permission to reprint material originally published in its journal *Modern Judaism*.

Manufactured in the United States of America

70 · 01 6-491

Library of Congress Cataloging in Publication Data

Eisen, Arnold M., 1951–
    The Chosen People in America.

    (The Modern Jewish experience)
    Bibliography: p.
    Includes index.
    1. Jews—Election, Doctrine of—History of doctrines—
20th century.   2. Judaism—United States—History—20th
century.   I. Title.   II. Series: Modern Jewish experience
(Indiana University Press)
BM613.E37   1983   296.3'11   82-49296
ISBN 0-253-31365-1
ISBN 0-253-20961-7 (pbk.)

2 3 4 5 6 00 99 98 97 96 95

For my parents

CONTENTS

PART FOUR: Conclusion

Acknowledgments

This study was prompted by three sets of questions. First, several years' work on secularization had piqued my curiosity as to whether we could actually see a religious belief changing "before our very eyes" under the impact of social and intellectual forces. Second, my life as an American Jew had caused me to wonder how American Judaism came to assume the character—all too often vacuous—presented to view in its synagogues and publications. Third, Martin Meyerson one day asked what I thought of the chosen people idea and whether anyone had recently written about the subject. A year or two later I decided on this response to his query, because it promised to help with answers to my own two questions as well.

I am grateful to Martin Meyerson for ten years of provocative questioning; to Professors Moshe Davis, Ben Halpern, Paul Mendes-Flohr, and Uriel Tal for directing my research into chosenness and criticizing the resultant dissertation; and, most of all, to my supervisor at The Hebrew University of Jerusalem, Professor R. J. Zwi Werblowsky. His erudition in the history of religions helped to make my research intellectually exciting, and his insights sustained me more than once as I worked through a seemingly endless succession of sermons.

The research was supported by the Lady Davis Fellowship Trust and the Danforth Foundation, to whom I stand indebted, as I do to the librarians of The Hebrew University Judaica Reading Room; Hebrew Union College–Jewish Institute of Religion in New York and Jerusalem; the Jewish Theological Seminary; and Columbia and Yeshiva universities. Rabbis Bernard Bamberger, Solomon Freehof, and Mordecai M. Kaplan received me graciously and helped me to understand the events in which they figured. Drafts of the book were read by many friends and colleagues, including Janet Aviad, Hannah Cotton, Michael Heyd, Paula Hyman, Gillian Lindt, Paula Newberg, Ari Paltiel, Wayne Proudfoot, Michael Rosenak, Michael and Ilana Silver, Robert Somerville, Michael Stanislawski, and the members of the Joshua Lipschitz Society. I thank them all. I am also grateful to Deborah Dash Moore for editing the final manuscript with care and sensitivity, to John O'Keefe for proofreading it diligently, and to Vivian Shaw for typing it valiantly. The "chosen of my heart," Adriane Leveen, bore with the final overhaul of the book without complaint. For this and much else besides, my gratitude.

Finally, the whole bears the imprint of three teachers who taught me—or tried—to read religious thought attentively and consider it with a sociologist's eye: Van Harvey, Philip Rieff, and Bryan Wilson. I hope I have applied their lessons well.

The work is dedicated to my parents, who enabled me to understand more than any theology, sociology, or ideology could what it means to live with the blessing and obligation of chosenness.

AE
New York City
Thanksgiving 1982

THE CHOSEN PEOPLE IN AMERICA

PART ONE

Introduction

I

A Part and Apart

JOSEPH JONAS, one of the first American Jews to journey west of the Alleghenies, has left us a tale from his travels that precisely captures the several dilemmas with which this study is concerned. One day in 1817, Jonas reports, he encountered an elderly Quaker woman who had never before laid eyes on a Jew, and was rather excited by the prospect. "Art thou a Jew? Thou art one of God's chosen people." She turned him round and round and at last exclaimed, with evident disappointment, "Well, thou art no different to other people."[1]

The Quaker woman was right, of course: Jonas was not appreciably different from other people—far less different, in all likelihood, than the Quakers themselves. Doors to Gentile society long closed to the Jews in Europe had opened early to the Jews of America, and opened widely; Jews like Jonas could and would rush through happily, to a degree of opportunity and participation never before theirs in all the centuries of wandering. "America was different," its Jews would soon proclaim, because, for the first time really, *they* were not. Yet, if that truly was the case, who were they? A people no longer set apart essentially from its surroundings could not invoke the self-definition of election which had served it for two millennia. It was one thing to call oneself a "chosen people" when religious barriers or ghetto walls reinforced the collective sense of being a "people that must dwell alone." But it was quite another to claim chosenness in the new chosen land of America, where Jews wanted nothing so much as the chance to be a part of the larger society. To describe oneself as "the Lord's special treasure" seemed absurd in such a context, and yet—here is the essential dilemma facing American Jews—what sense could Jewishness make without that inherited self-definition? To abandon the claim to chosenness would be to discard the raison d'etre that had sustained Jewish identity and Jewish faith through the ages, while to make the claim was to question or perhaps even to threaten America's precious offer of acceptance. This study is concerned with the ways in which American Jewish thinkers of the past two generations have coped with that dilemma, fashioning a new self-definition for their community through the reinterpretation of the idea of Jewish chosenness. It is this new understanding of self which continues to guide American Jewry in the 1980s.

While the history of that reinterpretation has until now not been charted, the dilemma which prompted it has been amply documented. Sociologists of American Jewry have made the Jews' adjustment to America the principal focus of their researches,[2] and more popular works have also treated the problem at some length.[3] Charles Liebman, in formulations particularly relevant to our own inquiry, has pointed to the conflicting desires of "the ambivalent American Jew" for integration into American society on the one hand and group survival on the other. Refusing to acknowledge that these values are in conflict, "the typical Jew" seeks "an ideological position which denies the existence of any tension," and, to attain it, must "blur reality, obscuring the real referents for those concepts which [Jews] find most attractive."[4]

Chosenness, the traditional vehicle for self-definition among Jews, became in America the single concept most often "blurred" and denied "real referents." In reflecting on American Jewish reinterpretation of the doctrine over the past half-century, I will "flesh out," enrich with data, and in some cases call into question, the generalizations advanced by sociologists and other concerning American Jewry's attempt to balance integration and survival. Detailed analysis of the ways in which Jewish thinkers have affirmed, denied, interpreted, and transformed the traditional concept of Israel's chosenness, against the background of identifiable social and intellectual pressures, will teach us a great deal about the character of American Jewish religious thought as a whole. It will also illumine the manner in which the community has been affected by the cluster of forces normally grouped under the umbrella of "secularization."

Chosenness, then, particularly as interpreted by the generation before our own, affords a lens for viewing these wider issues of American Jewish adaptation to a newly chosen land. It was during that "second generation" (ca. 1930–1955) that American Jewry and Judaism as we know them took shape, and a survey of Jewish religious thought in the period reveals chosenness to have been the single most popular theme of discussion. The literary critic R. W. B. Lewis has noted that

> every culture seems, as it advances toward maturity, to produce its own determining debate over the ideas that preoccupy it. As he examines the personalities and biases of the men engaged in debate at any given historical

moment, the historian is likely to discover that the development of the culture in question resembles a protracted and broadly ranging conversation: at best a dialogue—a dialogue which at times moves very close to drama.[5]

The "American Adam"—the new man uncorrupted by Europe's inherited sins—was the focal image of the debate of nineteenth-century America charted by Lewis. Chosenness played that role in the analogous conversation of twentieth-century American Jewish thought, as it fashioned a set of meanings and commitments for its religious subculture. Full clarification of the issues raised by the study of chosenness would of course require an exhaustive social and intellectual history of the period, if not a cultural history of America as a whole—for the Jews' search after themselves has arguably had a major impact upon America's self-definition as well. However, the shape of the Jews' essential dilemma—one still evident today—assumes unparalleled clarity if one moves outward from the point of "conversation" which they themselves made central.

One should bear in mind, before beginning this examination of American Jewish religious thought, that the views of rabbis and theologians are not representative of American Jewry as a whole. To be sure, the questions which made the issue of chosenness of immediate concern—how, why and to what degree Jews should retain a separate identity in America—were on the minds of laity and professionals alike. Ordinary American Jews, however, were probably not exercised by this or any other theological issue as such. Their theology remained inchoate, and their concerns were formulated less acutely. That is not to say that the laity was not influenced by the books and articles it read, the sermons it heard, and the prayers it recited in the synagogue, but only that our primary concern is with the authors of those books, articles, sermons, and prayers. They command attention both because of their influence on the laity, and because they provided the contours within which the forms and contents of religious American Judaisms are still to be found.

For the professionals, chosenness was of overwhelming concern, enjoying such centrality for three reasons. First, chosenness has always been central—an "unformulated dogma"[6] which, along with related concepts such as covenant and exile, has traditionally guided Jewish self-understanding. Chosenness marks the point at which the three lines of relation which define Jews—those binding them to God, to their fellow-men, and to each other—of necessity intersect. The people of Israel entered the world, according to its own sacred history, not through a natural growth from family and tribe, but suddenly, with a single event that they did not initiate: the covenant at Sinai. Jews were identified from the start as a "kingdom of priests and holy nation," paradoxically commanded to dwell apart from humanity in order to serve a divine purpose in which all humanity was somehow included. So they saw themselves and, for the most part, were seen. The vicissitudes of life in the many diaspora communities reinforced and enhanced this primordial self-consciousness, and only the integration into the modern gentile world which began in the late eighteenth century has presented Jews with a significant challenge to the assumption that they are meant to remain a people apart. Even so, that challenge has called forth reinterpretation of the idea of election rather than simple repudiation of it. For the exigencies of Jewish survival have continued to demand the explanation of identity which only chosenness could offer.

Secondly, chosenness engaged American Jewish thinkers because it touched directly and often painfully on all the matters which most concerned them. When European Jews suffered and died in the Holocaust, the question "Why us?" emerged as it had during previous persecutions. One could doubt that Israel had been singled out by God for reception of His teaching, but history's election of the Jews for suffering seemed indisputable. Anti-Semitism and economic discrimination here in America raised similar questions, as did the rebirth of the State of Israel and accompanying fears that American Jews would be charged with "dual loyalties." Even the Jews' rapid rise into the middle class and the professions provoked discussion of the special vocation and talents of Jewry as a whole. In short, history was over-full for the "second generation," which witnessed acculturation, economic depression, unparalleled social mobility, world war, Nazi genocide, and the founding of the Jewish state. The task which the generation faced was enormous: the fashioning of a Judaism that would be at home in the secular world and America, but that would retain the power to give meaning and motivation to the lives of American Jews. While it is still too soon to judge with any certainty the overall success of the generation's performance of this task, the endeavor did raise and provide an answer to the question of the Jewish role in American life. If the thinkers of the "third generation" have rejected much of the course set by their predecessors in the "second," they too have been driven by their historical situation to turn to the concept of chosenness as the means of understanding what it is to be a Jew in America. Indeed it was the success of their "parents" in achieving integration into America that lent still greater urgency to the question of what continued to set Jews apart.

There is, finally, a particularly American component to the dilemma of chosenness for American Jews. In choosing America the Jews had adopted a nation which, thanks to a Puritan legacy deriving from the

Hebrew Bible, has traditionally regarded itself as a chosen people and its bountiful country as a chosen land. Americans, Jews discovered, saw themselves as a people destined to build a "city on a hill" after traversing a great wilderness. Such notions harbored by the larger society ironically rendered the Jews' very similar claims both problematic and indispensable. On the one hand, it was distasteful—and certainly bad taste—to insist on one's essential difference from (if not superiority to) the society one so eagerly wished to join. On the other hand, what better way was there for the promotion of Jewish integration into American life than by trumpeting a symbolic definition of self which Jews and Americans shared? The problem was to arrive at a balance between exclusivity and participation, continuous with Jewish tradition and acceptable to America. Not surprisingly, then, the vehicle of solution most often proposed by American Jewish thinkers was reinterpretation of the idea which had served both Jewish and American self-definition for centuries. That presidential candidate Ronald Reagan continued to invoke the imagery of election in 1980[7] helps us to understand why a rabbi of a suburban congregation should do the same. The rhetoric still resonates deeply for both Jews and gentiles, anchoring Americans in a singular convenant with destiny and anchoring the Jews in America. It gives both a sense of being at the center of things, engaged in useful work which the Lord will watch over and bless.

The Generations and their Rabbis

The word "rhetoric" in the previous paragraph reminds us that the materials which we shall examine are neither timeless speculations by detached philosophers (if ever such existed) nor unsituated in the life of a particular people possessed of particular needs, interests, and aspirations. On the contrary: American Jewish thought is less an attempt (usually unsuccessful) at systematic theology, than an effort to make sense of a new and rather traumatic situation through the appropriation and interpretation of inherited ideas and images. The rabbis and theologians who have shaped American Judaism did not write for eternity, and not even for an audience of intellectuals. They wrote from within a community whose needs were immediate and acute. The conceptual rigor and system of, say, Maimonides, was therefore a less relevant model for them than the passion and impact of, say, Isaiah. This does not mean that we cannot judge these thinkers' efforts. However, we will not understand the particular style and content of any reinterpretation unless we attend to the special interests and background of both its author and its audience. American Jewish thought on election should be understood as "religious ideology" rather than theology, a conceptualization which, drawing upon the anthropologist Clifford Geertz, emphasizes the function of that thought in providing meaning to those who created and received it in the particular context of their time and place. Attention must be paid to the needs and situation of the "second generation" if the character of its religious thought is to be understood.

The generational terminology employed throughout this work is in one sense misleading and unjustified. Jews have lived in America since they joined Peter Stuyvesant in New Amsterdam in 1654, and the present institutional roots of the Jewish community go back at least to the mid-nineteenth century. That a Jew coming to maturity in 1930 could nevertheless be called "second generation" is a function of the massive immigration of Jews from Eastern Europe between 1880 and 1924 which raised the Jewish population in the United States from about a quarter million in 1880 to 4.2 million in 1927.[8] Such an influx could not but have an impact on existing Jewish institutions. These were in fact not merely changed but drastically overhauled, taking on the character by which we still know them today.

The Reform movement, for example, which recently celebrated the centenaries of its seminary and rabbinical organization, took on its current form only with the changes in style and outlook signaled by the adoption in 1937 of the statement of principles known as the Columbus Platform. Conservative Judaism, rooted in the "Historical School" of the previous century and nurtured by Solomon Schechter in the opening years of this one, likewise achieved its commanding institutional position only in the thirties and forties. Indeed, its current predominance really began when the children of the Eastern European immigration left behind the areas of "second settlement," to which they had moved from the immigrant ghettoes, and flocked with other Americans in the postwar years to the suburbs. Orthodoxy, present in America since the arrival of the first Jewish settlers, and the only available religious form until the rise of Reform in the nineteenth century, was also dramatically altered by the new immigration (and again by refugees during the Nazi period). It found articulate voice in the language and manner of America only toward the close of the "second generation." Reconstructionism, a new movement founded by Mordecai M. Kaplan, first appeared in these years, a "second-generation American Jewish phenomenon"[9] shaped, as we shall see below, by the period's intellectual, institutional, and communal currents. The "American influence," one sociologist has written, is present in the movement's "very marrow."[10] Finally, the various secularist Jewish ideologies, despite European roots, bear the imprint of the American experience in this period and reflect the strategies of acculturation and its resistance adopted by the immigrant community.[11] In the years following World War II a "third generation," which identified itself as such, inherited the forms of Judaism fashioned by the "second" and, through a combination of receptivity and rebellion, developed the current varieties of American Judaism.

Thus, the generational terminology now standard in the sociological literature on American Jewry is well suited to the present study of American Judaism, as is the sociologists' assumption that "the shared social experiences of age and peers are more critical in determining behavior than membership in the abstract category of generation of American nativity."[12] In other words, the phrases "second" and "third generation" denote a period and its population regardless of whether a particular thinker who joined in its debates and was subject to its influence was biologically its native son in the strict sense of the term.[13]

During the "second generation" those thinkers were almost exclusively rabbis. Considerable attention was given at the time to the alienation of lay intellectuals from Judaism and the Jewish community.[14] Except for rare articles, their voices were simply not heard in debates which, though they might have involved the destiny of all Jews, were especially concerned with the Jewish religion. Horace Kallen, Ludwig Lewisohn, Maurice Samuel and Hayim Greenberg—four of the more original thinkers writing during the period and figuring in the present study—were by default the only lay intellectuals to deal at length with chosenness or any other religious issue of concern to the community. Others did comment on issues of the day such as Zionism and the fate of European Jewry. Laymen, whether congregants or "organization men," also did not participate in debates on religious matters, or, at the very least, their contributions have gone unrecorded in the community's publications. No survey data documenting their opinions are available, and they did not write articles, even in local Jewish newspapers, which would give us a clue to their beliefs.[15] Discussions about "religion," quite simply, were left to the religious professionals. We can assess the opinions of the laymen only indirectly, and with great care.

However, while our ability to generalize about American Jewish opinion on the basis of the views of the rabbis is circumscribed, our focus on the rabbis has advantages which should not be overlooked. First, the "ambivalence" generated by the conflicting desires for integration and survival as Jews found clear expression among the rabbis, who after all represented American Judaism, and so symbolized the American Jew, not only to Jews but also to gentiles.[16] Indeed, the rabbi's position as spokesman to the gentiles—hardly a traditional rabbinical role—was in fact seen by many American congregants as a primary task of his profession. This point is of utmost importance, for the idea of chosenness presented rabbis with a critical problem in public relations at a time when their service as the community's principal "ambassadors" to gentile America was of great practical import. The materials to be examined here bear witness to those concerns. They must be read, almost always, as apologetic.

Second, though by default more than intent, the rabbis' task finds its place in the mainstream of Jewish thought in the modern period. The rabbis were with few exceptions not theologians, lacking both the tools to do theology and, one suspects, the inclination. They were college-educated when their congregants were not, but their backgrounds in Jewish sources were frequently minimal, and the age made performance of pastoral duties paramount.[17] Motivation had to be provided for Jewish identification, first at a time of discrimination and pressure to acculturate, and then during the trying years of Nazism and war. However, this emphasis on the practical is nothing new to Jewish thought in the modern period. Jewish thinkers since Moses Mendelssohn have been concerned both to describe a place for Jews in the modern social and political order and to conceive a Judaism suited to that order. Like many other Jewish thinkers in the modern period, the rabbis addressed the first task most insistently, and the second only in the context of the first. Their ideas of chosenness add a great deal to our understanding of American Judaism, but add precious little to our understanding of the meaning of chosenness. American Judaism has survived despite that signal failure—or rather (as we shall see) because of it. The nature of American Jewish thought as practiced by the rabbis thus teaches us a good deal about the predicament of modern Jewry.

Finally, with lay sources unavailable, the rabbis, as "middle-brow" thinkers, give us access to "a more popular sphere of thought" that we could not chart were we restricted to the writings of intellectuals.[18] The rabbis were of two sorts: those in congregations, large or small, whose views appeared occasionally in journals, rabbinical assembly proceedings, and the many published collections of sermons; and more well-known thinkers such as Robert Gordis and Abba Hillel Silver who were prominent in the Conservative and Reform movements, respectively, and the authors of longer works of some quality. These distinctions aside, however, the rabbis were a remarkably homogeneous group, and quite similar to their congregants. Most Reform and Conservative rabbis polled in a 1937[19] survey had been in the profession less than ten years, and most were native born (76 percent in Reform and 52 percent in Conservatisim, compared to only 21 percent in Orthodoxy). Both data of course testify to the second generation's quick rise to dominance in the American rabbinate.[20] The majority in all groups had earned a B.A. as their highest degree, by and large majoring either in philosophy or the social sciences. Only one-seventh of those polled professed belief in a God who had created the universe, while most of the rest assented to a less personalist definition of God as the "sum total of forces which make for greater intelligence, beauty, and goodness." Large majorities in Reform and Conservativism viewed the Biblical creation narrative as myth and held to a psychologized view of prayer as meditation. Even on Zionism, the differences of opinion were smaller than official Reform pronouncements questioning the wisdom of the Jewish quest for statehood might have led one to expect. On domestic American politics, the rabbis, almost to a man, were liberals on issues of civil rights, the economy, and collective bargaining. Perhaps most important of all, the rabbis were in agreement about the relative nonimportance of either theology or politics in their preaching. The former had been replaced by attention to a more general "philosophy of Jewish life," while the latter was precluded, in their view, by congregants' economic conservativism, vested interests, and careful consideration of the sensitivities of gentiles.

What this means is that we must look for the rabbis' thought—which comprises almost all of what one can call American Jewish religious thought in the second generation—not in systematic theological writings but in prayerbooks, articles, sermons, reviews, and proceedings of debate.[21] We can learn what the rabbis intended by their reformulations of the prayers or by their movements' statements of principles, because we have access to their debates on these matters. One cannot claim that chosenness was the rabbis' exclusive or even their primary concern. Among Reform rabbis (examined in chapter 3) the "Jewish mission" vied for preeminence with "god-concepts" and changes in the movement's attitudes on Zionism and ceremonial. Reconstructionists and their challengers debated chosenness more than any issue except perhaps Mordecai Kaplan's conception of God (chapter 4). In the Conservative movement (chapter 5) election was overshadowed by near-yearly debates on the reform of Jewish law and the need for a Conservative ideology, while the paucity of Orthodox comment on the matter (discussed in chapter 5) confirms the assumption that this movement, less concerned with secular philosophy or gentile opinion, would be less concerned to modify tradition.[22] All of that said, however, the profusion of articles, speeches, chapters, sermons and books on election—which far outweighs the attention devoted to any other single religious issue—does argue for the subject's importance to the rabbis, and, one suspects, to their congregants. It was the latter, after all, who listened to the sermons week after week, read the articles, purchased the books, and uttered the prayers which the rabbis so carefully reformulated.

In the "third generation" this situation changed dramatically. Theology emerged as a legitimate and respected enterprise of American Jewry. Jewish thinkers appeared who conceived of themselves as theologians, and journals proliferated in which the essays of such thinkers could be published. Congregational rabbis, faced with the competition of such thinkers (employed, often enough, by the movements' respective seminaries), have tended to leave chosenness and other matters of theology in the hands of the new professionals. The changed socioeconomic and political position of the Jews in American society, and the rabbis' new relation to their congregants (both analyzed in chapter 6) together militated against the sorts of efforts by rabbis so popular a generation before.

Rabbis and theologians alike now approached the issue with greater learning and sophistication, de-emphasizing its importance somewhat vis-à-vis the related ideas of Jewish tradition once more regularly discussed: revelation, messiah, exile, God's role in history (chapter 7). Yet chosenness was not ignored, but rather restored to a center made all the more apparent for renewed attention to its radii. The principal stimulus of rabbinic apologetic for chosenness in the "second generation" had been the charge that the idea promoted exclusivity or even racism. In the "third generation" Jewish thinkers responded more to a theological need: defense of a doctrine which, by their own admission, was and would forever remain a mystery beyond our comprehension.

Intellectuals, now included in these discussions, added a secular reinterpretation of chosenness which emphasized the Jew's role as perpetual critic and outsider. In the second generation such a stance would have seemed anathema to the rabbis, who invoked election precisely to make the chosen people of Israel insiders, for the very first time in history, among the other chosen nation of America. Now, however, Jewish involvement in America had become so complete that the ongoing need for a sense of what set Jews apart necessitated the self-distancing articulated, in part, by the intellectuals. This is the paradox decisive for the present situation of Jewish chosenness in America: that Jews so much a part of the larger society should still regard themselves as "ambassadors at home" and feel the need for distance; that the children of their parents' "half-way covenant" with tradition should find the need to embrace a mystery which reason and experience have rendered incomprehensible. It is a paradox not given to any but the most painful and unacceptable resolution.

The Ideas and Images of Election

The twentieth-century American Jews who have grappled with that paradox—whether rabbis or congregants, theologians or secular intellectuals—have approached it with a set of ideas and images furnished them by Jewish tradition. Like any generation in any tradition, they have been selective, emphasizing elements of their inheritance that seemed relevant to their own experience while downplaying or simply ignoring other elements important in other periods. More than any previous generation of Jews, however, they found the inherited tradition on election difficult to appropriate. It legitimated and even demanded an exclusivity which they had repudiated. It conferred a mission that they did not wish to undertake. It presumed a covenant with a personal God in whom they for the most part could not believe. If we are to make sense of their reinterpretations of election, we need to know something of the traditions which they reinterpreted, if only to see why they were forced to recast the tradition so dramatically instead of taking the easier course of subtle change through simple transmission and translation. I shall therefore sketch, in rather broad strokes, the principal notions of a people holy and apart which have animated—and often tormented—the imaginations of twentieth-century American Jews.

Every strand in Jewish tradition begins, of course, with the Bible; two contexts in particular are indispensable for understanding the concept of Israel's election. The first comes in the usage of the word *bahar* (chose) itself. The word appears in the Bible on some one-hundred-seventy-five carefully chosen occasions.[23] Its primary connotation is always that of setting apart for service,[24] as when Joshua is ordered to "choose" soldiers with whom to battle Amalek (Exodus 17:9) and Moses "chooses" men to help him judge the people (Ex. 18:25).[25] However, the word never denotes the mere sober consideration of alternative candidates and their merits. The antonym generally paired with *bahar* is *ma'as* which means to scorn or reject;[26] the consequences of choices indicated by the word *bahar* are always momentous. Chosen ones, moreover, are asked to signify their chosenness by choosing: by selecting that which God would choose—life, the good, the way—rather than the alternatives,[27] and only this rather limited set of nonhuman objects is ever said to be chosen by chosen ones. The usage of the word to denote persons is even more restricted. Individuals are called chosen only in one highly specific circumstance: where traditional legitimacy is overturned, a new authority is selected to supplant it, and the latter marks the start of a new hereditary succession. Judges or prophets (most notably Moses) are never said to be chosen, for they do not found a line. The word is reserved for kings and priests.[28] Chosenness, finally, is a status which can be withdrawn, and because the Chooser can and does reappear to choose anew if the behavior demanded of the chosen is not forthcoming (as when David supplants Saul as king), every moment when election is not withdrawn becomes a further confirmation, a resignification. Setting apart, service, a contract of reciprocity: these are the three elements of exclusivity, mission and covenant so crucial in the history of God's chosen "kingdom of priests." They are all inherent in the very word *bahar* by which kings and priests are said in the Bible to be chosen.

The election of Israel is announced immediately before the revelation at Sinai, when God declares (Ex. 19:3–6) that He has taken Israel out of Egypt in order that the people should become His "special treasure" (*segulah*) among the nations.[29] Israel shall assume that role if it agrees to "harken well unto My voice and keep My covenant."[30] The text does not clarify why Israel has been chosen, nor does it state the purpose of the election. In Deuteronomy 7:7–9 we learn that Israel had been chosen "because of God's love for you, and His keeping of the oath which He swore to your fathers." The purpose of this unique relationship is briefly set forth in 4:6: "The nations shall hear all these statutes [i.e., Torah] and say, 'Surely, this great nation is a wise and understanding people' "— and so be led to God and His law. However, the "mission" is clarified, and made a principal theme, only in the second part of Isaiah (42:1–7):

> Behold my servant whom I uphold,
> My elect in whom My soul delights.
> I have put My spirit upon him;
> He shall bring forth judgment to the nations . . .
> I the Lord have called you . . .
> and set you for a covenant of the people,
> for a light unto the nations,
> to open blind eyes, bring out prisoners from the dungeon . . .

This imagery culminates in the description of God's "suffering servant" (ch. 53), often held by later Jewish commentators—quite reasonably, given the refrain of "Jacob my servant, Israel whom I have chosen"—to refer to the Jewish people as a whole. "He is despised and rejected of men; a man of sorrow, and acquainted with grief."

In these verses from Deutero-Isaiah, which serve as the basis of much of the Reform Jewish thought which we shall examine, the universal thrust of election is accentuated in an explicit mission to the nations. "Behold, I have given him for a witness to the peoples . . ." (Is. 55:4). The emphasis has shifted from a covenant of commandments to be observed by and within the holy community, to Israel as the servant of mankind, which through Israel shall draw near to the God of Israel and all humanity. Israel's God will thus come to be worshipped by all as God. Moreover, suffering is pronounced the mark of election, rather than its discomfirmation, a feature crucial to American rabbinic interpretation.

It is worth giving some attention to the wider context of "Jew" and "gentile" as this is presented in the Bible through a series of stories and characters which have nourished the imagination of Jews—and powerfully shaped their self-identities—ever since. First of all, Israel's chosen-ness literally pervades the Biblical text. It constitutes the book's underlying raison d'etre, in fact, in a manner belied by the relatively infrequent recourse made to the word *bahar* itself. As we have seen, *bahar* depends for its power in part on that very rarity of usage; related words like *yada'* (knew), *kara'* (called) and *hashak* (embraced) are often employed in its place to convey Israel's special relationship with God. More importantly, however, the very structure of the text, and the character of its key personalities, lend a richness of meaning to chosen-ness that far outweighs that of the passages in which the word appears explicitly.

Consider, for example, the pace of Biblical history, racing over the hundreds of years between creation and the call of Abraham (Gen. 1–11), then slowing to a crawl (12–50) in order to detail the history of a mere four generations of patriarchs. The many failures to achieve human righteousness—Adam and Eve, Cain and Abel, the generation of the flood, the Tower of Babel—condition and, in fact, cause the attempt to educate the race to good through the descendants of a single man, Abraham. His rejoinder to God's call—"*Hineni:* I am here, I am ready"—whether voiced or silent, stands in pointed contrast (and is meant so to stand) to the evasions of the original parents or their heirs. The prehistory of Israel, then, is sketched not so much to explain creation or the diversity of humankind as to locate Israel on the map of humanity and thus to account for the sacred history which follows. Israel is to serve humanity precisely by separation from it. The nation's pre-history, described in these opening narratives, represents the sum of what Abraham leaves behind in order that the world may learn to join him, someday, across the river in the promised land. Israel's chosenness is fundamental to humanity's realization of itself according to God's plan. Separation from the gentile is, in a real way, the ultimate destiny of everyone—including the gentile.

The complexities of this separation for purposes of service are drawn most graphically in the stories of the text's principal characters. In Avimelekh's encounter with Abraham (Genesis 20), the Canaanite king, visited by God in a dream, and judged innocent of any wrong-doing, must nevertheless beg the Jew for intercession with God—for Abraham is "a prophet." Avimelekh prudently heaps gifts upon Abraham, and welcomes him to sojourn in his land: for the Jew is chosen, and he is not; the Jew is uniquely blessed, and so both dangerous and useful. Nowhere is this clearer than in the story of Joseph (Genesis 37–50), who turns every arena over which he is given responsibility, from the house of Potifar to the entire land of Egypt, into a further demonstration of God's manifest blessing. Joseph's unique usefulness to his ruler, combined with his ineradicable distinctiveness, confront him (as they would confront so many Jews in later generations) with the choice between survival through service to an exploitative power—or utter disappearance. Choosing survival, the Jews earn the wrath of subject populations, with the predictable outcome depicted at the start of the Book of Exodus. This too is the legacy of chosenness: a blessing and a curse served reluctantly and with devotion, involving social and political consequences that call forth the consolations of election all the more insistently, even as they call the explanatory power of election into question. It was a legacy inherited, in all its ramifications, by later generations denied the confirmations of election known to Biblical Jews: a tangible land flowing with milk and honey, a Temple in which the Lord of all the earth dwelt and could be found.

It was the loss of these that the writers of the rabbinic corpus (Mishnah, Talmud, and related works, both legal and nonlegal, dating from about the first to the sixth centuries) had to reconcile with their conviction of election.[31] Tales and parables that stressed the reciprocal obligations of Chooser and Chosen under the covenant implicitly offered the reassurance that, despite the destruction of the Temple, a faithful Israel need have no fear of abandonment by God. Other reflections emphasized that Israel was not a servant to be rejected by the Master at will but a favored son of a loving Father, or even the beloved bride of an always faithful Bridegroom.[32] God's love would thus endure forever, independent of all fluctuations in the merits of the beloved. Whether such affirmations came in response to specific Christian polemics challenging Israel's claim to chosenness,[33] or in reply to the more forceful challenges posed by historical events, their message was consistent. Israel remained God's "special treasure," and as such needed to have no fear of abandonment.

Two issues in particular were the focus of rabbinic concern in this connection. First, the rabbis were cognizant of what we would now call the tension between universalism and particularism. They were driven to explain that the Torah had been given in a wilderness so that no nation could conceive of God's revelation as its own exclusive possession; Torah had been revealed in seventy languages so that all the peoples of the earth could understand it.[34] However, " 'Moses commanded us the Torah' (Deut. 33:4): [This means that] this command is only to us, only for us."[35] The dilemma receives forceful expression in a well-known (and deeply ambiguous) midrash on Deuteronomy 33:2, which depicts God's offer of the Torah to various nations of the world. The children of Esau reject the gift because it prohibits killing, and their ancestor had been told "by the sword you shall live." The children of Ammon and Moab reject the Torah because it prohibits adultery, and they "are all products of adultery, as it is said, 'And the daughters of Lot became pregnant from their father. . . .' " Acceptance by the children of Ishmael is similarly precluded. Only Israel can accept the Torah, and does so even before hearing the terms of the offer.[36] Obviously, God's teaching was meant for them alone, and they could rightfully enjoy the benefits of having received it.

This tale, and others like it, set forth the confusing facts of divine-human relations as the Jews had come to know them. Unable to resolve the paradox of Israel's particular possession of a gift intended for all humanity, the rabbis merely restated that paradox in a way which articulated and contained their many doubts. Torah was a gift to all humanity, the world's first and only chance to hear God's word so directly and not be struck down by its awesome force. Yet the Torah had been offered mankind through the medium of the Jewish people, which had not set the terms for its acceptance but only accepted it, and, what is more, still sought to share the gift with all the world. Was it Israel's fault that the nations had refused, or was Israel to blame for pride in its unique possession? It had paid the price for that gift many times over. Particularity would remain in tension with universality. The covenant would go on.

This, however, was a resolution sorely tested by history. The rabbis denied that events such as the Jews' defeat by Rome vindicated the claims of Israel's enemies, and so needed to explain those events in a way consonant with their own claim to election. They could not account Israel's suffering as proof that God had abrogated the covenant made at Sinai, but neither could they absolve God of responsibility for history by blaming Israel's estate on blind fate. For the rabbis God remained the Lord of history. Some midrashim explained the destruction of the Temple as yet another chastisement of Israelite sin, others found the punishment incommensurate with the crime and looked elsewhere for explanation. In such tales Israel's continued faithfulness stands in implicit and reproachful contrast to God's apparent indifference,[37] or, more often, the seeming triumph of Israel's enemies is proclaimed an aberration that would one day be righted. The true meaning of Israel's history, and indeed of the world's, would be discernible only at history's consummation.[38]

Chosenness, we might summarize, is never explained by the sages, but only affirmed, and retained at the center of the set of ideas which locate Israel's place in the world: God, revelation, covenant, messiah, exile. Whether with the help of metaphors of covenant and love, or independently of such teachings, Israel was somehow motivated to hold fast to its relationship with God. Jewish law reflected and gave force to that affirmation, both in laws of holiness and purity which set Israel ritually apart, and in civil and criminal laws which prescribed very different rights and obligations for the Jew, the righteous gentile ("son of Noah"), and the idolater.[39] Until historical circumstances changed and God's universal intent was realized, Israel would remain steadfastly apart. One cannot gauge the price which this persistence in a separate course while awaiting ultimate vindication claimed from the Jews over the years. One can only speculate that the need to believe in one's chosenness became all the greater the more that history seemed to disconfirm such belief. Certainly the rabbis' vision has had enormous impact over the centuries and down to the past two generations of American Jews. They too invoked the rabbis' favored metaphors, wrestled with the paradox of universalism and particularism, and wondered how the Lord of history could permit a Holocaust to overtake His chosen people.

The tradition of thought surveyed thus far generally held sway throughout the Middle Ages, pervading Jewish liturgy and observance and providing explanation for Jewish apartness. Chosenness rarely needed or received explicit justification. The great philosopher Moses Maimonides (1135–1204) is thus typical of medieval thinkers in assuming election as a matter of course.[40] Yehudah Halevi (1075–1141), the exception to this pattern, argued for a notion of chosenness without precedent in Biblical or rabbinic sources: a hereditary capacity inhering in the Jewish people which uniquely prepared it for the reception of divine revelation. Israel was in this most concrete of senses "the pick of mankind."[41] Another version of this theory, brilliantly imagined, became standard in the mystical tradition (kabbalah) taught by Isaac Luria (1534–1572). In his teaching unique spiritual endowments are said to reside in Jewish souls. Indeed the unique goodness of Israel's primordial "sparks" and the fact that they are never trapped in the lowest dwelling places ("husks") of evil permit Israel, and Israel alone, to accomplish the restoration of God's creation to its original wholeness.[42] However, while such notions may have reflected and influenced the folk-imagination, the Jew uninitiated into kabbalah was more likely to learn about his chosenness from the separations of daily experience and the round of ritual observances. Both of these inculcated the notion of chosenness elaborated during the rabbinic period, rendering election the fundamental fact of Jewish experience—incomprehensible but undeniable.

It is worth remarking that in this context of symbol and rite, reinforced by the barriers between Jew and gentile, a Jew could hardly help believing in his or her own chosenness.[43] Every worshipping male thanked God daily for not making him a heathen. The Sabbath was ushered in with praise for God who "has chosen us and sanctified us from the nations," and ushered out with a blessing of "the Lord who makes a distinction between holy and profane, light and darkness, Israel and the nations." Such prayers made sense of a social reality of separations that in turn rendered the idea of chosenness self-evident. Why did Jew and gentile inhabit distinct worlds, with little but economic intercourse connecting them? Because the Jews were chosen, and gentiles had arrogated that chosenness unto themselves. How could one be sure that the Jews were chosen? One had only to look around; the facts were there for all to see. The problem remained reconciliation of these facts with other facts—Israel's suffering—and, as before, suffering became a mark of election rather than its disconfirmation. Indeed the Jews of Europe chose martyrdom in record numbers rather than suffer apostasy.[44] This became an integral part of the legacy of chosenness transmitted to later generations. Wandering and persecution, Jews knew, was the lot of God's chosen people.[45]

After their emancipation in Europe during the nineteenth century,[46] Jews could no longer assume chosenness as a given of existence challenged only by persecutions that became a further confirmation. The doctrine now had to be argued. Moreover, that argument had to be made in terms borrowed from and acceptable to the gentile world rather than in traditional terms of discourse. For Jews could no longer deny other peoples' equal access to divine truth, or propound a distinctiveness out of keeping with their aspirations to civic equality. The prayer book adopted by the Berlin Reform congregation in 1844 puts the matter well. The very first section of its introduction relates that changes have been made in all passages that mention Israel's election, for chosenness could no longer be viewed as a historic fact but only as "a subjective fact in the consciousness of the Jewish people." Israel had been more "enlightened" and "morally developed" than pagan nations, but

> the concept of tribal holiness and of a special vocation arising from this has become entirely foreign to us, as has the idea of an intimate covenant between God and Israel which is to remain significant for all eternity. Human character and dignity, and God's image within us—these alone are signs of chosenness.

Occasional references to the election of Israel had been retained only to "urge ourselves on to true humanity and brotherly love."[47]

The rationale for the survival and importance of Judaism, once chosenness had been rejected or de-emphasized, became the ongoing Jewish mission unto the nations. Reform Jewish literature for the next one hundred years overflows with references to that mission, conceived in the Idealist epoch, when national cultures were believed to incarnate eternal ideas, and quasi-racial theories of unique national genius were commonplace. The Reform historian and theologian Abraham Geiger (1810–1874) wrote that as the Greeks had had "a higher living sense for the Beautiful, the Harmonious, the Symmetrical, and the Pleasing," so the Jews were endowed with a "religious genius" which gave them unique insight into God and His teachings. Israel was charged with conveying this insight to humanity, and thus the "compact nationality" originally required for protection of the nascent idea had soon given way to a diaspora in which Jews lived among the nations whom they were destined to instruct.[48] Such notions were not limited to the Reformers. Nachman Krochmal (1785–1840), now claimed by Conservative Judaism as a forebear, stated in his *Guide for the Perplexed of the Day* that Judaism offered unique insights into the workings of the Spirit. It would thus survive forever, while the religions and cultures of other peoples followed the usual course of birth, maturity, and decline.[49] One finds numerous references to Israel's mission in the writings both of the neo-Orthodox thinker Samson Raphael Hirsch (1808–1888) and the (proto-Conservative) historian Heinrich Graetz (1817–1891).[50] Nevertheless, mission achieved centrality only in the Reform movement. When this movement was transplanted to America with the German immigration of the 1840s, the idea of mission seemed to find an even more suitable home.[51]

In America, Jews could believe they had found a new Zion, and Reform rabbis were fond of saying so. America was the ideal stage on which the mission to humanity could convincingly be proclaimed and publicly enacted. The two leaders of Reform in nineteenth-century America, David Einhorn (1809–1879)[52] and Isaac Mayer Wise (1819–1900),[53] both emphasized that mission and its new providential setting.[54] Kaufman Kohler (1843–1926), who guided the movement at the turn of the century, made Israel's mission the centerpiece of his systematic theology.[55] Non-Reform rabbis were more restrained. While the trope of mission often figures prominently in their work, Israel's calling remains the "inner-directed" work of commandment, rather than the dissemination of a specific set of truths outward to humanity.[56]

As the nineteenth century gave way to the twentieth, and the predominance of German-born Jews and their descendants to Eastern Europeans, the debate over Israel's mission and the "American Zion" came to symbolize a larger dispute over the definition of Judaism and the role of Jews in American life. Those who shared Kaufman Kohler's enthusiasm for Israel's mission were likely to believe with him that the words "American Judaism" "spell the triumph of the world's two greatest peoples and ideals,"[57] and so to urge the near-complete integration of Jews to the welcoming environment of America. Judaism would then be understood as a religion and not a national identity, a set of beliefs destined to converge with those of enlightened gentiles. Conservative thinkers such as Solomon Schechter (1847–1915), the organizing genius of the Jewish Theological Seminary in New York, gave far less prominence to the idea of mission and refused to see Judaism as merely a set of beliefs. They rather emphasized a Jewish peoplehood founded upon observance of the Torah's commandments, and sought a way for Jews to be both at home in America and apart there.[58] While no American movement or thinker denied the doctrine of election, then, each selected different aspects from the inherited tradition for emphasis.[59] All to some extent refashioned the traditional idea, and used that interpretation in defining the ideal shape of American Judaism.

The rabbis of the "second generation" faced three principal difficulties in appropriating the traditions of election just surveyed. First, the exclusivity heretofore attendant on Jewish chosenness now had to be discarded, in terms both of physical separation and of the distinct set of values which chosenness had helped to sustain before the modern period. The Jews were at home in America, or wanted and had a reasonable chance to be at home. To regard America as just another way-station of exile was to deny Jews could be at home there. Secondly, the notion of the Jewish mission to the nations was problematic, because it presumed that one people had the truth, and all others could but wait patiently to receive it. Such hierarchical ideas did not seem to fit a society which espoused egalitarianism; if all men were created equal, why did other peoples need the Jews in order to attain true knowledge of God? The search for ways of reconciling pluralism and election became a pressing task of Jewish apologetic. There was, finally, the matter of covenant: the set of obligations owed to the God who had chosen Israel "from among all the nations." By the time American Jews of the second and third generations came to ponder the idea of their election, two centuries of questioning had eroded belief by Jew and gentile alike in a God active enough in history to choose any people, and undemocratic enough to choose only one. What is more, the majority of Jews had ceased to observe or to feel bound by the covenant's original terms: Jewish law (halakhah). In many cases they substituted a set of ethical obligations shared by humanity as a whole for the particular regimen of commandments once believed to be incumbent upon the Jews alone.

In place of a view of self taken for granted, the American thinkers were faced with a set of nagging questions which could not be resolved merely by invoking the answers of tradition. What could chosenness mean, in the absence of distinctive and obligatory actions? How could Jews know themselves to be chosen, without seeing themselves acting out that election in any tangible way? How could Jews blur the line separating them from the nonchosen of the world, and still be sure they had not crossed it? Could they see the line connecting them with God attenuated or even cut, and still make sense of Jewish existence? Such were their dilemmas.

The solutions proposed were many and various; all, however, confirm the observation of a leading American Jewish novelist that "imagining what Jews are and ought to be has been anything but the marginal activity of a few American Jewish novelists." It is, in fact, the primary burden of American Jewish religious thought, which has attempted through the reinterpretation of a central theological idea and its associated imagery to describe what "the solitary being who has been designated Jew . . . is and is not, must and must not be."[60] That pursuit, as Philip Roth correctly notes, remains at the center of what American Judaism (and not merely American Jewish literature) has been about. The self-images of "victim," "assistant," "mama's boy" and, above all, conscience to a pagan world that fill the pages of American Jewish literature are part and parcel of an inherited self defined by the notion of election. Even secular Jews such as Roth continue to ground Jewish self-definition in a normative past, despite the profound guilt and ambivalence generated by the inability to bear the weight which the demands of that past impose. Such an effort cannot but be problematic. For the self imagined in these terms is too awesome in its holy ambition, and the self imagining too poor, limited as it is to the resources of the real.

PART
TWO

The "Second Generation"
(1930–1955)

II

"Nation, People, Religion—
What Are We?"

IN ORDER TO understand the second generation's reinterpretation of election, one first needs to examine the context in which it occurred, and the primary use to which it was put. Over a million Jews had poured into America in the decade before the First World War, following hundreds of thousands who had come just before them. Yet another quarter million would come soon after.[1] In the late twenties and thirties the children of these immigrants began to work earnestly at the task of being at home in America, and the doctrine of election was enlisted to serve that effort. More than any other idea, chosenness was employed to stipulate a bond between Judaism and democracy, and to define the role of the Jews in America—a chosen people in God's new chosen land.

This effort was without precedent in Jewish history for several reasons. First, there were no "ghettoes" in America to wall Jews out. Neither widespread discrimination nor voluntary residential segregation prevented the immigrants and their children from moving quickly out of the initial areas of settlement to new urban districts, and moving up from blue- to white-collar employment. Equally important, there was relatively little halakhic prescription to wall Jews in. The vast majority of the immigrants, and even more of their children, observed few traditional rituals, and absented themselves from the synagogue. The religion which had kept Jews separate for centuries seemed, in the words of one historian, on the way to "rapid dissolution."[2] Finally, there seemed little cause for separation, for the perceived values of America did not seem substantially different from commitments seen, often vaguely, as "Jewish." Certainly the surrounding American society, unlike those from which the immigrants had come, was not one to which Jews pondering their future as a distinct people could feel superior. On the contrary, they wished for nothing so fervently as to join it: to speak its language, adopt its styles, and attain to membership in its growing middle class.

This aspiration and opportunity to participate fully in American life only increased the need to explain what essentially separated Jews from other peoples. The more Jews could feel at home in America, the more they needed to be reminded why they should not feel too much at home. America's welcoming environment, then, exacerbated a problem with ample precedent in Jewish history: the conferring of meaning upon Jewish exclusivity. The American rabbis had the difficult task of reconciling two contradictory goals: helping Jews to fit into the surrounding culture and its mores, and seeing to it that, despite America's many comforts, the fit never became entirely snug. "America was different," they agreed, but the Jews' long exile had not ended. There was still a need for separateness; "integration" should not be achieved at the expense of "survival." The notion of chosenness served the rabbis well in balancing these goals. Its rhetoric linked Jews powerfully to America's own self-understanding, even as it proclaimed the message that Jews were by nature "a people dwelling alone"—and had to be so even in America.

Americanization and the "Jewish Problem"

In considering the rabbis' use of the election tradition, four aspects of the second generation's situation need to be noted: the extraordinary speed of its social mobility, the visions of acculturation which shaped its integration into America, the anti-Semitism to which it was increasingly subject, and the communal institutions which it developed.

Between 1920 and 1940, a first generation composed largely of small shopkeepers and manual laborers (many in the needle-trades) gave way to a second generation of businessmen, professionals, and white collar workers. So long as the gates to immigration remained open, new arrivals swelled the ranks of the working class; so long as the Depression gripped America, advancement into the middle class was slow. But already during the twenties Jews were laying the groundwork through intensive education for the rapid economic advance which would soon occur. A survey conducted in San Francisco in the thirties found that, out of every thousand employed Jews, eighteen were lawyers or judges and sixteen were doctors, compared to five in either category in the general population; in Pittsburgh the figures were fourteen and thirteen, compared to four.[3] According to a national estimate made in 1942, thirty-five to forty of each hundred employed Jews were in commercial occupations (compared to fourteen in the general population), only fifteen to twenty in manufacturing (compared to twenty-six), and ten to twelve in the professions (compared to seven).[4] The gap would quickly widen.

Life in the second generation communities reflected this generational mobility, combining, with no little strain, a "continued ethnic character" with the accoutrements and aspirations of a new middle class.[5] The first generation, according to one schematic summary, "pertains to that phase dominated by the immigrants and those old enough to have been affected directly by life in an Eastern European culture." The second, their children, "scurried between two worlds" and experienced the conflict of cultures which has left such an imprint on American Jewish literature.[6]

There was conflict within the Jewish community as well. German Jews were often uncomfortable with the new arrivals from Eastern Europe, perceiving them as uncultured and ill-mannered. Their discomfort was exacerbated by anxiety that gentile resentment of the newcomers would threaten their own acceptance in America as well. Class differences, too, played a role in dividing the two groups. German Jews had generally done well since their earlier immigration in the mid-nineteenth century, and now in many cases employed the East Europeans. Finally, Mordecai Kaplan, writing in 1933, pointed to "different class interests" among the East Europeans themselves. He attributed "professional careerism" and the "desire for social climbing" to the assimilationist policy of a "capitalist class."[7] Such an explicit discussion of the matter was a rarity, and the sources of strain are hard to pinpoint, but the divisions themselves are not. For one thing, higher- and lower-class Jews belonged to different social organizations. They also joined different synagogues, with those higher on the social ladder belonging (if they belonged at all) to Conservative or Reform rather than Orthodox congregations.[8] Jews who had advanced economically were more likely to meet gentiles socially, through organizations outside the Jewish community or participation in non-Jewish charities. The world of the second generation, in its opening years, was thus "highly stratified within a common minority situation," and, because of its ambiguous relation to the larger gentile world, "socially insecure."[9]

In part, that "ambiguity" stemmed from the efforts of their new host country to Americanize all its immigrants as quickly and as thoroughly as possible. "One-hundred percent Americanization" had become the marching order of the day following the outbreak of World War I. Professions of loyalty to the United States were demanded; propaganda and even coercion were liberally employed; and the immigrants were stampeded into citizenship, adoption of the English language, and unquestioned reverence for existing American institutions.[10] President Theodore Roosevelt's call in 1915 for the Americanization of the immigrants echoed that of the prominent educator W. B. Cubberly, who said that the aim should be

> to break up their groups or settlements, to assimilate and amalgamate these people as a part of our American race, to implant in their children the Anglo-Saxon conception of righteousness, law and order, and popular government, and to awaken in them reverence for our democratic institutions and for those things in our national life which we as a people hold to be of abiding worth.[11]

Jews along with other immigrants were sent to night-schools to study English, American history and civics; and, as long as the First World War lasted, they seemed to regard such programs favorably or at least to acquiesce in their imposition. They went to the classes faithfully, and dutifully marched in patriotic parades. After the war, however, the immigrants' resentment surfaced, at the very same time as the Americanization movement reached its zenith. By then, liberals who had turned antinationalist opposed Americanization as chauvinistic, but economic depression and the "red scare" of 1919–20 had increased the pressures for conformity. Nativist proponents of Americanization came to regard their effort as a failure, and instead of attempting to absorb new ethnic elements moved to exclude them. The resultant quotas reduced immigration sharply after 1924, just as the ideology of "100% Americanization" had begun to give way to the "melting pot" or even to cultural pluralism.[12]

The immigrants already here, however, experienced increasing hostility throughout "the Tribal Twenties," in which none were "subjected to quite so much hatred as the Jews."[13] As in a previous wave of anti-Semitism in the 1880s and 1890s, economic strains gave rise to social dislocations which in turn engendered a nativist and antiforeign sentiment directed particularly against Jews. While never as virulent as simultaneous agitation against Jews in Europe, anti-Semitism in this country did erect social and economic barriers to the Jews' rapid advancement.[14] Explicit quotas were placed on admission of Jews to colleges and universities, especially to professional schools. Medical-school admissions fell: 50 percent of Jewish applicants were accepted in 1927 compared to 20 percent only three years later.[15] The trend continued: according to one report, Jews made up 8.8 percent of the student body in American professional schools in 1935, but only 7 percent in 1946. Their representation in the nation's medical schools fell from 15.9 to 12.7 percent, and similar declines occurred in schools of dentistry, pharmacy, law, engineering, architecture, social work, and veterinary medicine.[16] Discrimination was not limited to the universities. One historian has estimated that in the late 1920s Jews were excluded from 90 percent of the general office jobs available in New York City.[17] Want ads commonly specified that Jews need not apply.[18]

Such restrictions were repeatedly justified on the grounds that Jews were untrustworthy, careless, and—most of all, it seems—too clannish.[19] These stereotypes had a long history of expression in American popular literature, as well as in the works of patrician intellectuals such as Henry James.[20] The conflicting images of the Jew which they contained—chosen yet unfaithful, resourceful yet cunning—now served to cast suspicion upon the "quintessential parvenus" who, unlike other groups, came to be disliked all the more as they made their way into and up in America.[21] The stereotyping had even achieved the legitimacy which comes of being woven into the fabric of language itself. *Roget's Thesaurus,* an indignant writer observed in 1930, offered these associations in the index entry for Jew: "cunning, usurer, rich, extortioner, heretic." He suggested in their place "monotheist, civilizer, People of the Book, brethren of Jesus, cosmopolitan, Torah bearer, Ten Commandments, Chosen People, benevolent"—a fascinating set of associations no less instructive in its imagery than the original.[22]

Ideological anti-Semitism, then, had ample material on which to draw when it reappeared in America in the 1920s, most notably in a series of articles in Henry Ford's *Dearborn Independent,* which featured accusations taken from the Protocols of the Elders of Zion.[23] During the war years, virulent hostility remained at low levels but stereotyping and "casual anti-Semitism" (for example associating Jews with cowardice in battle and lack of patriotism) grew. Whether because of Nazi atrocities or peacetime economic prosperity, such anti-Semitic sentiment dropped off sharply in the post-war years,[24] though as late as 1947 school principals in one city studied were reluctant to hire Jews in the public schools, and Jewish doctors could not practice at all in hospitals—examples far from unique.[25] The Jews' economic advancement, then, had not come without opposition, and opposition increased the more the advancement was remarkable and remarked.

Social mobility, the pressures of acculturation, and the existence of discrimination and anti-Semitism account for the insecurity among Jews, which both the rabbis who served the second generation and the sociologists who write about it have found pervasive. The philosopher Horace Kallen, writing in 1939, observed that "week in and week out young Jews come to see me," bewildered and angry that professional schools had no place for them, and in some cases resenting the Jewishness which they knew to be a handicap.[26] Mordecai Kaplan cited the "envy and resentment" which the "alleged advantageous position" of the Jew had provoked. He warned Jews that they could not look to gentiles for fellowship, because the latter resented the "cultural parasitism" of the Jews' readiness to abandon their own world for the gentile's.[27] Milton Steinberg, one of the finest minds of his generation of rabbis, wrote in 1934 that the Jews of his day stood between two worlds, one in which they could no longer live, the other of which would not admit them. "Only a people of acrobats could preserve a semblance of poise on a footing so unstable."[28] Seven years later he expressed concern that American Jews had become "apprehensive over their security as never before in their history. . . . A vast wave of worry has swept over them of late. They are still submerged beneath it."[29] The social psychologist Kurt Lewin warned that year of "Self-Hatred Among Jews" stemming from "life on the boundary" and the handicaps to which Jews were subject.[30] Descriptions of the Jews' "sickness" or "abnormality" or even "pathology" are quite common in the writings of lay and rabbinic observers alike.

If the strains upon the second generation did not significantly impede its socioeconomic advancement or diminish its desire to balance "integration" with "survival," much of the reason can be traced to the array of Jewish communal organizations which flourished in the twenties and thirties. Historians and contemporary observers of the community have both pointed to the tendency of second-generation Jews to congregate—first of all by continuing to live near each other in predominantly Jewish neighborhoods.[31] Even as they moved from one area to another, in flight from the immigrant ghetto, Jews sought out other Jews. Neighborhoods served as a bulwark against anti-Semitism as well as a barrier to assimilation. Communal agencies also served to counter the "anomie" and insecurity feared by the rabbis, and not only through the social services and defense against anti-Semitism which they provided. Equally important, they enabled Jews to meet each other, to express identity in a nonreligious setting, and to cultivate a self-image of activity and self-reliance rather than of victimization. Given discrimination at home and Nazism overseas, the importance of these functions should not be underestimated.

Jewish associations were of several sorts. Fraternal organizations claimed about 350,000 members in 1940. B'nai Brith had 150,000 members that year, and the Workmen's Circle, despite its roots in Yiddish and socialist movements which had suffered decline, retained 75,000.[32] As Jews entered white-collar professions such as education, social work, pharmacy, and law, they formed professional associations which sponsored meetings, published journals, and fought discrimination.[33] Activity on behalf of Israel was another unifying force, whether through affiliation with one of the Zionist organizations (Hadassah boasted 843 chapters in 1940)[34] or the simple possession of the blue collection box for the Jewish National Fund found in many homes. Local philanthropic agencies maintained about a hundred hospitals and clinics, directed relief efforts overseas, and participated in the upbuilding of Palestine. Three of the most prominent joined in 1938 to coordinate their fund-raising activities in a United Jewish Appeal.[35] Hillel Foundations with trained staff existed on sixty-two college campuses by 1942, while the *Menorah Journal* and the Menorah Association sought to retain the allegiance of Jewish youth through essays and lectures of high quality which stressed the richness of the Jew's cultural heritage.[36]

Synagogues, too, made an active effort to reach the young and the unaffiliated, through their transformation from places of worship into Jewish community centers. Small immigrant synagogues bound together by their members' common origins in a particular European community had given way previously to larger neighborhood institutions with American-educated rabbis. Now, in a further attempt to appeal to the young of the second generation, proponents of the Jewish community center such as Mordecai Kaplan sought to make it the focus of all the community's activities—social, organizational, educational, and recreational, as well as religious. Some centers accomplished the integration of function architecturally, dividing their spacious new buildings into three separate wings devoted to "shul, pool, and school."[37] Others merely sponsored a variety of cultural activities and invited existing organizations to use their facilities. In 1927 there were 47 such centers, with 100,000 members; by 1941 the number had risen to 234 with 435,000 members.[38]

Rabbis, in such a setting, required more than a mastery of English if they were to perform their new roles successfully. Given the achievements or aspirations of their congregants, a college education was essential. Sixty-four percent of the rabbis responding to a survey in 1937 had earned a B.A., 23 percent an M.A., and 12 percent a Ph.D. Their undergraduate fields of concentration tended to be in philosophy, psychology, or sociology, useful given the executive and interpersonal skills required for the chief administrator of a community center.[39] They needed to be good speakers, for it was the sermon in English—especially in newly popular Friday-evening services—that attracted large numbers of congregants less interested in Hebrew prayers and often unable to follow them. Appeal to the young was essential, for the programs of second-generation synagogues and centers were oriented toward retaining the allegiance of the third generation. A good public appearance in the gentile community was equally important, for the rabbi—especially with a variety of Jewish organizations housed under the roof of his center—was the principal Jewish representative to non-

Jewish America. The rabbis were well paid for meeting these demands, reporting a median yearly income of about $3700 in 1937.[40]

When asked in that same survey about likely solutions to the Jews' problems of adjustment, the rabbis placed their faith in education, socialism, and the "emergence of an international spirit" even more than in Zionism or a militant fight against anti-Semitism.[41] In this they articulated the sentiments of their congregants, who had embraced the belief that learning would translate into social mobility for Jews and tolerance on the part of gentiles, and had already "elaborated a form of liberalism as a distinctive American faith."[42] Jews supported candidates who seemed to promote urban welfare, civil rights, and internationalism. The first generation's support for the Bund and for socialist parties had given way to the second's adulation of Franklin Roosevelt, part of a larger synthesis between the values of an urban American middle class and commitments (perceived as Jewish) to social justice, progress, and international order.[43] This political culture was also a bond among Jews, a mark of distinction from the outside world, even as politics provided a means to move up in that world and use acquired power and influence for the protection of Jewish interests.

The communal loyalties thus formed and strengthened were sorely tested by the events of the Nazi era. *Fortune Magazine* undertook an investigation of the "Jews in America" in February 1936 because, in the view of its editors, Jewish apprehensiveness in the face of "Nazi barbarities" had "become one of the important influences in the social life of our time."[44] If a minority lives in fear of persecution, wrote the article's anonymous author, it becomes suspicious, defensive, and aggressive. Americans were troubled when Jewish neighbors took offense where none was intended. "Certain Jews carry their race like an Irishman's fighting shillelegh, while others resent, as though it were a deliberate insult, any reference to their blood, avoiding friends who speak of it, boycotting publications which publish it in print." *Fortune*'s own investigation found anti-Semitism to be declining, though it estimated that as many as half a million people might attend occasional anti-Semitic meetings. Asked if Germany, in the long run, "would be better or worse if it drives out the Jews," 54.6 percent replied "worse," 14 percent "better," and 31.4 percent "Don't know." The magazine cited the last response as "indifference—the most effective prophylactic against hate."[45] In a thorough and sympathetic examination of the Jews' role in American economic life, *Fortune* found few Jews in the leading banks, few in heavy industry or transportation, a large concentration in light industries and distribution, probable Jewish domination of the printing industry in New York, Philadelphia, and Chicago, and power approaching monopoly in television and the movie industry. "Half the opinion-making and taste-influencing paraphernalia in America is in Jewish hands."[46]

The Jews' undeniable economic concentration, *Fortune* concluded, like their position as scapegoat, could be traced to clannishness. For centuries Jews had refused to accept the cultures of their host countries and were unable to accept American culture, despite their will to do so, because the "habit of pride and stubbornness of their ancestors is too strong in them."[47] Here, where the article touches the issues of exclusivity and election most directly, the ambivalence evident throughout receives clear articulation. The same point is made, in virtually the same terms, by two authors writing in *The Jew in the Gentile World* in 1941. Chosenness, writes one, is seen by gentiles as an "expression of arrogance and contempt for other peoples."[48] The second, sociologist Talcott Parsons, asserts that Jewish claims to a special destiny, combined with the humiliations of Jewish existence, had created an ambivalent combination of humility and pride which "in extreme cases resulted in arrogance." The chosen people idea was a special source of friction, Parsons argued, because gentiles usually resented the arrogance of its claim that a group "who are in a sense 'guests' in their country" should claim a higher status than the host.[49]

The issue, then, whether for *Fortune* or Parsons, was the legitimacy of continued Jewish separation, symbolized for those who challenged it (covertly, to be sure, in the guise of examining anti-Semitism) by the doctrine of the chosen people. The rabbis of the period, seeking to define a place for the Jews in America, could not but confront the matter of chosenness at the very outset, for gentile opinion—no less than Jewish tradition—made the issue unavoidable. If the problems facing Jews promoted their cleaving to one another, outsiders would denounce them all the more for clannishness, and attribute that separatism to the idea of election. Thus, chosenness once more assumed its traditional roles: a principal element of Jewish self-definition, a guarantor of self-respect, and a focus of gentile attack.

One grasps the rabbis' dilemma still more forcefully if one examines the most important polemic with a Christian adversary in which they engaged in this period.[50] *The Christian Century*, principal organ of liberal Protestantism, was favorably regarded by Jews in the mid-1930's, because the weekly featured regular criticism of Hitler and of anti-Semitism in America.[51] However, Jewish "nationalists" were also favorite targets, linked by the magazine with the Jews who had crucified Jesus and even with the sin (chauvinism) of Hitler himself.[52] In this light the series of editorials which occasioned Jewish outrage in 1936–37 becomes, in retrospect, more comprehensible. The magazine was consistently intolerant of any group believed to threaten the cultural integrity which it held essential to the survival of American democracy.

Jews posed such a threat, in its view, when like the Reconstructionists they insisted that Jewish religion was "bound up indissolubly with its historical culture," thus defining Judaism in ethnic rather than religious terms.[53] A year later this critique of Mordecai Kaplan and his movement was expanded into a full-scale analysis of "the Jewish problem." "In the broad area of social intercourse which lies outside the domain of government," the Jew is treated not as a person but as a member of a particular race, and thereby denied full participation in the democratic process. This "Jewish problem" was at bottom the work of Jews themselves, specifically of their making "racial integrity" (the words were "used broadly in a non-technical sense") the "permanent basis of a distinctive culture." The fact that Jews were a hereditary group, and not only a religious one, was the basic cause of their problems with the gentile world, for it led Jews to "entertain no aspiration to universalize" their culture or their cult. The real question at the bottom of Jewish-gentile relations, then, embarrassing to both sides and therefore rarely stated, was this: "can democracy suffer a hereditary minority to perpetuate itself as a permanent minority, with its own distinctive culture sanctioned by its own distinctive cult form?"[54]

The question was of course rhetorical. While Christians were obliged to tolerate religious differences until the Judgment Day, Jews had no right to remove their faith from the normal influences of the democratic process by "insulating it behind the walls of a racial and cultural solidarity," and Christians could not guarantee their "Jewish brethren" that the prejudice "generated by their long resistance to the democratic process" would not result in an outcome damaging to the Jews, Christians, and democracy. Judaism, in refusing to yield to the essential process of democracy—the free interchange of values which leads in the long run to "new values and the higher integration of social relationships"—was bringing the Jewish problem on itself. The "root cause" of its refusal was

> the Jew's immemorial and pertinacious obsession with an illusion, the illusion that his race, his people, are the object of the special favor of God, who requires the maintenance of this racial integrity and separateness as the medium through which, sooner or later, will be performed some mighty act involving human destiny . . . what concerns us is the attitude which this obsession induces in the Jewish community, and the inevitable human reaction on the part of any general community to this attitude.

The Jews had to realize that their "martyrdom is in large measure self-invited," and that their "idea of an integral race . . . is itself the prototype of Nazism."[55] The magazine concluded, in a third editorial a month later, that

> the only religion compatible with democracy is one which conceives itself as universal, and offers itself to all men of all races and cultures. The Jewish

religion, or any other religion, is an alien element in American democracy unless it proclaims itself as a universal faith, and proceeds upon such a conviction to persuade us all to be Jews.[56]

The issue could not have been stated more clearly. A Jewish ethnic identity was illegitimate in democratic America; in clinging to the illusion of chosenness which demanded such an identity, Jews brought their sufferings upon themselves. The Jewish responses to the series of editorials were unusually vigorous, and extraordinarily revealing. While Hayim Greenberg, the editor of the *Jewish Frontier*,[57] Edward Israel, the leading figure in the CCAR's Commission of Social Justice,[58] and Philip Bernstein, another prominent reform rabbi,[59] all attacked the magazine unconditionally, two other parties to the debate did not entirely deny the *Christian Century*'s claims. In the sole response printed by the magazine, Rabbi Morris Lazaron, an anti-Zionist adherent of classical (Kohlerian) Reform, reasoned that Christianity, as a minority amongst the majority of unchurched Americans, submitted to the workings of American democracy no more and no less than did Judaism. He cited the Jewish customs and practices unique to America (and so a result of Jewish participation in the democratic process), and noted that Jews asked only those rights guaranteed by the Constitution, taking their chances, along with all other Americans, "in the give and take of American life." Lazaron accused the magazine of confusing the democratic process with American chauvinism, and then joined it in criticizing "secular Jewish nationalism"—a swipe at Kaplan and the Zionists—in the diaspora. Finally, he argued, the Jewish belief in God's special favor was no different from the Christian assumption of salvation through Jesus. Besides, Jews claimed no special favor. The phrase "God's chosen people" could not occur to Jews, having been denounced by Israel's prophets long ago.[60] In sum then, Lazaron condoned and even joined in the attack on a Jewish ethnic identity, restricting legitimate Jewish activity to the sphere of religion. He met the magazine's attack on chosenness with a dubious defense—its similarity to salvation through Christ.

Mordecai Kaplan, the founder of Reconstructionism, offered precisely the opposite response. The Christian critique of Reconstructionism, he wrote, was motivated by the traditional Christian hope that at some future time Jews could be completely absorbed by Christianity, a hope frustrated by the Reconstructionist denial that any religion possessed the truth "with a capital T." Reform and Orthodoxy could be tolerated, because they assented to that proposition, differing from Christians only on the question of who possessed the Truth. Rules of tolerance did not apply to Reconstructionists who refused to join the contest altogether, for example by Kaplan's frequently voiced repudiation of the doctrine of chosenness. Moreover, *The Christian Century* had reserved for itself the right to define the sort of religion to which the guarantees of the Constitution applied, thereby threatening not only "us, the religious culturists" but all adherents of secular Jewish culture.[61] Until men rejected the idea that there was only one path to salvation, he continued in a second article, and realized that different social groups develop "different instrumentalities for the achievement of this salvation," genuine tolerance was impossible. Precisely such a conception of religion was offered by Reconstructionism—but not by the branches of Judaism which held to the chosen people idea.[62] Kaplan thus turned *The Christian Century*'s objection to the doctrine back upon itself, using the occasion to undermine the Jewish positions which in his view had left Jews vulnerable to attack in the first place.

The magazine's thrust, then, had not missed the mark. It had uncovered the conflicts and weaknesses in the Jewish community's ill-defined position, thereby highlighting the need for a Jewish self-understanding compatible with and explicable to America. It had, furthermore, revealed the Jews' special vulnerability at precisely the theological node which had been the focus of disputation for centuries—Israel's chosenness. Apparently without his being aware of it, the magazine's editor had rehearsed in minute detail the traditional attacks on Jewish particularity which the rabbis of the early Christian era had confronted, and which Jews had faced repeatedly ever since. Only the idiom of the attack was new: where once the Jewish offense was couched in terms of "hatred for humanity," Jews now stood indicted for their refusal to join in the workings of American democracy. Particularism remained illegitimate. A religion, competing in the free marketplace of ideas, was acceptable; an ethnic group, perpetuated by blood and "clannishness," was not.

Such accusations, in a prestigious Christian journal held by the rabbis to be representative of many Christians, if not more liberal than most, explain the direction of the rabbis' efforts to demonstrate that Judaism was "democratic" and that chosenness was no bar to integration. Anti-Semititism in America, Nazism in Europe, potential charges of dual loyalty upon the creation of the State of Israel, and fears aroused by McCarthyism all lent added urgency to the task. At issue was the legitimacy of Jewish persistence in a separate identity—a problem symbolized in America, as throughout Jewish history, by the idea of chosenness.

At Home in the "New Zion" of America

The rabbis' primary strategy was to argue the compatibility of Judaism with democracy. Hymns to the ideals of America, and claims that the nation's political system was based upon the Hebrew Bible, were pervasive in the second generation. They were common to all four "denominations" of American Judaism, and cut across very significant differences in the interpretation of the idea of chosenness. The rabbis invoked the principal tropes of American rhetoric to argue the identity of American ideals with their own.

Leo Jung, the prominent Orthodox rabbi of the Jewish Center in New York, declaimed in a 1939 sermon entitled "Sinai and Washington" that just as Israel had once failed in its divine task by worshipping Baal, so Europe, meant to be an inspiration to the world, had now forgotten its appointed role.

> And the Father of man bethought himself, and sent men to look for the country of their dream where the song of the Lord might be sung in freedom, men with the courage of their vision and the endurance defying dark danger . . .[63]

Both the rhetoric itself and the theme appropriate what one critic has termed the central American myth. America was humanity reborn, a new Adam, in Jung's words mankind's "second chance." It was a nation with a mission, and should it live up to its calling and achieve economic and political democracy, Washington would be revealed as the echo of Sinai. The "voice of religion" rather than mere political ideals had been the crucial determinant in shaping America. Jung then described the vital principle of democracy as cultural and religious pluralism[64]—a notion which, as we have seen, the nation at large had not yet accepted. He later asserted that the fundamental tenets of democracy were based on the teaching of Torah.[65] Jewish observance (Orthodox, in this case) was precisely the contribution of American Israel to the American continent.[66]

That message was repeated in many other sermons by Jung[67] and, in the post-war years, by the president of Yeshiva University, Samuel Belkin. The greatness of American democracy, he wrote, lay in its belief that each individual and group could "contribute to the great American democratic symphony, in which every nationality is permitted—nay encouraged—to play its own intellectual instrument." Belkin, too, voiced the ideology of pluralism in its own favorite metaphor (coined by Horace Kallen) of the "orchestra." The special role for the Jewish "instrument" was the synthesis of Hebrew moral and spiritual values with the culture of the West. Because the American concept of democracy was deeply rooted in the "religious and spiritual democracy of historic Judaism," a call to renewed loyalty to the Declaration of Independence only echoed the "louder call for loyalty" to the fundamental principles of the Torah.[68] In another essay Belkin defended the idea which ordained

Jewish distinctiveness—chosenness—against those who opposed it.[69] His deft combination of reassurance to Jews and apologetic to gentiles is typical of the many essays and sermons on this theme throughout the second generation.[70]

Reform rhetoric was even more sweeping. In his full-length study of *The Democratic Impulse in Jewish History* (1928), Abba Hillel Silver, one of the most prominent rabbis of his generation, cited as proof of that "impulse" the distrust of royalty in ancient Israel, the exilic government by priests and assemblies, the system of ritual and prayer which rendered religious functionaries superfluous, and universal popular education. At the heart of Israel's commitment to democracy was a tremendous dogma, "an astounding ideological fixation, if you will, a spiritual 'fiction' of marvelous potency woven by the racial psyche and forever after inseparable from the life and thought processes of the people"—namely, that God had made an eternal convenant with the whole house of Israel, designating them His servant and emissary. Thus, Israel's mission—"the essential tradition of Judaism" and Reform's traditional variation on the doctrine of election—is here said to ensure the Jewish commitment to democracy, rather than to preclude it, as critics had charged.[71]

At a conference on "Judaism and American Democracy" held at Hebrew Union College in October 1945, the historian Jacob Rader Marcus criticized the "delusion" that democracy had always characterized Jewish political thinking in the past, but identified it all the more strongly with Reform Judaism. The French Revolution, he said, had first made it possible for the Jew to be a liberal. Isaac Mayer Wise himself had failed to realize that American democracy was more an ideal than a reality; the task of the American Jew was to bring America more in line with the American ideal, by expounding the truth that all men were created in the image of God. The Jewish commitment to democracy was founded in the fatherhood of God, America's in a "historico-philosophic concept of natural rights." Was he proposing "still another mission for God's Chosen People? Certainly: every people must have a mission if it is to live with dignity and self-respect."[72] Jewish chosenness was not merely compatible with American democracy, then, but essential to its realization.

His position received further articulation several years later in a speech before the CCAR by Nelson Glueck, soon to succeed Julian Morgenstern as president of HUC.

> Here in the New Jerusalem of America planned as a spiritual Zion by its founding fathers and brought into being by revolutionary patriots imbued with the God-inspired liberalism of the prophets of Israel, the concept of

this country as a citadel of social justice and warm-hearted humanitarianism was a natural one.[73]

Interreligious apologetic, in this address, has given way completely to intra-Jewish debate. Precisely because of the identity between Judaism and democracy, between the American and the Jewish missions, it was imperative to distinguish

> Reform from other less progressive Jewish movements. The intimate connection of our interpretation of Judaism with the meaning and goals of America, and the propriety of the association of the name of our country with the title and testament of our faith, lie in the atmosphere and attitude of the entire modern movement of Enlightenment and Liberalism and Rationalism, which are native to the development of each and mandatory to the mission of both. Out of this movement, which bears the imprint of the Hebraic spirit, the design of America evolved and the inspiration and purpose of Reform Judaism emerged. . . . The manifest appointment with destiny of American moral idealism and American Reform Judaism lies in their seeking the increase of human rights through the rationalism of the Enlightenment and the freedom of liberalism, through the laws and love of God.[74]

The factors provoking Glueck's address, we learn from the convention proceedings, were the threat posed by McCarthyism and calls by some within the Jewish community for the unity of its several branches.[75] Thus the identification of Judaism with democracy—so long as it was Reform Judaism. Glueck's out-and-out equation of the "Hebraic spirit" with the "meaning and goals of America" is striking, even given the rhetorical heights to which all such speeches tended. Rabbis who tended to scale those heights in the Reform movement were those who adhered to Kohlerian Reform rather than those who supported the movement's 1937 Columbus Platform (discussed below), with its advocacy of Zionism and its definition of the Jews as a people rather than a religion.[76]

Conservative Judaism's leadership, if more restrained, were likewise enthusiastic exponents of the "Judaism and Democracy" theme. Louis Finkelstein dedicated much of his time during the Second World War to the organization of a series of conferences on "Science, Philosophy, and Religion in their Relation to the Democratic Way of Life."[77] He also endeavored in his work on *The Pharisees* (1936) to show the identity between Pharisaic teachings and the Puritan ideas which were the basis of American democracy, and frequently adverted to this theme in his writings.[78] Simon Greenberg, in one of several discussions of the subject, wrote in 1945 that since the Bible's influence on American democracy was so well known, he would instead discuss "Democracy in Post-

Biblical Judaism." He focused on the central concept of God's justice, which "has prevented the Biblical concept of Israel as an *'Am Segulah,'* a 'treasured people,' from deteriorating into a blatant and destructive chauvinism."[79] Robert Gordis, the preeminent spokesman for the Conservative mainstream, repeated the theme on many occasions, reaffirming that the Bible was the "cement" of American democracy.[80] In 1963 he added that to say this was to ignore the full complexity of the Bible as well as the varied influences which had shaped the "American ideal"[81]—qualifications not voiced earlier.[82]

In fact, one seeks in vain through the entire record of the second generation for demurs by a member of any movement to the sort of statements rehearsed above. The editors of *The Reconstructionist* finally published such a rejoinder, entitled "Judaism and Democracy: 'Any Resemblance is Purely Coincidental'," only in 1956.[83] In the meantime Kaplan's own advocacy of the benefits of living in two civilizations—American and Jewish—only strengthened the impression of this "resemblance," as did his promotion of an American civil religion.[84]

Two related motifs strengthened the bond between Judaism and America as well. The first was the consistent denial by all but the Orthodox that the concept of *galut* (exile) had any relevance to the position of American Jewry.[85] On this matter Morgenstern, more moderate Reformers, Gordis, and Kaplan were all agreed.[86] The second motif was the purported existence of a "Judeo-Christian heritage."[87] That Judaism was identical to Christianity could not be maintained by the rabbis—for what then became of Jewish distinctiveness? However, they could and did argue that the two faiths were "fundamentally" alike. Finkelstein asserted that the Judeo-Christian tradition, "properly understood," was a single system of thought of which Judaism was the core and Christianity the periphery.[88] Similarly, Morgenstern claimed that the two faiths were "so intimate and insoluble" *(sic)* as to be basically one. Were the United States truly Christian, it would be truly Jewish as well.[89] When the wartime stimulus to such talk of a joint heritage disappeared, challenges to the idea multiplied.[90] The claim that American Jews were not in exile, however, remained virtually unchallenged until well into the third generation.

Two factors, we might summarize, impelled the rabbinic chorus of hymns to Judaic democracy. On the one hand, anti-Semitism and resultant Jewish insecurity made apologetic imperative, although in responding with the invocation of cultural pluralism the rabbis appealed to an ideology that most Americans, and certainly anti-Semites, did not accept. There was another reason, however, for the identification of Judaism with American values. The rabbis believed it. For all the discrimination and anti-Semitism, American rabbis and, *mutatis mutandis,* their congregants were at home in a gentile nation to a degree unknown to most of their parents, a fact certainly highlighted by the fate of European Jewry. For this they were grateful to America—"in love," as one leader of the Reform movement put it. For that very reason, the rabbis had good reason to fear that their congregants would come to feel too much at home. Once one was an American, why did one need to be a Jew, if the values of the two cultures were identical?

It was to this set of problems that the identification of Jewish with American values offered an apparent solution. It assured Jews that they were at home, that their affection for America was not misplaced. For their Bible was the basis of American democracy, and their dream of human fulfillment was also America's. The rabbis thus countered charges of disloyalty brought by anti-Semites, and reassured Jews that America was different, that "it could not happen here." Paradoxically, the identification of Judaism with America rendered the abandonment of Judaism—the rabbis' chief concern, then as now—unnecessary, even if it also made such "apostasy" more reasonable. The rabbis were arguing, in effect, that one did not need to seek outside one's Jewish identity for what was easily obtainable within it. By being a better Jew, one became a better American as well, and to be a better American was what the children of the immigrants most wanted. The rabbis expected their congregants to choose both Judaism and America; the danger that they would opt only for the latter was apparently a risk which it seemed worthwhile to take. The problem, as they saw correctly, lay elsewhere: in the definition of a Jewish role in America with which to navigate the difficult course they had charted between separatism and disappearance.

"Nation, People, Religion—What Are We?"

These dilemmas surfaced first within the Reform movement, in several addresses delivered in the mid-twenties before the Central Conference of American Rabbis (CCAR) and the corresponding lay organization, the Union of American Hebrew Congregations (UAHC). Rabbi Felix Levy (1884–1963), for many years perhaps the finest theological mind in the Reform movement, warned in a speech on "The Uniqueness of Israel" in 1923 that the Jews of his day were increasingly "lured by the charm of the world around us." Rabbis preached a "colorless universalistic liberalism" or a "Christless Christianity," and laymen, taking them literally, left the synagogue. Preoccupied with secular considerations, the Reform movement nevertheless flaunted its mission before others and itself. While that mission did exist,

> where are its apostles. . . . We cannot help ask ourselves if missionaries can flourish in the soil that produces department-store and factory owners, corporation lawyers, labor leaders, itinerant professional propagandists and high-salaried rabbis?

The belief in God "as one and not triune" was not enough to mark Jews as essentially different, and Reform's claim to be an "American" Judaism was perhaps meaningless: could there be a New York or an Illinois Judaism as well?[91]

At a UAHC conference on "The Perpetuation of Judaism" four years later, one of the most prominent members of the Reform laity, Judge Henry Morgenthau, demonstrated that Levy's fears were far from groundless. Taking Reform's universalism one step further, Morgenthau declared that Israel's election meant only that it had been the first to receive the divine message now available to all. Now that modern thought and science, new "revelations of the divine will," had made all claims to exclusive truth patently false, the "rivalry of creeds" should end.[92] Levy's concern that precisely that inference could be drawn from Reform's universalism was echoed at a second UAHC conference in 1929. There Rabbi Louis Witt argued, in a tone very different from any yet heard in Reform's official councils, that Judaism was the religion of a minority, one of the most "ancient, conspicuous, persistent, and particularistic minorities in all history"—and "a minority lives by virtue of its differences." The modern world was unfavorable to such distinctiveness, and America particularly

> by its very pleasantness and friendliness lures us away from our ancient loyalties. Its secularism is so delightful, its mutuality so penetrative, its universalism so enticing, that by a sort of sheer spiritual osmosis it incorporates us into itself and makes us look and become more and more like itself.

Jews had to resist, by seeing their history as consecrated and by attesting to the world the "lofty serviceableness" and "unique indestructibleness" of Judaism.[93]

Julian Morgenstern, a student of Kohler who succeeded him as president of HUC in 1921, rose to respond to Witt in terms which Kohler himself would have used. Jews were Jews by virtue of their religion and only their religion; that religion was universal. But Morgenstern realized that a change was underway inside his movement. It had, in his words, "put itself on the defensive" and begun to offer compromise, just when Conservatism and Orthodoxy were moving in its direction.[94] The shift to which he referred became the policy of the Reform movement in 1937, with the adoption by the CCAR, under Levy's direction, of the new set of "Guiding Principles of Reform Judaism" which became known as the Columbus Platform. Rather than accepting Morgenstern's definition of Judaism as a religion and only a religion, the Platform termed Judaism "the historical religious experience of the Jewish people." "We recognize in the group-loyalty of Jews who have become estranged from our religious tradition," it continued, "a bond which still unites them with us," though "we maintain that it is by its religion and for its religion that the Jewish people has lived." Most significant of all was the legitimacy granted to Zionism:

> In the rehabilitation of Palestine, the land hallowed by memories and hopes, we behold the promise of renewed life for many of our brethren. We affirm the obligation of all Jewry to aid in its upbuilding as a Jewish homeland by endeavoring to make it not only a haven of refuge for the oppressed but also a center of Jewish culture and spiritual life.[95]

Morgenstern, however, would have none of this. Throughout the Second World War he resisted the accommodation to Zionism, insisting at an address at HUC in 1943 entitled "Nation, People, Religion—What are We?" that "the true genius and destiny of Israel find expression only in its role as a religious people, the bearers of a spiritual heritage"—not as advocates of another petty nationalism.[96] As late as 1946 he declared that American Jews' unfounded fear of anti-Semitism, which amounted "almost to an obsession," showed only how ill at ease the segment of the community composed of immigrants still was. That group accounted for the over-emphasis on "survival" as the goal of Jewish existence in America, with its "corollary"—the retention (as "Jewishness") of "almost everything, good, indifferent, and bad which grew out of Jewish life in other lands." Such programs fostered separation, mistrust of the American environment, and the suspicion that American civilization would destroy Jewish values.[97] Here Morgenstern linked his paean to democracy with the particular definition of the Jewish role which he made it serve. Israel should define itself as a religion, and only that, and realize that only in America could its "eternal destiny" as a religion be fulfilled, its "god-inspired task," assumed consciously and wholeheartedly.

The "segment" of the Jewish population criticized by Morgenstern, that of Eastern European immigrants and their children, now comprised the majority of the movement's membership and perhaps of its rabbis. Reform's leadership was split on the matter as well. The conflict found expression in a debate in 1939, sparked by the remarks of Samuel Goldenson, a staunch adherent of the Morgenstern position and rabbi of the prestigious Temple Emanu-El in New York. Goldenson argued his position in terms of its exclusive compatibility with American democracy.

> If we insist, as I believe we should, upon the moral basis and universal validity of democracy, we should at the same time emphasize less and less the particularisms in our Jewish heritage, those particularisms that separate us from others, and stress the universal concepts and outlooks more and more.

Jews should stress the spiritual content of their thinking rather than the ethnic element of their background.[98]

Goldenson's colleagues were critical. "I believe that at the present juncture in Jewish history, when we are being accused by our detractors of being an exclusive and particularistic group, we ought to be on our guard against repeating the accusation ourselves," said one rabbi. Given that Jews had been found worthy to be the instrument of God, commented another, was it wrong to be conscious of and joyful in that distinction? A third reminded the assembly that universalism could not exist without particularism. Jews, like all men, were members of a group, not of society in the abstract. Samuel Schulman, a principal figure in the Morgenstern wing, responded with the assertion that the essence of the Jewish group lay "in a sublime self-forgetfulness," giving its teachings to the world and letting them speak for themselves, not in thinking of Jews as an "ethnos."[99]

American Jewry, however, seemed increasingly to take its status as an "ethnos" for granted. Eastern European Jews had brought to America, and expanded here, a legacy of secular culture (both Yiddish and Hebrew) and political activity (whether in the Bund, other Jewish socialist movements, or Zionism) that led them to see any exclusively religious definition of Judaism as irrelevant if not obsolete. The rabbis who emerged from their midst argued successfully that the conception of Jews as a people rather than a religious congregation should prevail, even if America still seemed unprepared for any but a religious definition of Judaism, and although the rabbis themselves had an obvious stake in the primacy of religion within Jewish life. Reform rabbis, like their Conservative colleagues, would soon acquiesce in a compromise definition developed in response to Kaplan's ideology of Judaism as a "civilization." That conception, in turn, was dependent on a theory of cultural pluralism which sought to legitimate ethnic Jewish identity in the face of the models of acculturation then regnant.

The principal theorist and chief exponent of cultural pluralism, both in the Jewish community and in America, was the philosopher Horace Meyer Kallen (1882–1974), who also merits attention here because of the unique rationale for Jewish distinctiveness which he proposed.[100] Born in Silesia of religious parents, Kallen lost his faith in adolescence to a combination of Spinoza and America, and regained it, he later confessed, only when Barrett Wendell at Harvard showed him the Judaic roots of the "American Idea." From William James, Kallen acquired the pragmatic approach on which his theory of social pluralism would be based: not the rigorous formulation which one finds in James's own work, but rather an orientation—a "preoccupation," in Kallen's words— with plurality, freedom, and functioning will.[101] Truth, for Kallen, was less the congruence between statement and object or fact (the "mean-ing" and the "meant" in his terminology) than a belief about the nature of things which is born of experience and validated by its consequences. Truth was the trustworthiness of an idea, its reliability when used.[102] Probes of the precise degree of relativism implied by such a conception were for Kallen beside the point. The only thing that mattered was the result which came of "betting one's life" on this belief or that: say, on cultural pluralism. For Kallen all philosophy was "ideology," an "instru-ment of adjustment," an "organ in the struggle to survive." Its goal was to wring a measure of satisfaction from life in an indifferent universe.[103] This "Jobian" determination to maintain the integrity of one's ways before an indifferent God, even unto death, was invoked so persistently in Kallen's work that one can only call it his life's credo.[104]

No one truth, then, could claim to be the exclusive truth, nor could any one group claim monopoly of the proper way to live. Humanity benefited when all learned from a flourishing variety of cultures and commitments, a possibility never before as achievable, in Kallen's view, as it was in twentieth century America.[105] In 1915 Kallen published a landmark essay in *The Nation* entitled "Democracy Versus the Melting Pot," and in 1924 a collection entitled *Culture and Democracy in the United States*, in which he first articulated his life-long challenge to the ideologies of acculturation known as "the melting pot" and the "genteel tradition." He called, instead, for the "orchestration" of the various ethnic groups in a harmony which would enable each to attain the cultural perfection "proper to its kind." America would thus move along the road of *e pluribus unum* marked out by its founding fathers.[106] In a volume published in 1954, after dozens of articles and addresses, little had changed. The charge by several respondents that Kallen had failed to explain how competing cultures could coexist and yet remain vital, or why diversity for its own sake was a good to be cherished, did not meet with any answer.[107]

In 1949 Kallen termed his pluralist American Idea the "democratic faith" and the "American religion,"[108] and in 1954 he argued, in a work entitled *Secularism is the Will of God*, that secularism—the recognition by all religions of the right of each to exist—was itself a religion "whenever a person, a church or any other society bets its survival and growth on this relationship with the divine." Faith, we recall, was not so much a "what" for Kallen as a "how." Since God, however defined, "signalizes a vision of hope whose substance is faith, an unseen Beyond, whose evidence is this vision," secularism would have to be the will of such a God, since it alone could preserve the faiths of all. Jefferson had noted that he who chooses a God for himself must allow the same free choice to others, thereby surrendering any claim to exclusive election and admitting the parity of all creeds. In this American religion God "would be a One-of-All and an All-as-One . . . an associative unity . . . a union intended and hoped for, whose godhood is in truth Deus Absconditus precisely because One, and one as mankind's ineluctable diversity of fluid, alternating faiths, working towards a free consensus."[109] In the total Kallen oeuvre this theme of "democracy as religion" plays only a minor role, while the call for a pluralism of ethnic groups is paramount.

The reference to Jefferson explains the virulent and persistent attacks on the ideas of mission and chosenness found throughout Kallen's earlier writings. Kallen believed that his own philosophy of "Hebraism" had been expressed most profoundly in the Book of Job, which in his eyes stressed the flux of life rather than its permanence, and recognized the "monstrous injustice" of the "cosmic elan." God, the dynamic life of all nature, was Himself a pluralist: He had no bias in favor of one way of living or another, and was "just" only because He regarded individuals with utter indifference "or, if you prefer, with equal care."[110] There was, clearly, no room for a doctrine of election in such a system, nor for a Judaism based on a relationship to or revelation from a God having the attributes of personhood. Hebraism consisted rather in the corporate life and ideas of the Jewish people. "What current rabbinism calls Jewish philosophy is not Jewish philosophy at all,"[111] and the purported mission of Judaism was but "the most insidious of all pretenses, that of altruism . . . the lupine nature under the wool."[112] Kallen repeatedly attributed the doctrine's importance throughout history, and its continued appeal, to the feeling of superiority which it gave Jews, especially necessary in a Christian world which had forced Israel into "a status of inferiority." Thus, in *Zionism and World Politics* (1921), Kallen wrote that "there are two types of prejudices about the Jews—those entertained by Jews and those entertained by non-Jews." The latter was anti-Semitism, and the former—chosenness—was a product of the Jews' need for psychological defense against their hardships in a Christian world.[113]

Kallen's Zionism, which he later termed "eager and intolerant,"[114] was as idiosyncratic as his Judaism, stemming as much from his commitment to the American Idea as from the predicament of world Jewry or the concerns underlying the principal Zionist ideologies. His vision, although it persuaded Louis Brandeis to join the movement and thus indirectly allowed millions of other Americans to do so as well, never found acceptance by the European mainstream. When European Zionists asserted control over the American branch of the movement soon after, both Kallen and Brandeis withdrew from its leadership.[115] Concomitantly, what Kallen called his "somewhat callow and hard realism" dissolved by the early thirties into a new sympathy for religion in general, and fresh attention to the problems of American Jewry in particular.[116] Kallen now asked in numerous papers and addresses delivered before Jewish educators, students, and community groups what "tune" the Jewish instrument could play within the great American orchestra. What, in other words, was the specific "habit-form" or "thought-form" which made something Jewish, and how could one motivate individual Jews to join in the preservation of their group life?[117]

Renouncing the advocacy of difference for its own sake, Kallen now stressed the contribution of each particular group to the larger whole.[118] Yet two obstacles stood in the way of identifying what the Jewish contribution might be. First, Kallen was an avowed secularist; second, anti-Semitism had in his view rendered the Jewish situation abnormal, thereby precluding any teaching that the Jews were only "a people among other peoples, no worse, no better, only different."[119] More was needed: "a core of inherited Jewishness" had to be discovered which would possess the capacity to grow and to include external activities, thereby rendered Jewish "in the sense that your dinner is made into you." Kallen lauded the Jewish "kitchen tradition" of dietary laws, and Kaplan's attempts to preserve them as a safeguard of Jewish identity.[120] He urged a cultivation of Jewish "knowledge, attitudes, and sense of history," of cultural habits ranging from the "specialties of the kitchen to the singularities of song and speech, of religious holiday and secular festival."[121] The values of this "Jewish spirit" would be vindicated in the interplay of cultures which it would enrich.[122]

The rationale for Jewish survival that Kallen offered, as we may piece it together from his writings, was threefold. First, Hebraism had made and would continue to make great contributions to civilization. The Jew aware (and thus proud) of the Jewish past would be motivated to remain within the fold and would be fortified against anti-Semitism.[123] Second, the "peculiarly American task of Jewish education" was the nourishing of the American pluralistic union, through the "liberation" of the powers of the Jews to contribute freely to it.[124] Kallen evidently felt that others would be moved as he had been[125] to retain their Jewish identity by realizing the service which Judaism had rendered and would render to America. The Jewish-American culture would make its contribution to the pluralistic whole. Third (and I suspect most important) was Kallen's credo: the determination to hold fast to one's integrity no matter what the price. A Jew, especially when life was difficult, could not surrender his or her Jewishness without the sacrifice of integrity. All three arguments, it should be noted, were common currency in all non-Orthodox American Judaism.

If such arguments found little sympathy among the rabbis, then, it was not because Kallen's rationale was so radical, as that it failed to take seriously what the rabbis, being rabbis, naturally regarded as most important: religion and God. One wonders, though, whether Kallen had given even secularists enough of a melody to play in the orchestra, or whether the Jewish instrument would not rather be drowned out, or rendered superfluous, if limited to such a banal and incoherent tune. Perhaps Kallen, in advocating a Judaism devoid of any real distinctiveness, was merely providing what he believed the Jews—and America—were prepared to accept. As it happened, his ideology of pluralism was accepted by Jews, as one critic has written, only when it proved "innocuous enough to become a general American, not merely American Jewish piety."[126] In the meantime, certain of its elements—including the emphasis on "Jewishness" and pluralism, and the related outright rejection of election—had come to be pillars of Reconstructionism, which chose to reinterpret the religious identity rather than to reject it. In that way Kallen came to influence the path taken by American Judaism as a whole.[127]

Mordecai Kaplan's program of Reconstruction, first set forth in a series of articles in the teens and twenties, was expounded at length in *Judaism as a Civilization*(1934), both his own most important work and the single most influential Jewish book of the generation. After analyzing the incompatibility of traditional Judaism with the modern state, economy, and science, and demonstrating the inadequacy of Orthodoxy, Reform, and the Conservative mainstream in resolving the resultant crisis of contemporary Jewry, Kaplan proposed a new understanding of Judaism. Rather than seeing Judaism as a religion, Jews should understand it as a civilization, comprised of "a history, literature, language, social organization, folk sanctions, standards of conduct, social and spiritual ideals, [and] esthetic values." The Jewish civilization, like that of any other people, was a creation of the people; being a human product and not divine, it naturally evolved over time in response to the people's changed historical situation and cultural environment.[128]

The American Jew, in Kaplan's estimation, moved in two civilizations,[129] and a way had to be found to ensure that the values of the two—which Kaplan tended to call their respective "religions"—did not conflict.

> Judaism, to evoke American Jews' loyalty, must be not only compatible with their loyalty to America but also corroborative of it. . . . America looks to the religious cultures which its various historic groups have brought with them, to give the individual citizen the moral stamina and sense of responsibility which are indispensable to national survival and health.[130]

Judaism, as in Kallen's thought and that of Reform, would be in service to America, yet with a significant difference. As opposed to Reform, Kaplan defined the Jewish group in ethnic terms, calling for the complete reconstruction of Judaism as a civilization in accord with his platform, and for the reorganization of American Jewry in local communities *(kehillot)* providing a range of services rather than in individual synagogue congregations. As opposed to Kallen, Kaplan accorded primacy to "religion" as he understood it, especially after colleagues in the rabbinate attacked him for failing to make that emphasis explicit. Like Kallen, however, Kaplan found "supernaturalist" elements in Jewish belief untenable as well as unsuited to pluralist America, none being so objectionable as chosenness. How, he asked repeatedly, could modern Jews possibly believe that God had actually descended to earth in order to "bear them on eagles' wings" to a covenant ceremony at Mount Sinai that singled them out for special blessing? Equally important, how could they hope for acceptance by America if they persisted in proclaiming a doctrine which, to Kaplan, so clearly connoted Jewish superiority over all other peoples? His persistent attacks on the idea are in no small measure responsible for making it the principal issue of theological dispute in the second generation.[131]

Kaplan failed to persuade his colleagues that election should be replaced by the more modest notion of "vocation." Nor did he win acceptance for his proposals to reorganize the Jewish community in *kehillot* and to promote an American civil religion in which Jews along with all other groups would join.[132] The former plan distinguished the Jews from America too sharply, while the latter identified Judaism with America too closely. Kaplan's positions on Jewish law, God, and of course chosenness only served to alienate rabbis of various persuasions even further. The Reconstructionists therefore failed to achieve major changes inside the other movements, and did not move to establish competing institutions until the 1960s.[133]

However, one need only recall Robert Gordis's authoritative definition of Conservative Judaism in 1945 as "the evolving religious civilization of the Jewish people,"[134] or the new Reform definition of Judaism in 1937 as "the historical religious experience of the Jewish people,"[135] to see the Reconstructionists' influence. Their position that Judaism included more than religion became the dominant one, even if other rabbis still insisted that the status of American Jewry was religious and not ethnic, and continued to employ the idea of chosenness (which the Reconstructionists, as we will see in chapter 4, took pains to renounce) as a principal prop of their self-explanation.

The result—which we must judge a success in winning the acceptance both of Jews and gentiles—was a Jewish group life officially centered in, and identified to the "outside" as, religion. Jews would find their place in the new "triple American melting pot" of Protestant, Catholic and Jew, even if they saw themselves, and were seen by others, as an ethnic group comparable to Greeks and Italians and blacks.[136] Reform rabbis, it is true, continued to place more emphasis on what they termed "religion," while avowed Reconstructionists emphasized what they insisted was a "civilization." Solomon Freehof, a leader of the Reform movement, was thus correct in pointing out that while all Jews loved America, "the love of America among Reform Jews is to this extent different, that it is virtually part of their religion."[137] If the Reconstructionists made a religion of America as well, it was because they understood Judaism, and religion itself, very differently. In the battle between these two movements, then, a battle helped along by Kallen's ideology of cultural pluralism, we have seen the progress of American Judaism as a whole toward the tentative definition of its status as a "people apart" in America. The declarations of chosenness by Reform, and the denunciation of chosenness by Reconstructionists, symbolized the larger contest between "religion" and "civilization," "Judaism" and "Jewishness." In this way, a model was provided for the integration with the American environment that was achieved, over the course of the second generation, along the lines which had been envisioned by Conservative thinkers such as Solomon Schechter a generation earlier.

Conclusion

One is struck—especially given the recurrent insistence in the literature of the period that "America is different," unique in the history of Jewish wanderings—by just how closely these developments conformed to the general pattern established in Europe with the emancipation of the Jews. Even the appeal to Judeo-American democracy, certainly a substantive element lacking elsewhere, had, in its form, ample historical precedent. Nathan Rotenstrieich has attributed the changes made in Jewish religion following the Emancipation to an attempt by Jews to "strike deeper roots" in the surrounding society and to win its complete acceptance. It was not enough, Jews recognized, simply to coexist as citizens or even to share in universalistic and abstract ideas of humanity. Jews had to adjust culturally as well, supplementing universal ideas with a harmonization to the particular culture in which they lived. One way to do so was to show that universalism itself, a value of the surrounding culture, was essentially a product of the Jewish prophetic tradition; another was the talk in America of a Judeo-Christian tradition. Repeatedly Jews attempted to convince gentiles and themselves of their shared culture. "There seems to be a kind of suspicion, vis-à-vis the Jews, that they have to be convinced of the identity between themselves and the surrounding world, lest they cultivate their own distinctiveness."[138]

In America, as we have seen, the primary effort at harmonization was not made in terms of universalism, or even of the "Judeo-Christian heritage," but in terms of democracy, a parallel harmonization which rendered the others, more useful in the past, somewhat dispensable. Jews attempted to demonstrate that democracy was a "transformation" or even a direct development of the Biblical-Talmudic tradition, and in making this particular attempt at harmonization the American rabbis had an advantage which their predecessors in Europe had not enjoyed. They could strengthen their argument both rhetorically and substantively through the use of what they knew to be a key element in America's self-image no less than their own: the nation's status as a providentially chosen people with a mission to all mankind.[139] America, too, saw itself as elect, and when articulating that election depended heavily on the symbols and concepts of the Hebrew Bible. This American idea of election, of special national importance at times of crisis such as the Second World War, more than anything else provided the "leverage" required to make the rabbinic argument convincing. In invoking it, the rabbis stood on solid ground.

For America, in Reinhold Niebuhr's words, "came into existence with the sense of being a 'separated' nation, which God was using to make a new beginning for mankind." It retained this religious vision of its innocence and destiny well into the present century.[140] Sacvan Bercovitch's study, *The Puritan Origins of the American Self*, carefully traces the development of "a central aspect of our Puritan legacy—the rhetoric of American identity." The key conception bequeathed by the Puritans was America's election, its status as the new chosen people; the destiny of "Christ's people in New England" was the destiny of all mankind. English protestants too had claimed that in their time and place sacred and secular history coincided, but in New England the Puritans claimed that the two histories were inherently one, and would continue such until the end of days which the New England settlement foreshadowed. They enjoyed the collective status of visible sainthood, and their land was chosen. "The subsequent impact of this concept," Bercovitch concludes, "cannot be overestimated."[141] One sees it most recently in the speeches of the successful candidate for President in 1980, who repeatedly asked Americans to join him in striving to become the "city on a hill" envisioned by the prophets.[142]

While resting on a Protestant transformation of a Biblical tradition, this American vision of chosenness was sufficiently similar to the Biblical tradition to provide the rabbis with a point of entry to the American symbols which they wished to make their own. Separation, covenant, mission, a sacred history, a messianic fulfillment—in short, collective election—were the key elements of America's self-understanding no less than of the Jews'. Taking Rabbi Solomon Freehof's observation that the Jews loved America several steps farther, we might say that the rabbis knew well what they loved, and that, loving, they wished to marry. The rabbis took the promise and promises of the American beloved seriously, accepting America's vision of itself as its true nature, believing that America would gather in the exiles of Europe and bless them with justice and opportunity, and seeing in America's claim to election a direct reflection of their own. Small wonder that the rabbis believed this "marriage of true minds" the surest way to overcome all remaining "impediments" to the desired union. They made what Bercovitch regards as the characteristic American rhetorical trope a principal theme of the sermons and essays meant to shape the self-understanding of their congregants.

Yet Freehof was correct: if all Jews loved America, Reform Jews loved it the most religiously, or at least professed their adoration most fervently. No one could possibly exceed Kaufman Kohler's praise of "the invigorating air of this God-blessed land of liberty";[143] certainly no movement exceeded Reform in alluding to America's chosenness. Yet of all movements Reform had the most trouble accepting the traditional belief in Jewish chosenness, because it had gone farthest in rejecting the assumptions and obligations on which that belief had always rested. Reform rabbis considering the doctrine thus faced a dilemma more acute than that of their colleagues in other movements. Detailed examination of the second generation's reinterpretation of election will therefore begin with the solutions which Reform thinkers proposed—and found wanting.

Reform Judaism and the "Mission unto the Nations"

THE PRINCIPAL theological legacy of nineteenth-century Reform Judaism—its notion of a Jewish mission unto the nations—was never without its vehement critics. Zionists repeatedly ridiculed the idea that the Jews' dispersion throughout the world had been a divinely intended device to bring the truth to all mankind, rather than a catastrophic historical accident which should be remedied; Orthodox Jews could not accept Reform's contention that Jews performed their mission by leading exemplary ethical lives rather than by obeying the "six-hundred-thirteen commandments" of the Torah. The loftier the heights of rhetoric scaled by thinkers such as Geiger and Kohler in extolling the Jewish mission, the more elevated was the ironic position from which scoffers could look down. "I frankly confess," wrote Israel Friedlander, a professor at the Jewish Theological Seminary in 1905, "that it costs me a considerable amount of effort to speak about it seriously."[1] In the second generation such criticism for the first time came as much from within the Reform movement as from outside it, and by the generation's close, after the rhetoric of mission had been sorely tested by Jewish suffering during the Holocaust, the trope of a "light unto the nations" had largely given way to another, more muted call. Jews were to cooperate with all like-minded men and women of whatever faith in working for the universal good, rather than leading them from the privileged vantage of a city on the hill.

This transformation—completing the earlier movement from particularist revealed religion to universalist rational ethics that the idea of mission itself embodied—was not without its price. Sufferings made more bearable when seen as the lot of the Lord's suffering servant remained utterly senseless when Israel's role was universalized. The persecution of the Jews, it seemed, had remained utterly particular. Reform's reinterpretation of the idea of mission, then, was tested at once by events which called every explanation of Jewish history into question. It was tested, as well, by the difficulty many Jews had in believing themselves "chosen" in any sense when they could not believe in either a choosing God or a moment of election such as Sinai. Our aim is to understand why Reform Jewish thinkers in this generation chose to see themselves as they did in spite of such difficulties, whether through the trope of mission or the vaguer sense of prophetic calling which superseded it. There was some self-deception in their rhetoric, we shall find, and no small measure of myth. Mission and chosenness comprised their essential themes because these ideas touched Jewish lives where they were most vulnerable, and so most needy of the meaning which such ideas, more than all others, promised to supply.

The Choosing People

For some, of course, the old myth remained sufficient. Julian Morgenstern, staunchly anti-Zionist until 1947,[2] inaugurated the first post-war academic year at Hebrew Union College with words which could have come (and did) from the lips of Geiger, Einhorn, or Kohler.

> We of the Reform wing conceive of Israel as a people, a chosen people, endowed from very birth with a genius for seeing God in every aspect of existence and of interpreting all of life, nature and history from the standpoint of the one, eternal God . . . chosen by God, therefore, to be His servant, the bearers of the highest knowledge of Him and of His way of life for mankind, unto all nations and peoples and throughout all time.[3]

The audience's discomfort at such talk, in the season given over to tallying the Holocaust dead, is palpable even now. Indeed, by the time Morgenstern gave this classic expression to the old formulae, opposition to them had been manifest for at least a decade in the literature of the Reform movement, and in its official platform.

One can discern the outlines of the new position as early as 1928, in an address by Rabbi Felix Levy of Chicago to the Society for the Advancement of Judaism, recently organized by Mordecai Kaplan in New York. Levy told the gathering that he favored retention of the chosen people idea and its "corollary," the mission of Israel,

> if by that we mean that Israel should consciously set itself up as a people that is to function as priests of the ideal, if we mean that in a world constituted like that of today, materialist, deterministic, and mechanistic, some group should stand for the idea of the world, not as it is, but as it might be.[4]

We note at once that Israel is said to serve "the ideal" and not the purposes of "divine providence," let alone a commanding personal God who could be said to have chosen it. Israel has been commissioned to stand for an unspecified vision of the world as it might be, rather than specific truths which previous generations had stated in the form of credos. Levy's new answers to the questions "chosen by whom, and for what?" came to distinguish his movement's position on mission a decade later. They found articulation in the debates of Reform's rabbinical organization—the Central Conference of American Rabbis—in 1936–37. Under Levy's guidance, the CCAR drafted a statement of principles for Reform intended to replace the Pittsburgh Platform.

A draft of the declaration, presented to the CCAR in 1936, averred that "revelation is a continuous and universal process confined to no one group and no one age." The Torah, however, made the Jews "an Eternal People—an *'Am Olam.'* " It granted the people of Israel and "its inspired teachers" a unique insight into the realm of religious truth—a claim to uniqueness which echoed that of classical Reform. The paragraph entitled "the Mission of Israel," however, represented a radical departure.

> The mission of Israel expresses our undying will to live a life of ethical and religious creativeness. Israel will endure as long as its destiny will be bound up with the destiny of faith, brotherhood, freedom, justice, love, truth, and peace. To cooperate with all forward-looking men in upholding these ideals as beacon lights to the nations, represents our mission as the servant people of the eternal. Ours has been the choice to serve God and to further righteousness. Our Messianic goal, envisioned by our prophets, is the establishment of the kingdom of God and of universal justice and peace on earth.[5]

The commanding God and His commandments are absent. Instead we find "Torah" explicated as peace, love, justice, etc. The careful phrasing—"ours has been the choice," "our undying will," "our Messianic goal"—stops short of actually declaring that Israel has chosen God and not the reverse, but that is its clear implication. Although the image of "light unto the nations" has been retained, the note of superiority so evident in Kohler's use of it has been muted by the emphasis upon cooperation with "all forward-looking men."

After this draft had been circulated among member rabbis and aroused widespread opposition (related more to its approval of Zionism and its attempt to impose any statement of principles than to the stance on mission), another was prepared. The latter was considered (against the wishes of half those present) at the 1937 convention.[6] The sentence affirming Israel's special revelation was retained, but the declaration on mission now read:

> Throughout the ages it has been Israel's mission to witness to the divine in the face of every form of paganism and materialism. We regard it as our historic task to cooperate with all men in the establishment of the kingdom of God, of universal brotherhood, justice, truth and peace on earth. This is our Messianic goal.[7]

The substance is identical to the previous draft, but the tone has been muted further and the text shortened. Israel is no longer called "the servant people of the Eternal." Even the ambiguous reference to election contained in the phrase "ours has been the choice" has been omitted.

In the discussion which followed, Samuel Schulman, rabbi of Temple Emanu-El in New York, demanded to know why the statement that Israel was chosen by God to witness to God and His Torah had been omitted. "Why is the word 'chosen' omitted? I am not afraid of the word."[8] In Schulman's own draft, which the conference on the advice of the platform committee refused to consider, chosenness was central. There Judaism was said to present "the most exalted conception of God, as this is taught by our Holy Scriptures and by the ideas developed from them by Jewish teachers."[9] Maurice Eisendrath, rabbi of Holy Blossom Temple in Toronto and another member of the Morgenstern wing, similarly called for greater emphasis on Israel's mission, in the face of the "masses" who "scorn" it, and despite the fact that some had labeled it "undemocratic."[10]

One suspects—although documentation is unavailable—that the word "chosen" had been omitted because it was troublesome, or rather, that it had been rendered dispensable because classical reform had always equated election with mission anyway. More important was the new direction of that mission: not to the nations but with them, against the forces of "paganism" and "materialism." Reform would now have none of the anti-Christian crusade so pronounced in the writings of Kohler, nor the elitism implicit in the sort of declaration which Eisendrath apparently favored. The statement on mission quoted above was approved, along with the rest of the declaration that became known as the Columbus Platform. The new view of Israel's election thereby became the official position of Reform as a whole.

Levi, who as president of the CCAR played a prominent role in the adoption of the Platform, once more gave voice to the new consensus. He named the "Four Permanent Values in Judaism" (ca. 1940) as faith in God, in the divine origin and destiny of man, in the meaningfulness of life, and in God's covenant "in a special sense" with Israel. Let critics denounce the last idea as "unhistorical and a fiction." America's vision of itself as the champion of democracy, and man's vision of himself as a moral creature, were no less fictitious. Both had become what they claimed to be by deciding to be such. Once a people consciously accepted a role and proceeded to play it earnestly, that role became its special task. Thus Israel had become a kingdom of priests, stamping the role indelibly upon its character.[11]

The function of myth-making had become conscious, then, and Levy knew just how far his movement had traveled both from rabbinic tradition and from Kaufman Kohler. For his claim to chosenness is purely historical. At a certain point Israel had chosen for itself the role of a kingdom of priests, and had remained dedicated to its task over the centuries. The covenant is indeed a covenant "in a special sense," since it has only one party. God is involved only indirectly, having inspired Israel to serve Him through ethical endeavor. In short, the claim that God chose Israel was now to be read as the recollection that Israel chose God—an inversion repeatedly affirmed by such rabbis as Abba Hillel Silver,[12] Samuel Cohon,[13] and Stephen Wise.[14]

This new formulation rather adroitly resolved the issue of Israel's relation to other nations, a pressing concern in the wake of charges by figures such as George Bernard Shaw and H. G. Wells that Nazi notions of racial superiority derived from the Jewish doctrine of chosenness.[15] However, the new position did not answer the related and equally pressing question of why Israel had again been singled out for suffering. This problem became more difficult to address the more one denied that Israel had been singled out in any other way.

One response—a variation on the tradition that Israel suffered "because of our sins"—was foreshadowed in a speech to the CCAR in 1936 by Rabbi Leo Franklin of Detroit.

> It is largely because the Jew has failed in his appointed task that mankind is without adequate moral leadership today, and the world despises us for that. As a priest people, we occupied a place of dignity among men, while stripped of the mantle of our office, we have come to be looked upon as drones in the beehive of humanity, idlers, and incompetents and satellites, deserving to be driven out by those who provide the things by which men live. It is because we seem to live without a purpose, and without a goal, and without a mission, and without a message, and without an ideal that is distinctly Jewish that we have become little in our own eyes and correspondingly so in the eyes of others.

Israel's existence was justified only by its status as "the people of Torah." Had the Jew not forsaken that responsibility, "it is unlikely that so dire a fate as confronts him even today in Germany and Poland would have been his." While the Jews might still have been "crucified for the sins of the many," Franklin continued, they eventually would have been hailed as the savior and redeemer of mankind.[16]

This severe chastisement was untypical even before the war, and the argument that Israel was to blame for its own suffering became untenable if not obscene as word of the Final Solution reached America. For the most part, the rabbis offered counsels of courage and perseverance in the face of the Nazi persecutions. They defended the chosen-people idea against charges that it had been the basis for Nazi racism, and cited the barbarism which the Nazis displayed as proof that the world stood more in need of Israel's ideals than ever before. This was the burden of several articles written for laymen in the late thirties and early forties. Many people besides the Jews were convinced they had a national mission, wrote one rabbi, and Israel had conceived the doctrine because "men who are obsessed with a great ideal, which they believe to be supremely beautiful and good," feel "under the spell of a higher power. They feel that they have a call to expound the truth." Chosenness had never implied Jewish superiority, but only that man's life was significant, "a sacred drama" in which each individual and nation was assigned a definite role.[17]

Israel's suffering, the article continued, supported its claim to election. It had been chosen by "deity or destiny" to bear the brunt of the pain and woe suffered by all who professed unwavering loyalty to universal and ethical principles. When the Jew was persecuted the freedom of all men was threatened. Jews therefore should not see themselves as martyrs set apart from the rest of mankind, but as individuals bearing the brunt of an assault against all free men, members of a company who could not "brook the arrogance of dictators" or the stupidity of their "uniformed lackeys."[18]

Another rabbi, claiming to translate the Biblical idea of election into the modern idiom, suggested that it meant that

> Israel chose God as his ideal of service . . . the province of religion and ethics and morality—all values emanating from God—as its domain of self-expression and self-realization. Israel chose God not as a matter of voluntary choice but as a matter of spiritual determinism. . . . It was not the result of trial and error . . . but of his native character and the natural bent of his spirit.

The idea needed to be retained, despite the misinterpretations to which it was subject, because "it renders our continued existence as a people meaningful to us and essential to the world."[19]

A third rabbi, writing in the *Congress Weekly* amid stories of the war and Jewish suffering, urged Jews to banish self-hatred by believing in Israel's holy mission. Only if they believed, as had their fathers, in the election of Israel would they be able to survive. "Faith in Israel's deathlessness and uniqueness transforms, heals, and becomes a source of

legitimate pride and inner power."[20] Two such articles were even accompanied by cartoons which depicted the world's "embattled peoples"
turning away from the Teutonic ideals of war and destruction and toward the sunburst and peace of Israel's ideals.[21]

These articles, remarkable in the explicitness of their message, are
full of pain and pathos. The rabbis had to deny Israel's chosenness and
uniqueness, lest people blame Jews for the Nazis—an unspeakable attack, given the circumstances. However, they affirmed that Israel did
suffer uniquely and urged Jews to bear that suffering by believing "as
their fathers did" in election rather than giving way to the indignity of
self-hatred. The eternity of Israel was to strengthen them in the face of
the death of Israel's current generation.

Yet how could it, given that Israel had chosen God and not the
reverse? At best Jewish destiny had been ordained by history. Why then
should the current generation allow "the crown of thorns [to be] forced
upon its unwilling head" in yet another repetition of the original mistake? One rabbi complained in a Rosh Hashana sermon in 1944 that
many Jews wished that God had chosen another people, or, if it had to
be Israel, that "he would grant us a little *Menuhah*, a tiny rest. We do not
consider ourselves the stuff of saints and martyrs." The rabbi went on to
explain that not every Jew needed to be a saint in order to exemplify the
task of the *am segulah*, for each made a contribution in his own way. If
one dealt equitably with employees, for example, he or she was fulfilling
Israel's mission, although if forced to choose between martyrdom and
betrayal of God, the American Jew was expected to choose martyrdom,
as Jews had done in Europe.[22] Yet why should Jews undergo martyrdom, if the role was completely of their own choosing and not divinely
decreed? And how could one talk of so mundane a matter as fairness to
employees in the same breath as a notion of chosenness far truer to
Jewish experience:

> These are the Chosen people. He has set
> upon their brow the diadem of thorn,
> The one imperishable coronet,
> The crown of pain, the briar branch of scorn . . .
> These are the chosen; He has named them all.
> None can escape the poison of His grace . . .[23]

The psychological dynamics were truly complex. Anxiety lest the
persecution somehow cross the Atlantic joined with survivor guilt because it had not. Doubts as to the legitimacy of one's own existence fed
on anti-Semitism in Europe and at home. The teaching of mission meant
to reassure Jews furthered the conviction that, as Franklin had put it in
1935, their right to existence depended upon fulfillment of their appointed role. Rabbi Leon Feuer of Toledo, Ohio, addressing these dilem-

mas perceptively in 1947, wrote that the "major fact of Jewish life today" was the hostility which Jews encountered everywhere they turned. They could not go on explaining, apologizing, "shrinking," currying favor. They had a right to whatever degree of difference suited them, and needed no rationale for being—certainly not mission or messianism. Jews in previous eras had not seen their role as one of wandering the earth to propagate religious ideas, or being the "Atlas" who bore the world's sins, or the Christ who suffered for the redemption of humanity. Let Christians spread universal ideals, proving their worth first of all in decent treatment of the Jews. By claiming a special mission, Feuer argued, Jews only reinforced the Christian notion that it was the Jews' duty to suffer for the rejection of Jesus. The Mission idea caused the ordinary Jew to feel that he had to be the moral superior of non-Jews and justify his existence by demonstrating that he was "about his Father's business." The only mission of Judaism, he wrote, was to the Jews and the Jewish people: to make of every Jew a God-revering person, and to found any Jewish society upon ideals of righteousness and justice.[24]

That Feuer's concern was far from academic is demonstrated by a high holiday *maḥzor* issued by the Reform movement a year later. One meditation in the book criticized Israel for the "prejudices, class enmities, and the envious conflicts for the prizes of worldly gain" which persisted in its midst. These failings were to its discredit as "ministers of the Lord, as a kingdom of priests and as a holy people, called by Thee to give light to the world." Israel's election had too often been

> turned by our erring minds into an excuse for our sins . . . to indulgence and self-justification. . . . Alas, we have contemned our holy heritage and made it minister to our own pride. . . . We have not made our sufferings a discipline for our souls. We have found excuse for our sin in the iniquity of the persecutor. We have lacked the moral power of our forefathers, even in the face of unjust hate, to say we too have sinned.[25]

This remarkable chastisement, incorporated in a service of confession only three years after the war's end, could not but have had a powerful effect. Israel is not only urged to accept its sufferings as the wage of sinfulness, but is also warned not to disclaim responsibility for the evil of its persecutors. The meditation's vehemence testifies to the depth of the need for explanation which its author, editors, and probably its readers had to confront.

The rabbis, then, faced a serious dilemma. If they chose to reinterpret the doctrine of election rather than discard it altogether, they faced the problems which this reinterpretation entailed. If they chose to repudiate the doctrine, they sacrificed the "positive religious values" which they perceived it to serve. Bernard Bamberger, a leading candidate to succeed Morgenstern as president of HUC, defended the doctrine of mission in 1946 through appeal to the "sense of consecration and responsibility"—as well as universalism—which it carried. The prophets who first expounded the mission had regarded the Jewish faith as "primarily a universal religion," which its adherents as a chosen people had a responsibility to propagate. Was not Judaism the message of God to mankind as revealed (by the mystery of Providence) through Israel? If so, one could not dispense with the idea of mission.[26] Three years later, in an address to the CCAR, Bamberger observed that "many of our people do not honestly believe" the idea of election; "not a few reject it and resent it." Yet even if "unto Jews a stumbling block and unto gentiles a foolishness," the idea was still central to Reform. "Belief in our mission may entangle us in knotty problems—but cutting the Gordian knot is less than the highest wisdom."[27] Bamberger went on to reject the scientific method as the "highest court of appeal" on matters of faith. Felix Levy, in a similar statement of the Reform dilemma regarding mission, likewise argued that one could not prove the claim to election on rational grounds.[28]

This postwar development in Reform thinking, foreshadowing the direction soon to be adopted by the third generation, was the rabbis' most significant rejoinder to Mordecai Kaplan and other critics of the ideas of mission and chosenness. Election could not be demonstrated, but only affirmed as a matter of faith. It was a mystery experienced by the Jew who felt himself party to a "covenant-relationship." Reform clung, however, to the belief that this mystery beyond demonstration consisted only in the work of furthering universal ethical ideals, in concert with others who were similarly minded. Thus, a Reform theological conference held in 1950 issued a statement on Israel's mission which called on Jews to implement their ideals "by supporting every progressive endeavor seeking to establish social justice in cooperation with all men of good will," and by promoting social-service projects within their congregations.[29] The new position was further communicated to laymen, and presumably impressed upon their minds, through a careful revision of the Union Prayer Book, published in 1953. The substitution of "who hast called us" for "who hast chosen us," first adopted in 1895, was retained in the prayer which begins, "You have loved us with a great love, O God." However, mention of Israel's "holy mission unto mankind" was replaced with the more traditional formulation that God has "called us and drawn us nigh to serve Him in faithfulness." In the prayer recited when a member of the congregation is called to the Torah, "who has called us" replaced the literal translation from the Hebrew "who hast chosen us from among all peoples," still employed in the 1937 edition. The concluding *Aleinu* prayer, with emphasis upon both particularism and universalism, was once again omitted.[30] In sum: ethical cooperation had decisively supplanted the elitism of mission. Chosenness had been reaffirmed, but drastically reinterpreted.

The principal "knotty problem" to which Bamberger referred when defending the idea of mission was what precisely the idea might mean, now that it was bereft both of the substance of commandment and the rhetoric of light to gentile darkness. Reviewing Abba Hillel Silver's book-length exposition of the new Reform position, a masterful polemic entitled *Where Judaism Differed* (1957), one critic within the movement asked the same question. Silver did not much seem to care, he wrote, what Jews actually did in their mission. The author was apparently as content with a minimum as with a maximum of Jewish observance.[31] And yet, we might add, Silver had argued in an earlier essay that if Reform's claim concerning Israel's mission was "an absurdity," the whole life of Israel was "one stupendous absurdity."[32] What could set the Jews apart in our day or furnish the basis for the distinctiveness which Silver urged, and on which the very meaning of Israel's existence depended, barring equation of contemporary Christianity with the paganism that Israel had fought in the past? Levy too had failed to escape the clutches of this dilemma. The divine sanction to Judaism was gone, he said in 1959, and nothing could take its place. Perhaps the day would come when Jews would freely opt for God and the tradition, but in the meantime only "ethical aspiration" was left them. Ethics was and had to become "the dominating determinant of Jewish personal and social being."[33]

Once more, in this farewell message of a generation, Levy had hit the mark squarely, identifying the other reason which, along with the Jew's changed position in gentile society, had necessitated the rethinking of Israel's chosenness. The problem, quite simply, was God—by no means a problem limited to Reform rabbis in our period, but most acute among them. For they persisted in raising theological questions when other movements did not, and in answering those questions with doubts that took them outside the inherited wisdom of Jewish tradition.

The Non-Choosing God

Whether because of an antipathy to systematic theology, which some rabbis defended as but one more point of intersection between Judaism and the American environment,[34] or because many rabbis simply did not believe in a personal God and so preferred not to discuss the subject, the second generation rabbinate for the most part avoided the difficult problems arising from the claim that God had chosen Israel. The incursion of the transcendent God into human history, His revelation to a particular people at a particular time and place, and His selection of a small group for a task upon which the salvation of all mankind depended raise questions about God's nature, transcendence, and justice which the generation rarely addressed.[35] Classical Judaism too had rarely posed the questions systematically, and had refrained from essaying conceptions of the divine nature. But it had raised the matter of divine choice in *aggadah*, and affirmed through midrash what it could not pretend to explain. Revelation took its place at the midpoint of a sacred history begun with creation and directed towards redemption. In America, by contrast, the Sinaitic revelation was discounted by many rabbis, and belief in the messiah had given way to trust in a continuing progress to be accomplished by humanity alone. As a result the questions which were asked about Israel's chosenness were often posed in a conceptual vacuum. Most accounts of election presumed a certain sort of God, without ever stating how or if He could be said to have chosen Israel.

Reform rabbis, as noted above, in fact devoted more time to theology than their colleagues in other movements during this period, and logically so.[36] If, in the words of their platform, "the heart of Judaism and its chief contribution to religion" was "the doctrine of the One living God, who rules the world through law and love,"[37] then Judaism could perpetuate its distinctiveness only by speaking of that God to the world. Having collapsed Judaism to religion, and religion to belief, Reform had to confer on belief a richness that would enable it to bear the burden which Reform imposed: the survival of the Jewish people. However, the very same paragraph which proclaimed Israel's "god-concept" to be the source of its uniqueness revealed how indistinct a "god-concept" Israel's now was. Did the reference to "law and love" constitute a rephrasing of the traditional divine attributes of justice and mercy, and so a testimony by Reform to belief in a personal God who displays those attributes? Or did "law and love" merely express the sentiment that God revealed Himself through human law and love as, in a subsequent paragraph, He was said to reveal Himself in nature and "the human spirit"? Did the statement that "in Him all existence has its creative source and mankind its ideal of conduct" intend to make the traditional claim that God is man's Creator and Commander? Or did it seek to ennoble human creativity and morality with the adjective "divine"? Finally, did the affirmation that God "is the indwelling Presence of the world . . . whom we worship as Lord of the universe and as our merciful father"[38] intend to affirm His personal involvement in human affairs, or merely to assert His general immanence and describe a mode of relation to Him? The credibility of Reform's reaffirmation of election depended on the underlying connotations of its declarations about Israel's Elector.

Samuel Cohon, principal author of the Columbus Platform and professor of theology at HUC, may be taken as representative of his movement's position on God's role in choosing Israel.[39] A study of the contradictions in his theology reveals the problems of the Reform position generally. Cohon regarded the difficulty of "some moderns" with the idea of a chosen people as semantic, and proposed what he considered a purely verbal solution. Henceforth, Jews would think of themselves as a "god-choosing" people.[40] He denounced concern with such "non-essentials" as messiah and resurrection, which in his view had been invented "to brighten the gloom" of a despairing people.[41] Yet he affirmed the unique character and mission of Israel, claiming (in the words of the Platform) that Jews had "achieved unique insight into the realm of religious truth." He even asserted that Judaism would continue to exist as a distinct faith once the Kingdom of God had been achieved.[42] One finds a consistent contradiction between what Cohon said God could do, and what he said God had done.

Both in his tracts for laymen and in his historical theology, Cohon affirmed that God is both cosmic and personal, immanent and transcendent. He is the principle on which the universe rests but is not reducible to the universe. There is, at the heart of things, something akin to the mental and spiritual sides of human nature. God could not be unrelated to man, even if the attributes of personality which we ascribe to Him are only inadequate attempts to comprehend Him. He is personal in a nonanthropomorphic way, embodying in complete and perfect fashion attributes shared to a limited degree by human beings: unity, rationality, ethical consistency, and purposiveness.[43]

Revelation, to Cohon, was "the unquenchable fire of God disclosed to the inner eye of faith, the manifestation of imperishable truths written in rock and star."[44] It was not a clear message communicated to a person, but the stimulation of his or her spirit, a stirring in the consciousness of "spiritually endowed individuals." Revelation is, in fact, the working of our reason and our genius: "a progressive process whereby the Creator's activity, thought, and purpose are disclosed to spiritually gifted souls."[45]

The vision is Kohler's. Particular transcendent revelations such as that at Sinai are precluded. Revelation comes only to particularly gifted individuals; Israel's unique insight into divinity is attributed in the Columbus Platform to its "prophets and sages," thereby reaffirming Kohler's Pittsburgh Platform. However, where Kohler could still speak of such genius in the absence of Sinaitic revelation, because of his belief in a national genius of the Jewish people, Cohon had no such basis for his position. He persistently spoke, not of God, but of belief in God. The latter stimulated personal and social well-being and regeneration, inspiring men with patience and courage.[46] God was what belief in God accomplished. This is surely no mere semantic quibble. Given that God's "personal" revelations come only to individuals of special sensitivity, and even then as a product either of reason or genius, it is not clear how this God is at all involved in the coming of His kingdom. He is neither active from without, like the God of Jewish tradition, nor active from within, like the God of Spinoza. Aside from indirectly revealing Himself and inspiring us to bear with the infirmities caused by His concealment, His activity is left unspecified. The space for it has been severely contracted. It is also not clear how Israel can lay claim, through its prophets, to a "unique destiny," or how its idea of God could "embody the very substance of the Jewish spirit"—claims which permit Cohon to regard Israel as the "channel of God's revelation."[47] This argument partakes both of Mordecai Kaplan (whom Cohon paraphrases)[48] and Yehudah Halevi (whom Cohen cites),[49] without the consistency of either. His argument for Jewish uniqueness is nowhere grounded in his rather eclectic "god-concept."[50] When Cohon goes on to assert that Israel will exist forever, his faith in the people and its destiny has once more overstepped the bounds of his theology.[51]

Abba Hillel Silver, far more consistent in his thinking, refused to repudiate election, but reduced it to a description of Israel's precocious historical development. Silver described God in a sermon as the

> creative energy of the universe, the source of all that is and is to be, the substance and the form and the purpose of everything. I think of God as the personality of the universe, whose wisdom integrates the world, holds it together, directs it to His own ultimate purposes. I think of God as of the omnipotent goodness, as of the ultimate and absolute truth, as of the moral ultimates, the best in the universe.[52]

Silver's aim in the sermon was no doubt the edification of his congregation rather than theological precision. Yet the general approach, adhered to in his other writing, is clear. Unlike Cohon, Silver did not claim a unique divine revelation to Israel, for his God could not grant one. God has personality, but is not really "personal." Rather He is the "creative energy" which guides the universe with its wisdom. The prophets who had endowed Israel with the "god-idea" that still distinguished it had simply been uniquely insightful. "Israel was a chosen people only because it was within Israel that the idea of the one spiritual God was manifest."[53] Silver did not speak of personal providence, and left open the issue of immortality—a belief Cohon had seemed (however tentatively) to affirm.[54] For Silver, the special meaning of Israel's destiny, and so of the life of the individual Jew, lay only in the burden which Israel had undertaken by its own choosing, and in the superiority of its ethical monotheism. By affirming far less than Cohon, Silver could argue his faith more convincingly. He purchased that consistency, however, at the expense of literal belief in Israel's election.

No other position is ever seriously argued in the many Reform writings of the period which talk of God.[55] One rabbi did propose in a 1931 debate that the CCAR should omit all mention of God in a proposed declaration of principles, lest it impose its thinking on members who might disagree.[56] Another rabbi, a year earlier, complained of Jewish humanists who "vacillate and equivocate . . . negate the cardinal affirmations and attitudes which religion demands or implies, and yet . . . persist in using the term God." He called upon the CCAR to affirm belief in an "Infinite, Eternal, but Personal God."[57] As we have seen, his colleagues stopped just short of that in the platform cited above, and the "humanists" whom he denounced ceased in a few years to be a factor in the CCAR. The rabbinate's collective position on the matter of God, therefore, certainly permitted no stronger affirmation of the chosen people idea than the one actually adopted: that Israel had chosen God and not the reverse.

This historicized notion of election, and the concomitant transformation of belief into ethics, were by no means original with American Reform. They were part of its legacy from German Reform and from post-Enlightenment religion in general, the space carved out for religion by the philosopher whose critique of metaphysics had displaced faith from its previous arena of authority. Immanuel Kant had left God the guarantor of ethics, and thus had made of ethics a realm for faith which was safe from empirical challenge, "a residual content for Judaism the validity of which was unassailable even after the demolition of metaphysics."[58] The second generation now pressed chosenness into the service of universal moral ideals, through a reinterpretation that purchased conformity with modernity's "religion of reason" at the expense of traditional belief in God's election of Israel at Sinai.[59] Once more the America which the rabbis held to be "different" only conformed to the general post-Emancipation pattern.

One suspects that Reform laymen were quite content with these developments, the challenge to faith passed on to the rabbis having become part of their cultural inheritance as well. Where were they to find the God of their ancestors, after all? If human beings do indeed require "plausibility structures" to inform their world views with the air of factual reality,[60] then plausibility must surely have been lacking to the ideas of God the chooser and His chosen people Israel.[61] The Jewish mission unto the nations lay buried, now quite literally, under the ashes of European Jewry, while the flight from immigrant neighborhood to suburb, via areas of "second settlement," had only acted out the conceptual move away from the particularity demanded by Israel's mission. One could simply not say as much as before. The hesitancy or even contradiction of Reform thinking on God and chosenness seemed plausible where less equivocal affirmations were not. The rhetoric of mission was no longer a meaning to conjure with, and the fact that no other meaning seemed available could not hide the fact that another myth was urgently needed. These were the realities—inchoate to be sure, but no less inescapable for that. The rabbis, casting about unsuccessfully for a new purpose to Jewish existence and a new guarantee for that purpose, probably responded accurately to the deep-felt needs of their congregants. Israel's mission was one more inherited truth—a crucial one to their self-understanding—in which many Reform Jews could no longer literally believe.

A Rhetoric and its Functions

Why, then, did they continue to talk about it—rabbis (and perhaps their congregants) retaining mission and chosenness as the centerpiece of the "broken myth" they did construct, "broken" in that its postulates had been denied?[62] Why not simply find new symbols, or at least forget about this one as they had the messiah, the exile, and the personal God? The reasons, I think, are tied to mission's rhetorical function in the synagogue and its suitability as an ideology capable of undergirding Reform Jewish liberalism. Mission brought together what the Reform Jew did in everyday life with the Jewish people's eternal task, uniting the two, making the self whole, in a way which no other symbol could.

Let us recall, first of all, the principal location of the rhetoric of mission: its service as subject of the weekly synagogue sermon. Alexander Altmann has shown how, under the influence of Protestant developments, the sermon took center stage in the synagogue services of German Reform. From the traditional homiletical *derashah* on the portion of the Torah read that week in the synagogue, the sermon evolved into an address designed to uplift or inspire or inform or "mysteriously excite" the congregation of worshippers.[63] In American Reform, the sermon retained this central place. Many of the generation's leading rabbis (one thinks of Abba Hillel Silver and Stephen Wise first of all) achieved fame by their oratorical skills, preaching sermons known to last for hours. Mission was the single most popular religious theme of Reform sermons in the generation, yielding first place to communal concerns such as anti-Semitism, Hitler, and Zionism, but far more popular a theme than any other which touched the Jews' destiny as a people of God.[64] The Jews who listened to such sermons, furthermore, were unlikely to have any other religious observance during the week and, even during the synagogue service, were likely to participate far less than fellow-Jews in Conservative or Orthodox synagogues. Except for several hymns sung in unison with cantor, organ, and choir, and responsive readings together with the rabbi, the congregation was quiet throughout the service, an audience coming to the synagogue for inspiration to be provided by its professionals. Finally, as Solomon Freehof observed in a lecture on preaching to students at HUC, the sermon could no longer take its traditional form because those who heard it were unfamiliar with the Biblical text upon which rabbis in the past had built their homilies.[65] Upon what theme could the rabbi preach, then, in hopes of inspiring and uplifting his congregants and motivating their continued identification with Judaism?

Mission was ideal for several reasons. It elevated the audience from humdrum daily life to the eternal work of God, even as it distilled the essence of Judaism into a prophetic concern for justice and brotherhood. Moreover, it gave the rhetorical illusion of activity to congregants whose role both inside and outside the synagogue was largely passive. It is a rhetoric of movement above all else, of doing and working together and reaching out to a waiting world. To Jews who could no longer point to commandments done, as Jews, because this was what Jews did, mission confirmed that activity which the congregants undertook in any event was the proper expression of Jewish commitment. Charity, social justice, group life—this was the stuff of Judaism. The struggle for progress on these matters was truly divine service. The rhetoric of mission, then, moved with the compelling rhythm of the real, providing an order lost to Jews long freed from the sterner metronome of the law.

The sentimentality which afflicts so much of this rhetoric was of course not unique to Reform or to Judaism. It had come to pervade American Protestant churches in the late nineteenth century as well. Rationalist religions of eternal truth gave way to a religious life believed to reside in the emotions, and do-gooders of various sorts undergirded their philanthropic activity with the notion that their work constituted a "mission" from on high.[66] Salvation Army "missions" in the slums were only the most obvious example of the general case. The social gospel was carried forward by American Protestants under the same banner that had sent missionaries to spread the original gospel around the world, and that now speeded nation-states on their way to unification and imperial conquest. In fact, the religious users of the rhetoric drew on its more tangible employments for much of the power of their message; the sentimentality of the rhetoric in church and synagogue consisted in large measure in the contrast between the heroism of the metaphors and the harmlessness (not to say banality) of the religious enterprises which they served.

Reform Jews, in adopting this rhetoric to their own ends, drew on both the Protestants' and the nationalists' usage of mission, but to differing degrees. Their effort closely paralleled that of the church (even, as we shall see, to the development of a Jewish social gospel). But whereas nineteenth-century nationalists such as Fichte in Germany or Mazzini in Italy had invoked the mission of their respective peoples in order to spur on their quest for independent nationhood,[67] Reform Jews continued to use this same rhetoric as their ancestors in Germany and America had: to espouse an essentially antinationalist universalism. They thus turned the principal trope of romantic nationalism—a force which had retarded Jewish progress towards Emancipation in Europe—to the service of Enlightenment ideals which had initiated that progress. It is not surprising, then, that adherents of the classical Reform position, such as Morgenstern, attacked the Zionists' use of the Jewish mission to support a Jewish national movement. Nor is it surprising that the Zionists for their part continually ridiculed the notion of a Jewish mission which presumed and even glorified existence in the diaspora.[68] American Reform rabbis—most of them Zionists by the second generation, but Zionists committed to remaining in America—clung to their movement's inherited rhetoric but did not direct it either against the movement for a Jewish state (as Morgenstern did) or for a nationalist definition of Jewish existence (as did the Zionists and Kaplan). Instead they adopted the course we have examined, invoking the prophet Isaiah in the name of a cooperative effort with all people of good will to achieve universalist ideals.

This rhetoric, I believe, was extremely well suited to the political liberalism to which most American Jews and their rabbis of whatever "denomination" inclined during the second generation. When the CCAR had first begun to evince concern for social issues during the teens and twenties, the rabbis had followed the lead of Christian organizations in adopting a somewhat radical social gospel which put them at odds with many of their wealthier congregants.[69] In the name of Israel's mission unto the nations they joined, for example, in achieving an end to twelve-hour workdays in the steel industry and in securing parole for members of the IWW arrested in a clash with American Legionnaires in 1919. The rabbis supported labor's right to collective bargaining, called for prohibition of child labor and more equitable distribution of the wealth, and advocated workmen's compensation and better housing for the poor. During the thirties, the rabbis endorsed or went beyond the policies of the New Deal, consistently occupying ground to the left of the political center.[70] As we might expect, these particular applications of the teaching of Israel's mission did not sit well with some Reform congregants. In 1936, Morgenstern noted to his colleagues in the CCAR that the breach between laymen and rabbis on social issues was growing "wider and wider,"[71] while Felix Levy complained in his presidential message the next year that the Temple had become a "rich man's club."[72] One sees the conflict clearly in a debate between Rabbi Barnett Brickner and a prominent Reform layman before the movement's lay organization, the Union of American Hebrew Congregations, in 1939. The latter wondered aloud whether it was helpful to have rabbis in the forefront of controversial issues at a time of anti-Semitism, and argued that rabbis should consult their boards of directors before pronouncing on such issues from the pulpit.[73] If published sermons are any indication, his view prevailed. Rabbis preached time and again on the theme of Israel's mission, but drew upon it to argue particular political or economic stances that were controversial only in their conventions and not in their congregations. Abba Hillel Silver thus had good reason for his acerbic remark that the mission to save the world espoused by Reform had too often become, in the persons of the rabbis, "a rocking-horse race."[74]

In the course of the second generation the issue lost its urgency, for about the time of the war rabbis and congregants seem to have been brought together in support for the New Deal. Jews as a whole now voted, writes one historian of the New York Jewish community, for a blend of social reform and internationalism, supporting gentile candidates who supported these positions even against Jewish politicians who did not.[75] The source of this internationalism may have been concern for Jews abroad, while discrimination against Jews at home perhaps supplied the impetus to Jewish concern for civil rights. In some cases, too, the socialism of immigrant parents no doubt left its mark on their middle-class American children and inclined them to liberalism. Regardless of how one accounts for this distinctive voting pattern, one can see how successful the rhetoric of mission might have been in undergirding it with religious meaning. For mission urged Jews to work for the progressive improvement of the general welfare (as opposed to advocating its radical improvement, or inviting contentment with the status quo, or acquiescing in purely particularist concerns). Jews were to work for the day when universal faith and brotherhood would render Israel's religious distinctiveness unnecessary. They could and should do so by joining general movements, such as liberalism, which were directed to these ends; in joining such causes they performed a distinctively Jewish mission. As one leading member of the third-generation Reform rabbinate would put it, Judaism became a way of life "which the decent, liberal, New York Post-reading citizen would live even if there were no Torah."[76]

Non-Reform Jews of course shared this political orientation, and often associated it with Jewish religious ideals such as the tradition's concern for social justice. Their rabbis did not emphasize the notion of mission or make it a primary trope in their rhetoric, however. It had simply not been part of their specific heritage. Even Reform rabbis, as we have seen, invoked the Jewish mission less and less in the postwar period. Its elitism grated more as Jews identified themselves more completely with American society, and its bombast had gone out of fashion. One suspects, as well, that mission eventually proved dispensable because the situation once explained and legitimated by it no longer obtained. American Reform Jews did not stand where their ancestors had, nor did they share the ambiguous position of their parents. Those one short step from complete assimilation had taken the leap, while those still identifiably Jewish had a clearer relation to gentile America and enjoyed its qualified acceptance. They could rest content with the "quieter," less definitive accounts of chosenness which thinkers of the third generation would soon proffer.

In the meantime, however, mission seemed to link the political and social commitments of Reform Jews to the demands of Jewish tradition, through a rhetoric that is striking in its power. One wonders, then, about the psychological effect which persistent invocation of Israel's mission might have had on the Reform believers: the guilt imputed to Jews by Leo Franklin or the 1948 *maḥzor*, for example, or its repudiation by Leon Feuer.[77] An even graver problem was suggested by one of the most famous rabbis of the day, Joshua Loth Liebman, whose combination of Judaism and psychology proved so appealing that his book, *Peace of Mind*, became a national best-seller. Rabbis who dwelt on the mission of Judaism, he wrote in 1949, made the mistake

> of dwelling so much in the realm of pure "essence" as to ignore the realm of "existence." It is a kind of "thanatopsis"—a contemplation of death—to be so concerned with the goal and purpose of Judaism as to be oblivious of the material, organic and concrete welfare of the agents who alone can bring that purpose to fulfillment.[78]

Liebman unfortunately did not elaborate on this fascinating suggestion. What he seems to be saying is that by its location of meaning in a bare-bones abstraction rather than in the flesh-and-blood particularity of lived life, Reform had placed its believers in the shadow of the final end to particularity, death. We might take the connection further still. Mission was by definition directed ever forward, toward a consummation which no Jew now alive would ever witness. (Belief in resurrection had of course been abandoned.) The mission thus could have no credible relation to the daily life of the individual in the here and now. It offered no divinely-established rhythm (such as the commandments) through which the Jew could step into eternity. Nothing stood between the Jew and death, nothing ordered his days and activity, except a mission which pointed beyond him, his days, his activity, and his death. Mission left the believer face to face with infinity, a danger which earlier preachers such as the Puritans intended to combat when they admonished their own "men of vocation" to remain within the ordered confines of their calling, where they could be safe from the evil without. "The care of the work belongs to you, and the other is not your care."[79] Mission took away the work, leaving only the care. It is worth noting in this connection that Reform sermons dealt with death more frequently than sermons by rabbis of other movements—perhaps because of a greater honesty, or (in the early years of the generation) a more highly-educated membership. There may have been another factor, however: that death loomed especially large once the traditional beliefs which had lent assurance and the traditional activities which had ordered daily life no longer played their assigned traditional roles. This of course must remain a speculation and only that.

One thing is certain: the rhetoric of mission was obsolete by the close of the second generation, and Reform rabbis no longer defined their community in its light. For its universalism, the third generation would substitute out-and-out progressivism, and declare this the distinctive mark of Jews;[80] for its sense of purpose and meaning, they would fall back on inherited images in which they no longer quite believed: covenant, Torah, suffering—the mythic stuff of chosenness. No longer exactly a "chosen people" (for whom had God really chosen?) or even a "choosing people" (for whom among them had actually chosen God?), they would, nonetheless, continue to claim an election of sorts, as their "parents" in the second generation had claimed a mission.

The degree of "bad faith" attaching to such claims has apparently remained a price which Jewish thinkers are willing to pay, given the perceived alternative of breaking faith with the self-definition of their ancestors. All the more reason, then, that we turn our attention to Mordecai Kaplan's unceasing demand that Jews repudiate the idea of election, on the grounds that they could no longer believe it in good faith. For far more was at stake in this quarrel over chosenness than the doctrine itself—far more, even, than alternative definitions of Judaism as a "religion" or a "civilization." The issue, ultimately, was the nature and place of Jewish theology, once the guiding assumptions of Jewish tradition had been discarded. Kaplan's rejection of election, we will find, was an integral part of his program for the wholesale "reconstruction" of Jewish faith.

IV

Mordecai Kaplan and the New Jewish "Vocation"

T HE PRINCIPAL THEORIST of American Jewish identity throughout the second generation, and the principal critic of the doctrines of mission and chosenness, was also the period's most influential, prolific, and incisive Jewish thinker. Turn where one would in those thirty years, one found Mordecai Kaplan with a critique of the traditional idea of election as he understood it, or of one of its many outfittings in modern dress. Turn the election idea as one would, so that a more pleasing side of it faced the modern audience, and Kaplan was there to brush away the cosmetic and show that even in this aspect the idea just could not be countenanced. If American Jewish thinkers of the second generation spent so much time reaffirming, reinterpreting, reexplaining, and simply pondering the doctrine of Israel's chosenness, the reason was in no small measure that Kaplan spent so much time in attacking it. Chosenness, he insisted, unlike the rest of Jewish tradition, could not be "reconstructed," but only repudiated.

My concern in this chapter is to document that singular refusal to reconstruct, to explain it, and, most important, to chart its implications for the self-definition of American Jewry. Kaplan's disavowal of election in favor of an idea of "vocation" was far from idiosyncratic. It was, rather, essential to the entire enterprise of Reconstructionism as Kaplan envisioned it, and to the concepts of God and Judaism which he proposed. It was also particularly well suited to the altered socioeconomic character of the community to which it was recommended, and expressed rather precisely the dilemmas of the rabbis who were, in the beginning, its principal audience and supporters. The nuances of Kaplan's attempt to reformulate the symbols by which American Jewry defined itself to itself and to gentile America take us to the heart of what American Jewish thought in the second generation is really about.

Chosenness as a Vocation

Because so much that is crucial to American Jewish life began with its publication in 1934, one tends to forget that the author of *Judaism as a Civilization* was far from the beginning of his own career when the appearance of the book gave that career dramatic new impetus.[1] Born in Lithuania to a distinguished Talmudist in 1881, Kaplan had come to New York at the age of eight, attended public school and *ḥeder*, spent nine years at the Jewish Theological Seminary, and received a B.A. from City College and an M.A. from Columbia University. The biographical details are telling: first because the late nineteenth century left its mark on Kaplan's thought, second because he pioneered a path, vocational and intellectual, that would prove well traveled in the generation to whom he spoke most directly. Kaplan's influence can be traced in part to this personal acquaintance from experience with the dilemmas of his students. While serving as rabbi of a prestigious Orthodox congregation in New York in 1909, Kaplan was invited by Solomon Schechter to head the recently established Teachers Institute at the Jewish Theological Seminary. A year later, he became professor of homiletics at JTS as well, successfully turning the teaching of sermon-giving, held in low esteem at the institution, to the matter of sermon content, and thence to the need for a sweeping redefinition of Judaism that would enable rabbis to reach their congregants more effectively. In 1921 Kaplan left a second Orthodox rabbinical post in order to found his own congregation, the Society for the Advancement of Judaism, which (borrowing a term from Ethical Culture) he served not as rabbi but "leader." In the interim, Kaplan had resigned and regained his position at JTS, declined Stephen Wise's offer of the presidency of the Jewish Institute of Religion, and attracted many young rabbis, educators and Zionist intellectuals to the branches of his Society that had by now been formed in cities of the East and Midwest. Kaplan's ideas on the rejuvenation of American Judaism were appearing regularly in such periodicals as the *Menorah Journal* as early as 1910. It was their systematic recapitulation in *Judaism as a Civilization*, however, that gave the impetus both to Kaplan's own intellectual production and to the growth of his movement. Reconstructionism now had an ideology, an orientation vis-à-vis the Jewish past, and a detailed program of action. Despite variations within the ranks over the next several decades, especially regarding Kaplan's controversial "god-concept," the thinking of the First Reconstructionist can safely be taken for the stance of the movement as a whole. In tracing the movement, therefore, we shall follow previous students in focusing almost exclusively upon the development of Kaplan's personal thought.[2]

Kaplan's starting point in *Judaism as a Civilization* was the crisis in the Judaism of the day, especially manifest in Jewish self-hatred. At the very outset Kaplan introduced a reading of history crucial to his entire enterprise of reconstruction. Before the Enlightenment, he argued, Jews as much as Christians had conceived life primarily in otherworldly terms. Jews had overcome centuries of earthly ill-fortune by centering their thoughts upon their destiny in the hereafter, and this prospect of bliss had constituted their salvation. But

> now that the aura of divine election has departed from his people, and his Jewish origin brings with it nothing but economic handicaps and social inferiority, the Jew rebels against his fate . . . [he] is maladjusted morally and spiritually as a result of losing the traditional concept of salvation. He has to evolve some new purpose in life as a Jew, a purpose that will direct his energies into such lines of creativity as will bring him spiritual redemption. That purpose will have to constitute his salvation.[3]

Kaplan here and throughout his works assumed otherworldly salvation to have been the true reward conferred on the Jew by election, the real meaning of chosenness for the ordinary Jew. This is a point brushed aside by other rabbis of the period, on the grounds that according to rabbinic teaching the righteous of the nations of the world had no less a share in the world to come than the Jews. For Kaplan the theological niceties mattered less than how the doctrine actually worked in practice. The point, therefore, was election's clear implication that "other things being equal the Jew . . . stood a far greater chance of attaining salvation than the rest of the world."[4] Since such salvation was in modern times no longer available (for Jews, he felt, could no longer believe in it), the Jew was in need of a new purpose to replace it, one which Kaplan felt he could supply.

Adopting the medical imagery of which Kaplan was fond, we might say that his first objection to chosenness lay in the need of the doctor thoroughly to convince the patient both of his sickness and of the recommended cure. Again and again, one finds Kaplan complaining that many Jews continued to rely on their chosenness to save them, when only this-worldly salvation could possibly do the job.

What is more, Kaplan continued, election was incompatible with the civic status of the modern Jew. In apparent endorsement of the charge of dual loyalties often leveled against Jews since Emancipation, Kaplan argued that citizenship in a modern state precluded allowing "the interest of any outside group to influence [one's] political action." The interests of a chosen people, however, "would surely take precedence" over the national interest, especially given belief in the eventual return of the entire Jewish people to Palestine. Clinging to the doctrine of Israel's election barred "complete self-identification with the state." Discarding that belief, though, meant that a substitute motivation "for Jewish solidarity" would be needed to provide the sense of "a social unit making history . . . [the] sense of augmented power" previously evoked in the Jew by chosenness.[5] Kaplan of course believed he had found it.

Once more we see him standing apart from his contemporaries, this time in perceiving and openly stating the political implications of belief in election. As a concept inseparable from *galut* (exile), chosenness entailed a self-distancing from the reigning political order and, unlike the modern nation-state, conferred on the Jewish individual a sense of his own power in the world. Kaplan's verbatim repetition of the charge of dual loyalty is striking, especially given his own call to the American Jew to live in two civilizations. Finally, one observes the dilemma which Kaplan would never quite escape. Reconstructionism, unlike chosenness, could save Jews, but how, without chosenness, could Kaplan persuade Jews to turn to it for their salvation?

His third objection to chosenness concerned its incompatibility with "the modern ideology." The scientific world-view had rendered belief in supernatural revelation and a supernatural order impossible. Moreover, given modern ideas about justice and equality, it was inadvisable "from an ethical standpoint" to perpetuate the ideas of "race or national superiority" inherent in election.[6] Kaplan had collapsed two arguments: the inability of the idea of chosenness to function as it once had, and its unsuitability on ethical grounds even if it could function. He argued, unlike his colleagues, that chosenness does imply a claim to superiority. Kaplan would continue to emphasize the distasteful implications of election, the better to argue for its disavowal. Once bereft of the consolations of election, Jews would be forced to seek a new purpose to Jewish national life which "would be the equivalent of the traditional belief" and therefore its "functional revaluation."[7] Salvation, meaning self-fulfillment, would then come through "living the civilization" of one's people, and the people would be enabled to provide such fulfillment through Reconstruction.

In sum: chosenness was unacceptable for reasons of strategy, politics, ethics, and rational belief. Reconstructionism was explicitly meant to replace chosenness, both as the source of pride in Jewish identity and as the purpose for which the Jewish people actively worked.

In the next major work, *Judaism in Transition* (1936), Kaplan observed that belief in election justified Marx's view that religion resigns the downtrodden to their lot,[8] and attacked the claim to superiority inherent in election as a cause of "hatred and strife," an incentive to "religious imperialism." Even secular nationalists such as Ahad Ha'am had been guilty of chauvinism in their claim that Jewish civilization was ethically superior to all others. Rather than believing in a divine revelation of truth, as did Christianity and traditional Judaism—a belief "incompatible with tolerance"—Jews should seek awareness only of their privilege in having been gifted with a civilization that spells salvation for them, without any implication that other peoples have not received similar revelations of the goodness and sacredness of life which spell salvation for their own adherents.[9]

Other peoples had in fact received similar salvation. Religions could not be understood apart from the civilizations in which they developed, Kaplan explained, and "always express the collective personality" of these civilizations. They were "as non-transferrable and incommunicable as is individual personality." Every civilization had a religion, since each people possessed a collective personality, and every religion constituted a "unique" (and equal) "manifestation of the divine." The subjection of the various religions to a common standard of measurement was thus impossible, and so the conclusion that one was superior to the others, more true, "chosen," was also impossible. What was true for one people in its situation might not be true for another.[10]

This Durkheimian presentation of religion as *conscience collective*— the shared beliefs and practices of a community—rendered election unacceptable on two new grounds. First, the doctrine was unnecessary. Every civilization "spells salvation" (provides meaning) for its members, and so the salvation believed to accrue to Israel through election was provided by Jewish civilization as a whole. Second, the claim to election was meaningless, since all civilizations by definition perform the religious function and all perform it equally well—an assumption which would be questioned in future works. Chosenness, then, contradicted the very nature of religion. Not surprisingly Kaplan insisted that all passages which made "revolting" claims to Jewish superiority be stricken from the prayer book.[11]

Durkheim had figured heavily in *Judaism as a Civilization* as well, and it is worth noting just how crucially Kaplan's acceptance of the sociologist's premises affected his vision of Judaism and fixed his own future agenda. For Kaplan, Durkheim was not merely one thinker among many, but the man who had "stated the attitude of science toward religion with matchless clarity." One might argue with opinion, but not with scientific fact. This did not mean, Kaplan explained in Durkheim's own words, that science would deny religion's "right to exist," but it would deny religion's "right to dogmatize upon the nature of things and the special competence which it claims for itself for knowing man and the world." Religion "does not know itself. It does not even know what it is made of, nor to what need it answers. It is itself a subject for science."[12] Sociology, then, would explain religion's existence and the particulars of its belief and practice by showing their function in integrating the lives and consciousness of communities. It could thus judge the truth-claims of individual faiths by assessing their success in generating and maintaining the *conscience collective*, by making this "general will" felt in the minds of individuals. Religion's "right to exist" has been affirmed and justified by appeal to its function, but—a consideration not mentioned by Kaplan—religion has been reduced to that function.

The usefulness of this approach for Kaplan is clear. Quite simply, in his words, "the question of 'why be a Jew?' loses its relevance. If Jewish life is a unique way of experience, it needs no further justification." Nor would one need any further justification for tampering with tradition to help it better serve the modern Jew. For, as Kaplan explains in a passage remarkable for its candor,

> attachment to Judaism has always been derived from just such an intuitional attitude toward it. The various interpretations of Jewish doctrine and practice, the abstract values and concepts, are but the formal afterthoughts of that intuitional attitude. The recital of the Shema Yisrael was traditionally one of the most dramatically meaningful practices of Judaism, not because of the abstract idea of absolute monotheism which it is supposed to express, *but simply because it provided an occasion for experiencing the thrill of being a Jew.*[13]

It is a telling passage. The truth-value of the essential credo of Jewish faith, uttered by every traditional Jew with the last breath of life, has been reduced to its function in generating what for Durkheim was the quintessential religious experience: the consciousness (and accompanying thrill) of group belonging.[14] The belief itself is irrelevant. Much more than the chosen-people idea has been rendered dispensable by this approach, and Kaplan found no problem with such reductionism. It made the scope for reconstruction all the wider.[15]

Two implications of this borrowing from Durkheim would persistently claim Kaplan's attention. First, the elements of civilization enumerated by the two thinkers presupposed "the life of a group which contains enough social machinery to articulate the general will."[16] They were, in other words, a desideratum in the modern world, and not a reality. Indeed, the raison d'être of Durkheim's entire sociology lay in his conviction that the anomie of modern society derived from the loss of the sort of "mechanical solidarity" idealized in *Elementary Forms*. The Jewish group too had largely disintegrated, for many of the same reasons. How then could the Jewish "general will" be reconceived, as Kaplan wished, let alone internalized by individual members so as to provide them with salvation? Kaplan did cite internal and external "factors of conservation" making for the preservation of the Jewish collectivity, but he also recognized that Jewish identity in his day rested upon "little more than a blind urge to live as Jews."[17] If Kaplan was to motivate such loyalty, and not merely provide a rationale for those already motivated for other reasons, he needed nothing less than a reconstituted Jewish community of the sort never achieved in the post-Emancipation diaspora. To achieve that community, however, he needed the *conscience collective* which only the functioning group life could provide. Durkheim's theory, as has often been noted, is only adequate to a situation of stasis in which group life and group consciousness reinforce one another. Losing one of the two, one inevitably loses the other as well.

Durkheim sought to break out of this circle through a renewed solidarity, "organic" in his terms, which could be rationally constructed on the basis of two existing group identifications: occupational guilds on the one hand, and the nation-state on the other.[18] Kaplan, however, had no use for the first suggestion and ridiculed the "spiritualized patriotism" of the second as the sort of exaggerated loyalty one would expect from an assimilated French Jew.[19] The point was crucial. For if religious beliefs and practices existed to serve the function of strengthening group identity, and "a blind urge to live as Jews" was not an adequate substitute, what was? Chosenness had worked by taking the chosen people beyond itself and grounding its existence in transcendent purposes. A viable "substitute" for election would have to do that also, yet what, short of God, could the grounding be? To fall back on God was to reject the Durkheimian model which was the theoretical underpinning of Kaplan's entire effort. To accept the model was to doom that effort to certain failure.

This is the second implication of Durkheim's theory which would continue to occupy Kaplan throughout his works. Durkheim was an atheist. Kaplan, as we will see below, was not. He severely criticized that "science of religion . . . which, by trespassing upon fields of inquiry beyond its scope, presumes to explain away the reality of God." However, he saw no problem in a science which "confines itself to the task of explaining how the God-idea has functioned in history."[20] As it would so often in the future, Kaplan's eclectic spirit found it possible to differentiate between a theory or a language of analysis and the presuppositions on which it rested. Durkheim's assumption that God was nothing more than the consciousness of the group, symbolically represented (and thus dispensable when another symbol could serve the same function), was to Kaplan's mind neutralized by his own Idealist notion of the group as one of the many arenas in which God was immanently manifest. Indeed, God was present in "that very reality which serves as a criterion for rejecting as illusions the traditional or conventional ideas of God,"[21] such as Judaism's. Yet how could we be sure of this reality? On what could this "criterion" rest, unless it was intuitive, now that we as moderns were aware that "god-ideas" come and go rather frequently, and that the act of belief is at bottom only another "expression of man's will to live?" In the end, Kaplan found personal belief to rest on a prerational will, precisely as national loyalty did, in his view. In neither case, he recognized, was the grounding satisfactory. Two tasks confronted the Jews, then: the providing of a new purpose to Jewish existence, replacing chosenness, and, in that connection, the conceiving of a God at once modern, functional, compelling, and real enough to replace the Chooser of Jewish tradition. Only with this "glue" of a reconstructed *conscience collective* in hand could one set about putting a shattered Jewish community back together.

We will take up momentarily the "god-concept" at which Kaplan arrived in his next major work, *The Meaning of God in Modern Jewish Religion*(1937). Suffice it to say that Kaplan proceeded to apply his functionalist approach to Jewish belief and practice through imaginative assignment of new meanings to traditional Jewish group observance. For example, the Sabbath's primacy in Jewish life testified to its function in symbolizing "the most significant and comprehensive spiritual purpose which the Jewish religion sought to help the Jew achieve." What more comprehensive purpose could there be to human life than "the complete and harmonious fulfillment of all the physical, mental and moral powers with which the human self as a social being is endowed?" This, in traditional parlance, was called salvation, and hence the task was to reformulate salvation for the modern Jew and show how the traditional observances associated with the Sabbath expressed this conception symbolically.[22] Chosenness, in this context, was utterly psychologized: it represented "the typical self-assertion of the personality that is haunted by an inferiority complex." Where Jews of old had believed that their superiority consisted in possession of the Torah, the modern Jew who no longer believed in revelation at Sinai was reduced to hunting in newspapers "for success stories of Jews that might serve to bolster up his pride in the face of the sense of inferiority that his position as a Jew imposes." Jews should rather eradicate the inferiority which at present possessed their minds through a new notion of what it meant to be a holy people. Their covenant with God should signify the nation's consecration to universal ideals and "an integrated cooperative human society." The resultant individual salvation would be no more and no less than the resources offered by every group to those who partook in its life.[23] No development in Kaplan's thinking on election is evident here.

In *The Future of the American Jew* (1946), by contrast, Kaplan makes an original contribution to the conception of chosenness. First, after urging Jews to be faithful to Judaism "because it is ours, the only religion we have,"[24] he makes a crucial concession in the hope of motivating such loyalty. He now concedes that "if we wish to foster Jewish group solidarity, we must live up to a higher ethical standard than the average.

No other justification for our remaining an identifiable minority will avail."[25] As Kallen had done before him, Kaplan has retreated from the advocacy of difference for its own sake. As Reform had moved from chosenness to ethics, and stressed Jewish service to America and the world, so now did Kaplan. Judaism would strengthen the morals of America's Jews, and achieve a "religious orientation" which might prove of great value to the "religiously starved mankind of our day."[26]

Kaplan then devoted a long section to the enumeration and refutation of all possible reinterpretations of the doctrine of election. Racial theories were groundless. Other peoples had made equal or greater contributions to the world. To say that Israel possessed the highest religious truths was impossible, for truth was a "dynamic concept," ever changing. Finally, election should not be confused with mission, derided by Kaplan as "the subject of less than a dozen passages in the second part of Isaiah." Reinterpretation of election was thus not viable, and the traditional version could only be, "ideologically, a definite hindrance." "Rationalist" Jews would be lost to their people as Felix Adler (the founder of the Ethical Culture movement) had been, because of their inability to embrace belief in election. "Romantic" Jews content to accept election as a figurative truth would thereby "paralyze all spiritual initiative" and lull the Jews into a "dangerous somnolence."[27]

The only alternative lay in reconceiving election as *vocation*. Jewish religion should be refashioned to enable Jewish civilization to enhance Jewish life and the life of mankind. The Jew would then be able to "live the civilization of his people in a spirit of commitment and dedication;" to

> live with a sense of vocation or calling, without involving ourselves in any of the invidious distinctions implied in the doctrine of election, and yet to fulfill the legitimate spiritual wants which that doctrine sought to satisfy.

Distinctions were not entirely lacking even among vocations. A janitor was not a president. But neither did the latter thank God daily that he was not the former (a reference to the morning benedictions in which the Jew thanks God that he is not a gentile).[28] Finally, to those who might object that vocation was a Christian idea, Kaplan replied with a citation from the Talmud (*Berakhot* 17a) which reminds us that work in the field is equal in value to work in the Torah, so long as "each directs his heart to Heaven."[29]

There is much here to which we shall return presently. Since further works added little to the conceptualization of chosenness and Jewishness now in place, I will round out the picture by considering those later works before taking up the notion of a Jewish vocation in detail. First, we should note the ironic exchange of essays which Kaplan conducted with the Christian theologian Franklin Littell in 1947. Littell equated the communal self-consciousness which Kaplan at times termed "religion" with "self-adulation," and asserted *pace* Kaplan that, far from breeding intolerance, the chosen-people idea was "dialectically related" to a universal dream. Kaplan in reply repeated the arguments which we have examined. He was placed in the position of telling a Christian in favor of ecumenical relations between the two faiths that the chosen-people idea, which the Christian defended, precluded Jewish respect for Christians—surely a prerequisite of Christian toleration for Jews.[30]

In his autobiographical essay, "The Way I Have Come" (1952), Kaplan confessed that the question of election "forced itself upon me" in this form: how could Jews "accord religious significance to American sancta [i.e., that which the nation held sacred] without giving up the claim to being God's chosen people?" They could not, in his view. Integration into American civilization and the very definitions with which Kaplan worked (namely, that all civilizations provided salvation) demanded that American "sancta" be accorded religious significance. If all peoples were chosen, as one Conservative rabbi had maintained, then chosenness was meaningless; one might as well do away with it, especially since it constituted "the main obstacle . . . [to] universalizing the method and the secret of Jewish religion": the use of a people's "sancta" as the "frame of reference for its moral and spiritual values."[31] Here chosenness is explicitly denounced for its particularity, the problem which Reform thinkers had been having with it all along.

In *Judaism Without Supernaturalism* (1957) all the previous themes are reiterated, and their underlying assumptions become manifest. The definition of religion upon which Kaplan had been insisting for over a generation is now explicitly said to serve the purpose of outreach to disaffected Jews. "We must learn to redefine the term 'religion' in such a way as not to be put in a position of having to declare as irreligious or anti-religious, not only the intellectual elite, but virtually most healthy-minded persons."[32] Kaplan now juxtaposes his insistence that religions be the unique creations of national civilizations with the recognition that religion in the West and Near East, for the past two thousand years, had not followed that pattern. The latter, he concluded, had "been thrown out of kilter," and the renascent Jewish national religion would set things right.[33] Moreover, the Jewish contribution is now explicitly said to be the sole legitimation of a Jewish presence in America:

> The only kind of contribution of a high order that Jews as a group can make to American culture is that which reflects their group individuality. Hence, only if Jews would excel in the field of religion, would they have reason to feel that, in the one boat in which they find themselves with all their fellow Americans, they pull their own weight culturally and spiritually.[34]

That the Jewish people more than any other approached the ideal religious form "is a fact that hardly needs laboring," Kaplan continued, for other nations were at present far short of the capacity to offer their members salvation. Only Christians came close. The Jews, by discarding their supernaturalism, would be able to "universalize the acceptable implications" of their traditional interpretation of Jewish history. Their particularism would be understood "in the sense of providing a specific example of what is involved in a people's dedication to the service of God."[35] This too, on the face of it, is a formulation that might have come from Kaufman Kohler.

It raised, furthermore, precisely the same question. Why remain Jewish, if the universal elements in Jewish religion could be incorporated in American institutions? "Why bother about maintaining the Jewish group individuality and the specific Jewish form of religion?" Once more, despite all the attempts to formulate a transcendent purpose for Jewish group life, Kaplan replies that the reason to stay a Jew is "as ultimate a matter of feeling as the will to live." Only once imbued with this will did one seek a rationale for it in "some universal purpose that might enhance American civilization."[36] Kaplan here attempts to reconcile his call for Jewish difference for its own sake with his vision of a purpose to Jewish existence which the collective life of other peoples could not offer. The Jews were to take the lead in promoting American religion, but were to remain Jewish for reasons (including that contribution to America) which were to be sought only after the decision to remain a Jew had already been made. At another point Kaplan suggests that the individual best serves humanity through his own group, the Jew by placing his particular tradition at the service of all humanity. Near the close of the work he explains that the problem is to provide the Jew who identifies with his people a "valid justification" for doing so, now that the belief in a chosen people no longer sufficed.[37] This is precisely where he—and we—began, and where we may conclude, since later works add only a presentation of traditional teachings on election less distorted by Kaplan's need to refute them,[38] but no further reinterpretation. It is time to consider what Kaplan's far-reaching attempt at reconstruction had wrought.

The "Power, not Ourselves" and Civil Religion

What Kaplan had attempted might best be described as a semantic coup. "Vocation" connoted the call of individual and group to a particular task, issued by a divinity certainly no less vague than the God imagined in much of non-Orthodox theology. It laid no claim to either superiority or exclusiveness. The frequent attempts in his day to argue that the Jews were chosen, but so was everyone else, were doomed to failure by the meaning of the word "chosen" itself, whereas the word "vocation" presented no such stumbling-block. "Many are called, but few are chosen." That verse (Matthew 22:14) and Kaplan's explicit denial of vocation's non-Jewish provenance suggest that perhaps far more than a semantic alteration was involved. Kaplan, we shall find, had not simply imported a word, but rather a concept, not to say a world-view. The problem is endemic to his eclecticism. In this case the echoes of the Puritan idea of the calling reverberate with such force that the entire thrust of the traditional idea is altered: a consequence not unintended by Kaplan, I believe. The Puritan idea, then, merits closer examination.

As set forth by William Perkins in his *Treatise of the Vocations* (1603) and subsequent works, the calling is threefold. The individual is called to reorder the private realm of behavior in home and work. He is called as Christian to aid in the purification of the church. As citizen, he is called to fight for the reordering of the commonwealth against an unregenerate king. Sin and licentiousness were to be expelled from one's thoughts, one's home, one's labor, one's church, one's country, and a space created in which God's will alone was performed.[39] Kaplan borrowed the threefold scheme, lessening emphasis on the individual, as befit a Durkheimian view of collectivity and religion. The individual Jew was to live the civilization of his or her people, filling home and life with meaning. The Jew was to reorder Judaism, transforming it from a burdensome religion to a civilization capable of providing meaning. This reconstruction was explicitly referred to as the individual's "vocation," even his or her "salvation."[40] Likewise, the American commonwealth had to be transformed so that it, like all ideal nation-civilizations, could provide salvation for its members. It was no coincidence that Kaplan called for social and economic reforms at the same time as he urged—along with Horace Kallen and long before it became fashionable—the formulation of an American civil religion.[41]

In a word, just as the Puritan's "inner-worldly asceticism" took the man of vocation out of the monastery and set him to work in and on the world, so Kaplan took the Jew out of the *halakhah*'s "four ells" and set him or her to work in and on the Jew's world, on the Jew's two worlds. Recalling Kaplan's reading of *Berakhot*—that work in the field is equal in worth to study of Torah—we might say that where Reform had substituted an ethical mission for the traditional curriculum of Jewish practice, Kaplan now gave full credit for fieldwork. The change in direction—from an inwardly directed regimen of *mitzvot* to an outwardly directed program of activity—is as significant as the transformation from a call to specific, prescribed activities, as in *halakhah*, to a more generalized call to action that left full scope to individual initiative. The Puritan achieved this room for maneuver because his God was a *deus absconditus*, who left earthly battles to mortal agents. Similarly, if we are to grasp the full significance of Kaplan's replacement of election by vocation, we need to examine the relation between vocation and his concept of the divine.

Kaplan's many works offer a variety of formulations of his "god-concept," but for our purposes the idea is sufficiently lucid and consistent: "a quality of universal being, all the relationships, tendencies and agencies which in their totality go to make a human life worthwhile in the deepest and most abiding sense."[42] God is the totality of forces which render life worthwhile,[43] the "aspect of reality to which we react with a sense of life's unity, creativity and worthwhileness,"[44] the aspect of reality which confers meaning on life,[45] and "the Power that endorses what we believe ought to be, and guarantees that it will be."[46] Kaplan, we should note, never reduces God to a human projection or ideal. Rather, God remains an objectively real process which, working through us but transcending us, renders life worthwhile by furthering the causes of freedom, salvation, social regeneration, the regeneration of human nature, human cooperation and righteousness.[47] Meaning to life, then, comes from knowing of the perfected unity for which God works, and from joining in that work. Only our faith in its accomplishment enables us to join the work, and only our agency accomplishes it.

The work is, above all, the ordering of chaos into unity. God provides (this-worldly) salvation, Kaplan writes, by functioning as a totality to make the world into a totality, an "organic unity." God labors constantly to enlarge that portion of being which partakes of godhood, or unity, rather than non-godhood, or chaos. "It is sufficient that God should mean to us the sum of the animating, organizing forces and relationships which are forever making a cosmos out of chaos. This is what we understand by God as the creative life of the universe." God, with our help, was still creating the world. Evil merely testified to the "chaos still uninvaded by the creative energy, [the] sheer chance unconquered by will and intelligence."[48] The "man of vocation" served this work of God by perfecting his small area of being, thus creating a microcosm of the larger whole to come and contributing to its achievement. He created unity where chaos had been, and testified to the reality of the invisible God of process at work transforming that which is by means of individuals such as himself. Ultimately, the individual fulfilled his or her self by losing it:[49] that is, sacrificing it to the cosmic process constructing wholes out of parts. For the present, his or her own salvation through unification, insofar as it was attainable, prefigured the world's.

One might think, given this logic, that the particular might serve better by disappearing straight off: the Jew, in this case, working for universal rather than particular ends. Kaplan, however, has two overriding concerns, and it is the vocation idea which enables him to reconcile them. The first, sketched above, is the salvation of the Jew, who must be saved as everyone (e.g., a Frenchman) is saved, by being part of a nation-civilization that offers fulfillment. The second goal, however, is the revitalization of the Jewish people, the existence of which was at first justified by Kaplan only by the prerational "will to live" of its members.[50] The Jew could be saved only by a revitalized Judaism, and not by America, because at present Judaism's "god-consciousness" was "the distinctive achievement of the Jewish spirit."[51] The Jewish nation, therefore, was uniquely equipped to provide salvation. Its unique "god-consciousness" enabled its members to experience "the reality and meaning of Divinity" more than any other people.[52] All vocations, we may now summarize, were not equal; one was far "more equal than others." Judaism was uniquely able to save: for historical reasons, to be sure, and only for the time being, but still. Chosenness, ushered unceremoniously out the front door, was in more modest dress smuggled in through the back.

Its Kaplanian outfitting was rather traditional: the uniform of service which we have seen time and again in our survey of chosenness and its reinterpretation. The Israelites of long ago, we might say, had been provided with a ready-made space for the labor of their vocation—the Land of Israel. Other nations, observing Israel's successful pursuit of its calling, would be moved to exclaim upon the wisdom of its laws and Lawgiver—and then do likewise. Kaplan, following the Puritan model of threefold calling to God, church, and commonwealth, was enabled by Durkheim's sociology to adapt the traditional Jewish conception to the American diaspora. He made of every human space a potential promised land in which one did the work which truly was God's own. America was Zion, though for reasons which Kohler could not have grasped. True to all three of his models—Deuteronomy, the Puritans, and Durkheim—Kaplan could not conceive of religion as (in the words of a theologian whose view of God is quite similar to Kaplan's) "what the individual does with his own solitariness."[53] Rather, if men were to perform their divine labor of constructing order from chaos, they needed political worlds in which to build. This the notion of civil religion could provide as no other, even as it served to legitimate the Jewish presence in America.

One finds the concept adumbrated as early as *Judaism as a Civilization.* Every civilization, Kaplan wrote, would "ultimately . . . organize its own sancta into a collective religion to fill the void left by the shrinking of Christianity." Jews in America would "share with the civic community the task of meting out salvation." Patriotism—loyalty to one's civic community—and religion—loyalty to one's "historic community"—

would be seen to work together, once the individualistic conception of religion still predominant in America had been abandoned.[54]

However, the idea is fully developed only in *Future of the American Jew*, once the two more basic ideas on which it rests—God and vocation—have been put in place. Kaplan argues, in a chapter entitled "Education for Democracy," that in the modern world religion had come to be secularized, and, conversely, nationhood had been "religionized." States were now concerned with promotion of the public good. They asserted "the sacredness of the human soul and its dignity," and regarded men as "endowed by their Creator with . . . unalienable [*sic*] rights," etc.—the reference to the Creator here expressing a "profound religious evaluation of human life." After heredity, nationality was "the most decisive influence in a person's life," and it was, therefore, imperative that nationality be shaped as a means to salvation. In America this had already occurred. "Democracy is to us Americans nothing less than a method of this-worldly salvation." It should therefore be possible to teach about God "with the aid of American sancta, like the great texts, events and personalities of the American people." There would always be a need for the historic religions of Judaism and Christianity, whose "larger perspectives" would preclude the abuses to which the "religionizing" nationhood was subject. Christianity should use its influence to encourage the emergence of an American religion, "with democracy as its way of salvation." Jews should recognize that "the American religion of democracy has room for Judaism, and Jewish religion has room for American democracy."[55]

Some of Kaplan's colleagues were not so sure. When Ira Eisenstein, Kaplan's chief disciple, successor at the Society for the Advancement of Judaism, and son-in-law, urged the American civil religion upon his colleagues in the Conservative rabbinate in 1949, they were not receptive. One wondered if democracy would not come to be a greater goal than Judaism. A second noted Eisenstein's failure to mention the goal of Jewish survival. A third criticized his use of the word "religion," and urged Jews to insist on their separate existence as both ethnic group and religion in a society becoming less and less pluralistic. Eugene Kohn, another Kaplan disciple, responded that the tendency to a national religion already existed; "shall we plan it or not?" Eisenstein remarked that any civilization had a religion when it became aware of its deepest aspirations and expressed them in terms of human life. From "the social and psychological point of view, what was the difference between Passover and the Fourth of July?"[56] Precisely. Civil religion would not win the rabbis' adherence.

Two years later, Kaplan, Kohn, and J. Paul Williams published *The Faith of America*, a collection of prayers to be recited on New Year's Day, Lincoln's Birthday, Arbor Day, Flag Day, etc. Independence Day would be dedicated to reflection upon the uses of freedom, Arbor Day to thought upon the responsible use of natural resources. On New Year's Day, Jews would reflect upon the ideals of America, a singular people, a "one new Man" composed of "the most vigorous scions from all European stocks." Columbus Day would be devoted to "an appreciation of the exploring and pioneering spirit."[57] And so on.

As Robert Bellah's enthusiastic declaration of American civil religion in 1957 was influenced by a Durkheimian view of religion and meant to serve the purpose of religious and national revitalization,[58] so was Kaplan's a generation earlier. His proposal had one further motivation, however. Civil religion would resolve "doubts concerning the legitimacy of Jewish corporate life in America." Genuine democracy would always "give Jewish life free rein." Furthermore, "by fostering those interests which unite American Jews with the Jews of the rest of the world, we are helping to effect that division of function between the nation and the trans-national group which is indispensable to the life of the democratic state."[59] Jewish ethnic loyalties too are thus part of the Jews' service to America—this according to the Mordecai Kaplan who had denounced chosenness because it precluded "complete self-identification with the state." America, it now turned out, could be persuaded to accept less than that, by learning to see itself as more than merely a state. Making his adopted nation religious, the Jew could persuade it that his own national religion was legitimate and even necessary. Kaplan's strategy here parallels rather precisely the "Judaism is Democracy" offensive, examined in chapter 2, which as we recall he was the first to condemn. Judaism was not identical to democracy—but it could serve the American "religion of democracy." That was precisely the civic component of the Jews' threefold-vocation. Kaplan has been led by his own logic and, rather more importantly, by the position of American Jewry, to a strategy very similar to that of his opponents, precisely as he was led by that same situation to an affirmation, however tentative and qualified, of the uniqueness of Israel.

One can make still more sense of these twists and turns if one recalls the two figures accounted by Kaplan himself to be the most influential on his thinking on the matter of election, and one whom he significantly does not mention. His entire concern with chosenness, Kaplan recalled in 1952, arose only after he had come under the influence of Ahad Ha'am and—rather more surprising at first glance—Matthew Arnold.[60]

The latter, whose early and profound influence on Kaplan is not often noted, conveyed far more to him than the terms "power (not ourselves) making for righteousness" or "method and secret" of religion. Arnold's *Literature and Dogma*, which Kaplan cited approvingly, is a plan not unlike Reconstructionism for recasting an inherited faith in naturalist and national terms.[61] Moreover, for all that *Culture and Anarchy* found "Hebraism" in need of correction by a healthy dose of "Hellenism," Hebraism is one of the two elements of healthy civilization, and is credited with a unique insight into the ways of God.[62] Just as Kaplan sought above all else a God who could serve as the basis for moral action and guarantee the achievement of a perfect moral order, so Arnold had discerned in ancient Israelite religion—and praised—a unique belief in the "not ourselves" who would guarantee that happiness will flow from "right conduct." Israel, after all, had called its God Jehovah, the Eternal. What did they mean by that? "The Eternal cause? Alas, these poor people were not Archbishops of York. They meant the Eternal righteous who loveth righteousness."[63] This scorn for metaphysics, of course, resounds in Kaplan as well. His only criticism of Arnold, perhaps following John Dewey's in *A Common Faith*, concerned Arnold's narrow definition of "power not ourselves." The power worked for other values than righteousness, Dewey insisted, such as beauty, truth, and friendship.[64] However, while Dewey's influence on Kaplan—and especially on his "god-concept"—seems indisputable, the philosopher represents only one more contributor to Kaplan's eclectic mix, and in the matters of vocation and civil religion cannot compare in his impact on Kaplan to Arnold. Nor does Kaplan mention Dewey explicitly. Arnold, like Ahad Ha'am, evinced a concern for national culture, for Jewish culture, and for the ongoing Jewish role in the world not found in Dewey. They were, moreover, practitioners, possessed of a sense for the flesh-and-blood of religious culture, which Dewey could never match. Arnold's most dubious legacy to Kaplan may have been a faith in and regard for the virtues of "sweetness and light" which Kaplan refused to renounce even after the terrors of the Holocaust.

In a way, one suspects, Arnold served primarily to legitimate the legacy of Kaplan's principal master, Ahad Ha'am, through advocacy in the wider, gentile world of the path which the Zionist thinker urged for Jews. Ahad Ha'am, chief proponent of cultural Zionism, principal opponent of Herzl within the Zionist movement, and the architect of a secular recasting of Judaism as national culture, provided Kaplan with his model of two sorts of Jewish civilization.[65] In the land of Israel Jews could fashion a complete national civilization, receiving salvation from their revitalized Jewish civil religion, while in the diaspora they would participate in (and be enriched by) two civilizations, the Jewish and, e.g., the American. To the question "why be a Jew?" Ahad Ha'am had answered: as well ask why be your father's son. He derided mission and election as symptoms of an inferiority complex. Yet he went on to ascribe a different moral sense to each people and a superior one to the

Jew. Kaplan, through concepts of God and vocation unavailable to his teacher, was able to go further, offering a transcendent purpose for Jewish culture that would promote the national revival which Ahad Ha'am had sought. In short, Arnold gave Kaplan a model of national religion applicable only to a homogeneous or majority culture. Ahad Ha'am, however, provided a model of diaspora culture centered on the Jewish homeland, though he could not envision healthy integration in two civilizations. Arnold could "religionize" the American in the Jew; Ahad Ha'am could revitalize the Jew in the American. Kaplan hoped, with Durkheim's help (and God's!), to put them together in the form of a new Jewish vocation.

It is useful, when one considers the possibilities for success of that venture, to note that the first thinker to pose the question of the Jewish vocation in the modern world is rarely mentioned by Kaplan. For Spinoza, unable to answer the question to his own satisfaction, had recommended a naturalist faith and civil religion very similar to Kaplan's, along with what he took to be the inevitable consequence of his logic: the quiet disappearance of the Jews. It was Spinoza, in fact, who had set the agenda for modern Jewish thought, insisting that the "theological" and the "political" be considered together in order to locate the proper role of religion in the modern state. Not at all by coincidence, then, the first several chapters of his *Theologico-Political Treatise* are devoted to refutation of the Jewish idea that had joined the two spheres most irrevocably: Israel's chosenness, which Spinoza calls "The Vocation of the Hebrews." The terminology, too, is not an accident. The Bible, Spinoza attempts to demonstrate, never claimed any greater faculty for the Jewish prophets than especially vivid imaginations, nor any more special status for Israel than election to "a certain strip of territory, where they might live peaceably and at ease." How could Israel or anyone else have been chosen, when "by the help of God" we could mean only "the fixed and unchangeable order of nature or the chain of natural events?" This God—the sum of all that is, operating in accordance with natural laws—could not "choose" anyone. Israel, then, had been no more and no less chosen than any other people. "All nations possessed prophets and the prophetic gift was not peculiar to the Jews." Israel might have a vocation, a place in the order of things, but could not be chosen; since that place was a certain strip of land at a certain time, it pertained only to the Hebrews, but by no means to an ongoing people called the Jews. Hence the chapter's title, and its conclusion that continued Jewish existence was unwarranted.[66]

Spinoza's stated intent in the work is to demonstrate that freedom of conscience is compatible with, indeed essential to, the welfare of the modern state,[67] and he does so by arguing that religion can claim no independence from the dictates of reason or from the nation-state charged with securing the well-being of its citizens. Certain religious beliefs (chosenness first of all) were incompatible with that end, and, lacking any access to God through revelation, which was unavailable to reason alone, religion could hardly claim exemption from the rational verdict of the state regarding religious doctrine. This was true also because the very purpose of religion—furthering piety, obedience to the laws of God—was now the province of the state. Thus, freedom of conscience would be permitted: for, if one's beliefs fell outside the domain policed by state control, conscience could safely be assumed to be innocuous. The state would demand belief within its domain, specifically in "a Supreme Being, who loves justice and charity, and Who must be obeyed by whosoever would be saved:" who is "One," "Omnipresent," and "forgives the sins of those who repent."[68] Presumably, the philosopher would understand these last dogmas symbolically, for God could in no way forgive or not forgive, but only accept one into the sum total of all that is, while the masses' literal belief would help to safeguard the public good. This is civil religion indeed, in the tradition of early modern political thought: a set of dogmas deemed essential to the securing of public order.[69]

One cannot help but wonder, like the Conservative rabbis who quarreled with Eisenstein, how successful propagation of an American civil religion, complete with a "god-idea" not all that different from Spinoza's until one delves into subtleties beyond the range of most laymen, would have allowed the room for Jewish existence that Spinoza's conception did not. Kaplan, I suspect, would have responded pragmatically to this question. The Jews could cross that bridge when they came to it. In the meantime, the project could serve two immediate goals: revitalization of American Jewry, and integration of the Jews into America. It was not so much that the Jews would be in service to America, as that the idea of that service would enable the Jews to serve themselves—that is, their survival as Jews in America. The answer is not convincing, however, because far more was at stake here than one or another idea or program. Kaplan had fashioned an ideology which he believed had unique appeal to the Jews of his generation. Had they chosen to accept it, their definition of self to themselves and the rest of America would have been very different from what it remained—and much more compatible with what they actually believed and were.

An Ideology and Its Functions

We have, thus far, noted two respects in which the repudiation of election and the substitution of vocation were essential to Kaplan's entire program. First, Reconstructionism was to replace chosenness as the motivation for and purpose of Jewish identification. Jews would not turn to the tasks necessary for their survival, enumerated in the Reconstructionist platform, so long as they trusted in election to save them and provide them meaning. Reconstructionism was thus superfluous so long as chosenness was affirmed. The repudiation of election was critical to the very existence of Kaplan's movement as he understood it. Second, the new motivation for and purpose to Jewish identification which Kaplan proposed relied for its integration in American life and its transcendent grounding in God on the notion of divine vocation which Kaplan elaborated. Unless Jews were called to their particular labor, there was no ultimate point in performing it. Unless Americans were equally called to theirs, Jews would not be permitted to undertake their own. Unity of the two callings would provide optimal integration and maximum survival—the two poles between which, as we have observed, American Jews found themselves oscillating. Vocation would resolve the dilemma for which no other solution was in sight.

There was, I would suggest, yet another factor motivating Kaplan's persistent attacks on chosenness: the need to differentiate his movement from the branch of American Judaism to which, by the late 1930s, it was most similar. Kaplan's persistent attempts to persuade the Conservative movement to follow his lead should not blind us to the fact that the real object of Kaplan's polemic, the group whom he had to answer, his true "reference group" in sociological terms, was in fact not Conservatism but Reform. Time and again Kaplan denounced Kohler and the Jewish mission. Until the present he has refused even to recognize the changes that have overtaken Reform since Kohler's day, symbolized in the Columbus Platform. This stance becomes comprehensible, rather than merely idiosyncratic, if one grants the conclusion apparent from Kaplan's treatment of election. He intended to take the Jewish response to Emancipation represented by Kohler and carefully turn it on its head.

Both classical Reform and Kaplan, we might say, found the traditional notion of the chosen people unacceptable. While Reform accepted chosenness in the form of mission and denied Jewish peoplehood, Kaplan did precisely the opposite. He accepted peoplehood and denied chosenness. Reform, in the second generation, discarded the still-too-elitist notion of mission in favor of an ethical universalism. Kaplan for his part wrote that "the purpose in the various attempts [i.e., his] to reinterpret the God-idea is not to dissolve the God-idea into ethics. It is to identify those [in part ethical] experiences which should represent for us the actual working of what we understand by the conception of God."[70] God would not be reduced to ethics, rather ethics would be elevated to God. Finally, if Reform in its Kohlerian recension rendered Judaism a part, in service to the larger whole, Kaplan now rendered the status of part in larger whole the source of salvation both of part and whole.

Kohler too, after all, had introduced Protestant terminology, and particularly the concept of vocation, into his work on Israel's election, and had pointed Israel's mission outward to the world. It should hardly surprise us, then, to find that in the Reconstructionist prayerbook, "all references to the Jews as a chosen people, the concept of revelation of the Torah by God to Moses, the concept of a personal Messiah, restoration of the sacrificial cultus, retribution and resurrection of the dead were excised."[71] The list is precisely the same as Reform's, with the single notable exception which heads it: Israel's chosenness. Kaplan's views on election, then, are comprehensible only in the context of Reform, for that context defined his problem, channeled the course of his innovation, and in part secured his unconfessed assent.

There were two key differences. First, Kaplan insisted that intellectual honesty, if nothing else, mandated the elimination of a term—chosenness—which symbolized beliefs that Reform too no longer held. Second, while both he and Reform pointed election outward rather than inward, they did so in very different ways. Reform asked the Jew to remind the world of its obligations before the One God or to live up to a high ethical standard. Kaplan turned outward by turning inward, asking the Jew to "cultivate his own garden" so that other peoples, looking on, would begin to cultivate theirs, and so contribute to the flowering of the whole earth.

But these are minor points, the turning of Reform on its head without substantial alteration. By moving later to accept the uniqueness and primacy of the Jewish vocation, Kaplan only mirrored Reform's eventual reacceptance of peoplehood. In both cases a somewhat unique Jewish people was discreetly remarried to a God to whom it stood in special relation. Julian Morgenstern was thus correct when he asserted in 1945 that what distinguished his Reform movement from Kaplan's Reconstructionism was above all the chosen people question.[72] As Kaplan was later to confess, had the Zionist Bernard Felsenthal, rather than Kohler, been head of HUC at the turn of the century, Kaplan might have gone there instead of to JTS[73]—in which case, presumably, nothing would have separated the two movements, for Reconstructionism would never have been born. As it was, the chosen-people idea served to draw the line between the two movements much more clearly than ideas of God (on which most Reform and even Conservative rabbis agreed with Kaplan)[74] or even positions on Zionism, once Reform's new platform and the flow of events had rendered Morgenstern's opposition to it obsolete. Chosenness served to focus the larger issues of Judaism and Jewishness, religion and civilization; the debate thus served ideological as much as or more than strictly theological purposes.[75]

This is generally true of Kaplan's thought. He himself stressed that all beliefs are ideologies: to be judged by their function for a group rather than their conformity to some putative objective truth. Milton Steinberg was thus not entirely wrong when he wrote that Kaplan's theology, lacking a metaphysics, was itself "really not a theology at all but an account of the psychological and ethical consequences of having one."[76] Kaplan does venture metaphysical judgments, if only by ruling out the possibility of contrary assertions, such as claims for God's personhood and special providence. It is true that Kaplan has been unwilling to "recognize the logical implications of his postulates,"[77] ascribing purposeful intelligence to his "force," for example, or seeking to avoid transcendence on the one hand and Spinozism on the other through the ill-defined category of the "trans-natural."[78] Kaplan does have a metaphysics, then, and yet Steinberg's critique holds nonetheless. For to Kaplan the substantive content of his "god-concept" is always secondary to the function which belief in it performs for the group and the individual. He invites (and deserves) judgment on theological terms for speaking of that which, by his own lights, should have been left to silence. However, we mistake his meaning if we quibble with this or that formulation. The words are not meant to be true. They are meant, rather, to work: to do the job assigned them, whether this be the motivation of Jewish identification, the integration of Jews in America, or the differentiation of Reconstructionism from kindred movements.

In this light, we can better understand another function assigned the notion of vocation by its author: outreach to American Jews and to their rabbis first of all. As the sociologist Charles Liebman has demonstrated, Kaplan's initial supporters were largely rabbis and other Jewish professionals such as educators and social workers.[79] These were people whose beliefs were no longer Orthodox, but who desired to retain their affiliation with, to serve, and even to lead, the Jewish people. Kaplan legitimated that service by explaining that religious beliefs were subservient to (and a function of) Jewish group life in any case. Changing the instrumentality, the better to achieve the end, was only good sense. How much more meaningful that message must have been, we can now add, when couched in terms of vocation. For the concern of the Jewish professionals to whom Kaplan appealed was precisely the legitimacy of their chosen vocational role, given their failure to "qualify" for it according to inherited norms. In applying Robert Lowry Calhoun's reformulation of personal vocation[80] to the collective vocation of Israel, Kaplan was really addressing the concrete needs of individual readers much more than the rather abstract (and in his eyes secondary) issue of their beliefs.

It has been suggested that for an individual to experience the presence of God in his life as a divine calling, he has to meet the following conditions: He has to be engaged in doing needful work, work that calls into use his best powers and encourages their development, and, finally, that enables him to contribute his share to the welfare of mankind.[81]

To young rabbis uncomfortable with the theology of their teachers, and about to undertake a role without traditional precedent, the words must have offered real consolation. They conveyed the very same sense of service which the calling to the priesthood (or the kingdom of priests) had provided in the days of their ancestors. Kaplan's next sentence takes on new meaning if we read in the individualist connotation. "If Jews wish to feel a sense of vocation, all they need do is apply themselves to the tasks which would be most likely to meet for the Jewish people the foregoing three requirements . . . outlined in Chapter II—Reconstruction: A Program."[82] Kaplan offered no abstract, universalist mission, but rather a concrete and particular vocation—to precisely the same effect.

Similar considerations might have been expected to apply to lay American Jews. Kaplan, after all, invoked the word "vocation" on behalf of a generation characterized socioeconomically, as we have seen, by its rise into the professions. Talcott Parsons and others have pointed to the new role which the professions have assumed in American society as a primary source of ultimate meaning to their practitioners.[83] Doctors, lawyers, and scholars may be said to serve the highest values of our secularized society—life, law, and knowledge—at a time when those less privileged, now as before, can merely work. The sense of service or calling continues to set apart those blessed with its distinction, even though few such professionals or professors actually profess belief in a calling God (or, given their goal of value-neutrality, in anything else). Jews have no doubt been attracted by this religious dimension to career as much as anyone, anchored as it is in their own traditional values. Indeed, one might argue that they required it all the more, having lost the meaning which used to come through their collective service as the chosen people. The meaning which used to be inherited, collectively, now had to be earned, individually, though the hunger for it was transmitted no less than before. Vocation may have provided a solution of sorts. As Israel had once legitimated its collective presence among the nations by appeal to its election, individual Jews could now justify their new participation in American society, as individuals, by appeal to their personal service in their professions. The boundary between Jew and gentile would be drawn, as before, in terms of service; one stood apart, as always, by laying claim to the highest values which joined one to those whom one served.[84] What Reform had hoped to achieve in the nineteenth and twentieth centuries through "mission," then, Kaplan could reasonably hope to achieve through "vocation."

It is therefore surprising that his notion of vocation, the most original definition of Jewish identity proposed in his generation, died still-born. Virtually no one inside or outside the rabbinate adopted it, and other movements, no more convinced of Israel's literal chosenness than Kaplan, chose to reconstruct the belief rather than reject it. Liebman, attempting to explain this puzzle, has speculated that Reconstructionism articulates the basic "values, standards, and attitudes of American Jews": integration into America, separation of church and state, Jewish peoplehood, the irrelevance of theology, the survival of Israel, the belief that "Jewish rituals are nice, up to a point." His empirical survey demonstrates, however, that while American Jews of all persuasions "agreed with the Reconstructionist rabbis on those statements which came closest to expressing behavioral norms," they took more traditionalist positions on "statements expressing definitions, or rationalizations of behavior." In short, "American Jews may act like Reconstructionists, but they neither think nor talk like them."[85] Liebman theorizes that Kaplan articulated in "elite" terms (systematic, coherent, intellectual) the "folk" religion (unformulated, inchoate, expressed through rite and symbol) of American Jews. He was especially able to do so, as we have seen, because his emphases were theirs: observance and loyalty, rather than belief. Yet folk religion in elite terms may be unrecognizable to the folk, and, what is more, the folk may not want its own religion to supplant the norm. It may want elite religion to survive, and may even recognize the elite's right to set norms for folk observance. Norms honored more in the breach than the observance are norms nonetheless, and honored nonetheless.

The analysis is suggestive, and bears extension on the basis of the examination presented above. Kaplan failed precisely where one would have expected him to be most perceptive: on the symbolic level at which American Jews continue to affirm and practice Judaism. What vision of self and Jewishness did he propose, after all? A Jew, according to his teaching, was heir to no special learning and participant in no unique adventure. He or she could not claim a distinction beyond membership in one ethnic group among many, and had to disavow previous claims to more (the faith of parents or grandparents) as so much chauvinistic superstition. At present, this legacy largely outmoded, the Jew was called to a task of wholesale reconstruction, with little to prop up shaken faith except the reassurance that the "blind urge" to live as a Jew somehow served the purpose of the Power not ourselves at work, for good, in the universe. It sounds so bare, robbed of borrowed imagery and denuded of all symbolic resonances, and that is precisely the point. Kaplan, for all his emphasis on symbol, took on the role of truth-teller to American Jews. In order to assure their future, he felt impelled to burst in with the long-suspected but never uttered news that the Emperor had no clothes. Or, rather, that He needed new ones, and that, luckily, Kaplan had arrived with, if not exactly a wardrobe, a pattern for constructing one.

But could he, really? The enormity of the task of weaving new meanings out of whole cloth called his optimistic appraisal of the possibilities for Jewish life into question, and his own literalist approach to the matter of chosenness caused him publicly to discard the only fabric out of which he might reasonably have worked. The notion of vocation offered Jews nothing more than what they already had. This was in fact its appeal: the confirmation that more (such as the "more" one's grandparents had enjoyed) was not needed, that the work before one was sufficient. Apparently, it was not, even for Kaplan. And in order to undergird Jewish activities and commitments by appeal to a God in harmony with the latest in modern science, Kaplan further weakened his case—by precluding appeal to a God who could actually be counted on, even if one did not quite believe He was really there. If Passover really was the same as the Fourth of July, in other words, there was no point in Judaism, and the Emperor stood exposed. If the civil religion of America was equal in its saving power to the religion of the Jews, the latter had been trivialized and psychologized without ennobling the former. Jews wanted to be part of America, and yet apart. Kaplan, by pronouncing them an ethnic group and not a faith, set them too far apart, even as, in calling for a shared civil religion, he made them more a part than they wished to be.

Religiously identified American Jews, rather, would be an ethnic group that retained the consciousness of being something more and lay claim to a calling different from all others, even if they could not explain, justify, or account for it. They would act like Reconstructionists and, at one level, even believe like them, but would reserve the space for symbolic affirmation that Kaplan's literalness on the matter of chosenness denied them. Through Reform and the other movements, they would retain chosenness precisely as a symbol which gripped through the power of its resonances and not as a concept expounded coherently. It was thus Kaplan's agenda, outlined above—the ideological needs of his movement for existence and distinction—and not his god-concept or any idiosyncrasy in his thought that precluded the affirmation of election, while other movements, lacking such an agenda, were able to affirm it. His position on election was rejected by others, similarly, not because it had been refuted, but because it could not do the job which the resonances of election continued to perform, in the third generation even more than the second, even for those who were otherwise quite unreconstructed unbelievers.

V

Conservatism, Orthodoxy, and the Affirmation of Election

THE "UNRECONSTRUCTED" of the Conservative movement—the source of Kaplan's special frustration and ever the butt of his sarcasm—engaged throughout the second generation in an often futile search for middle ground. Kaplan at times exaggerated the evasions and confusions attendant on their effort: "on the one hand," he would say, "you had Reform. On the other, you had Orthodoxy. And on both hands—the Conservatives."[1] However, Conservative interpretation of chosenness does lend credence to Kaplan's conviction that the hoped-for terra firma simply could not be discovered. Conservatives could not stand for Reform's reinterpretation of election as universalist ethics or merely historical uniqueness. The Conservative commitment to *halakhah* as law, revealed, in some sense, by God to Jews and only Jews, was the movement's proclaimed reason for existence. Neither, however, could Conservatives stand with Orthodoxy in silent affirmation of election, assuming the doctrine on every page of commentary as "unformulated dogma" in need of no justification. Indeed, Orthodoxy was distinguished from all other movements in this period by virtue of being an insular and predominantly first-generation community, and as such largely immune to the external pressures upon chosenness that affected other movements. Even when "modern Orthodox" spokesmen such as rabbis Joseph Ber Soloveitchik or Samuel Belkin felt constrained to legitimate Orthodoxy in terms of philosophy or America, Hasidic and other "ultra-Orthodox" Jews did not. Against the dramatic foil of Orthodox silence, then, Conservative rabbis practiced and repracticed the art of cautious reaffirmation through manifold reinterpretation. They ended up nowhere in particular, but somewhere in-between.

That was precisely the point—and not only for Conservatism. With the elite at the Jewish Theological Seminary seeking to retain loyalty to *halakhah* while achieving greater flexibility in its revision, and congregational laymen seeking to adapt Orthodox forms and observance to their new urban and suburban environments, the Conservative aim was more to stake out such middle ground than to build upon it according to a carefully conceived blueprint. One had to be seen—and to see oneself—as standing between the extremes. In the second generation in general, what had been a rather systematic theology of chosenness in Jewish tradition, and remained so for the Orthodox, became what we have called a rhetoric in Reform, an ideology in Reconstructionism, and something of all three among the Conservatives. Before proceeding to the latter's attempts to locate a via media on the issue of election, I want to consider in some detail the language in which their reinterpretations of chosenness, like those of non-Orthodox rabbis generally, were couched. Having done so, we will be able to examine the sermons and essays of the rabbis with greater understanding.

The Language of American Jewish Thought

We misread American Jewish thought on chosenness if we regard it as an attempt at theology: the systematic elaboration of tradition in carefully formulated concepts, rigorously argued claims, and ideas logically interrelated one with another. For reasons already noted, theology was not possible during the second generation. Nor, with few exceptions, was it even contemplated. Coherent answers to the questions on the rabbis' minds were simply not available at a time of such social and philosophical upheaval. Reform, reconstruction, and selective conservation were strategies of response, barely adequate to the drastic changes in Jewish life that had provoked them.[2] They could not offer new visions of Jewish life for laymen, undergirded by cogent philosophical argument for the elite. Nor could the rabbis, few of whom were well trained in philosophy, and many of whom lacked adequate grounding in the halakhic and philosophical materials of their tradition, have provided sustained theological argument in the best of times. They certainly did not seek to do so now. Their first priority was not to produce theology but to address, in the most effective way possible, the immediate needs of their congregants, needs which congregants confronted as human beings (e.g., sickness and death), as Jews, and as American Jews subject to the particular political, social, and intellectual pressures of their troubled time and place.

Theology, then, was not the rabbis' principal tool, and indeed it has not been the predominant means by which any of the world's religions, including Judaism, has ever engaged the awesome questions which threaten human meanings in any time and place. Other, more powerful resources have been available—less discursive and more imaged, less conceptual and more symbolic, less a logical set of ideas than a series of pictures for the instruction of the mind. On these the rabbis drew as well. While this distinction between the conceptual and the symbolic is not without its own problems—concepts, indeed words, are certainly symbols—I think it serves us well in describing the language of the rabbis.

Throughout this analysis, for example, I have labeled the rabbis' words as rhetoric: speech, in Cicero's classic definition, that is "designed to persuade."[3] The forms which encased this rhetoric in the second generation were many, but all were designed explicitly to persuade: sermons, debates, apologia, polemics, and tracts. In chapter 2 we noted the rabbis' attempts to convince Jews and non-Jews alike of the Jews' legitimate place in America, by appeal to values ("democracy") and indeed to ideas and symbols ("chosenness") which were the joint patrimony of both parties.[4] We then noted (chapter 3) the attempt by Reform rabbis to imbue their congregants with a sense of purpose in their Jewish identity, through appeal to a mission that Jews carried out simply by being and doing what they would have been and done in any event.[5] Kaplan's attentiveness to the function of religious language and his insistence on the primacy of symbols over propositions led him to describe all religious thought as ideology (chapter 4). I adopted that term in its everyday usage ("a partial, hence to a degree deceptive, view of reality, particularly when the limitations can be attributed to 'interest-begotten prejudice' "[6]) to indicate the particular denominational interests served by Kaplan's elimination of the idea of election and its replacement by the idea of vocation.

What I would like to add now is another usage of the term ideology to which Kaplan's stress upon the symbolic nature of religious language points, a usage elaborated by the anthropologist Clifford Geertz. Ideologies, he writes, "transform sentiment into significance" through their use of hyperbole, symbol, imagery, and even self-contradiction. They are thus able to "grasp, formulate, and communicate social realities that elude the tempered language of science." Ideologies are able to guide us through "problematic social reality" at times of stress when the normal "maps" provided by tradition are inadequate.[7] The second generation was such a time, and chosenness was such an ideology. It remained indispensable because of and not despite the contradictions which it embodied, permitting the rabbis to address questions which lay outside the circle of their beliefs and enabling them to contain rhetorically the questions which had so urgently demanded their response. The resonances of election—love, needed work, a place at the center—continued to hold Jews, even when the beliefs upon which the idea of election rested—God, revelation, commandment—no longer enjoyed their assent.

One could of course overdo this dichotomy. Every corpus of religious thought includes both the more conceptually rigorous and systematically articulated elements of theology and the symbolic images and resonances of what we should term religious ideology. One can distinguish in Judaism between the system of Maimonides and the less disciplined imaginings of midrash. However, one can also distinguish between the midrash of the rabbis of the Talmud—grounded in a carefully worked-out system of life and thought—and the sermons of American rabbis ungrounded in such wholeness. The latter, I believe, practiced a mode of religious ideology unprecedented in the history of Judaism.

When we look at Conservative materials, then, we are largely looking at religious ideology, at times in the guise of theology; the rabbis' sermons, debates, and tracts served to keep the image of election alive, even in the face of a disbelief which all the sermons in the world could not assuage. Such considerations, relevant to all the non-Orthodox movements, are especially applicable to the Conservatives, because it was they—closest to Orthodoxy—who felt and manifested the distance which they had traveled from Orthodoxy most acutely. This becomes even more clear if we examine the Orthodox materials themselves. For they represent a mode and a substance of religious discourse which Conservativism never lost sight of, often sought to emulate, but was never able to adopt—that of the tradition and its theology.

Chosenness and the "Man of Halakhah"

Samuel Belkin, president of Yeshiva University from 1943 to 1975, put the Orthodox position concisely when he averred that the Torah, as God's law, must be scrupulously obeyed. Its truth and wisdom, the highest possible, are sufficient for all time.[8] No more needs to be said. The authority of the Chooser, the uniqueness of the Chosen, and the content of the chosenness are all affirmed unequivocally. Still, while other Orthodox Jews, less responsive to the gentile world and Jewish doubt, saw no need to justify the doctrine of chosenness, Belkin took pains to defend it.

> Our entire concept of election, of distinctiveness and separation, is based upon the greater degree of responsibility which the Torah places upon each one of us. . . . Those who have, therefore, stricken the *"atah bahartanu"*—the

avowal of the doctrine of "chosenness"—from our prayer book, have denied the raison d'être of the Jewish people as revealed in the Torah, and misinterpreted the Torah concept of distinctiveness or "chosenness" which has nothing to do with superiority of race. It is rather a greater dedication to the moral precepts of the Torah, and the endeavor to live a highly disciplined spiritual life, which is the Jewish essence of *kedushah* (holiness).[9]

Belkin's stress on the "moral" and "spiritual"—rather than on the ritual enforcement of "distinctiveness and separation"—seems well attuned to the objections to election which his defense sought to meet. While his rhetoric could be Reform, the content varies considerably from Reform's "mission" or Kaplan's "vocation" or the adherence to tradition carefully navigated by the Conservatives. The burden of chosenness is simply and precisely defined: obligation by and to the *halakhah* which Jews received at Sinai.

One sees this clearly in the first major essay undertaken in America by the intellectual and spiritual guide of modern Orthodoxy, Rabbi Joseph Soloveitchik (1903–   ). The scion of a long line of Lithuanian rabbis known for immense learning and rationalist faith, and himself receptive to an extraordinary degree to the values as well as the challenges of secular science and philosophy, Soloveitchik has sought to "interpret his spiritual perceptions and emotions in modern theologico-philosophical categories."[10] He is by no means typical of his generation of Orthodoxy, yet he is the acknowledged spiritual leader of that branch of Orthodoxy—the "modern"—affiliated with Yeshiva University and the Rabbinical Council of America. "The Man of Halakhah" (1944) captures the psychology of Orthodox self-conscious commitment brilliantly.

Soloveitchik distinguishes his archtype from the non-Jewish "man of religion" as well as the nonreligious "man of knowledge." Unlike the latter, the "man of *halakhah*" stands before the mystery of God's universe in a wonder only deepened by his knowledge; unlike the former he is commanded to transform his world rather than to escape from it, to pull the ideal world of *halakhah* down to earth rather than to ascend from the earth to an ideal realm beyond it. No phenomenon in the natural and social worlds can be strange to the "man of *halakhah*," for all has been accounted for in the law and becomes known to him in the relation which the law has commanded. Like the "man of knowledge," he must know the world, the better to help God create it with the reason given him for just that purpose. Soloveitchik denounces liberal religion for its distinction between moral and ritual holiness, both orderings of creation commanded by God. He is especially critical of liberal Judaism, which he accuses of banishing God's presence from the house of Israel, "and setting aside a place for it in a palace (Temple)." He rather holds fast to the traditional paradox that transformation of the world is to take place in the world and yet never leave the confines ("the four ells") of the *halakhah*.

This religiosity-cum-creation distinguishes Judaism from other faiths, and that particularity in turn guarantees the reality and ultimate importance of the finite human individual in the face of arguments that only the eternal, the infinite, and the universal can be real. Man's special status in the order of creation, the special attention given him by God, and the life awaiting him (and no other creature) after death are all bound to the unique and particular function which man performs on earth as partner to the Creator. Only because he has been singled out from the rest of creation can man hope for eternal life, and only because the Jew has been singled out from the rest of mankind can he (or anyone) know what to do during earthly life. In fact, the "man of *halakhah*" clings passionately to this life and does not wish for life eternal, because only in this world can he serve God through performance of the commandments.[11]

If any but the Jew, singled out at Sinai, can join in the partnership of creation, we are not told of it in Soloveitchik's essay. Rather, humanity is free to create only if it stands under the authority of *halakhah*, where the Jew of course stands alone. In another essay Soloveitchik writes that two covenants distinguish Israel from other nations and bind it to God: a covenant of fate and a covenant of destiny. The former consists of shared history, shared suffering, mutual responsibility, and cooperation, all imposed on the Jew by the world. The covenant of destiny and purpose, by contrast, is a way of life voluntarily assumed and directed by *halakhah*, through which Jews are to realize the full potentiality of their existence.[12] The occasion for the homily is as traditional as the midrash itself: reflection on human and Jewish suffering. One can remain passive in the face of suffering, seeking to master the evils which befall us by comprehending them. This quest is futile, and does nothing to ease human misery. Or one can act to reduce suffering, through transformation of the world according to divine direction. *Halakhah*, then, does not explain why suffering exists, but tells us what we can and must do to reduce it. It transforms humanity from creatures of fate to creatures of destiny[13]—and once again the possibility of that transformation is vouchsafed only to Israel. The suffering to which all nations are subject is likewise represented and indeed multiplied in the unique suffering of the Jews.

I have dwelt on Soloveitchik's essays at length because they bring out the ways in which Orthodoxy pays obeisance to the tradition's authority through commentary on traditional texts. Soloveitchik does not argue for chosenness, because he does not need to. The coherence of his statement derives in large measure from his conformity to the entirety of a tradition which his non-Orthodox colleagues could accept only in part. Indeed, until recently American Orthodoxy refused to acknowledge its status as a movement within American Judaism, claiming rather, because of its embrace of the tradition, to represent the totality of authentic Jewish life in this country. Its institutions were in its eyes not Orthodox, but simply Jewish.[14] Soloveitchik in particular, and modern Orthodoxy in general, were exceptions only to a degree.[15] Only after the war would the American environment begin to impinge on Orthodoxy as it had on the other movements a generation earlier.[16] Even then, chosenness would be a doctrine more assumed than argued, and would thus serve not only to distinguish the movements of American Judaism each from the other, but to separate Orthodoxy, which blessed the doctrine with its silence, from all the rest.[17]

Approaching the "Sea" of Tradition

Conservative rabbis, unlike their colleagues "on the left hand" (Reform and Reconstructionist), were perpetually concerned about the Orthodox opinion to their "right," for two reasons. First, as Marshall Sklare observed in his pioneering analysis of the movement, Conservatism developed in America as a function of "Orthodoxy in transition." Simply put, the children of immigrant parents left their home neighborhoods for the outer-city areas of "second settlement," and then for the largely non-Jewish areas and suburbs of the "third settlement." They took with them a reverence for the Orthodox forms of their parents, tempered with less than punctilious observance of the details.[18] On Friday night, for example, one lit candles, and observed the Sabbath with a special meal. At Passover, there would be a ritual *seder* with friends and family. On Saturday morning, the family might go to *shul* (synagogue), one where women sat with heads covered, and men put on not only a yarmulke but also a *tallis* (prayer-shawl). It would not be a full-length *tallis* like those which had covered one's father and grandfather head to toe, but a smaller one that wrapped conveniently about the neck and shoulders. The *seder*, while it employed the traditional *haggadah,* was not as complete as the traditional service. One might ride to the synagogue, in defiance of traditional prohibitions, especially given the greater distances of the suburbs, just as one might or might not eat kosher food outside the home, as a concession to gentile America, while maintaining two sets of dishes within as the law demanded. This, in sum, was the tenor of Conservative accommodation: forms remained, but were shaped to fit the new content poured into them by the new context for Jewish observance.

The cost was a studied inattention to the sorts of intellectual rationales demanded by Kaplan in the name of integrity, a function of the split between "elite" and "folk" religions that has characterized the Conservative movement almost from the outset. The young rabbinical students at the Seminary had left the immigrant Orthodoxy of their parents, were secularly educated, and aimed at a balance between their homes and America. They were destined for congregations that at best observed some traditional forms and, as the decades went by, grew more and more to resemble Reform and Reconstructionist counterparts. Yet the Seminary that trained them was staffed by a faculty that by and large maintained Orthodox observance rather scrupulously, along with the bulk of traditional beliefs. Though fundamentalist adherence to Sinaitic revelation and personal providence might be questioned, strict Sabbath observance was enforced, and even the prayerbook developed by the Rabbinical Assembly for use in Conservative congregations was judged too heretical for use in the Seminary's services. To this day it is not employed. Rabbinical students bound for congregations known even half a century ago for their mixed seating of men and women still pray while at the Seminary with men on one side of the room and women on the other. Unlike the leaders of other movements, then, many Seminary faculty were not truly leaders of a movement at all. They continued to see themselves as the only rightful heirs and transmitters of Jewish tradition, rather than as reformers or "reconstructors" who felt the need for a clean break and courageously made it. The Conservative lay movement, in their eyes, had ceased to "conserve" enough.

Thus, while Orthodox disapproval on some points of adjusted *halakhah* could be dismissed as benightedness or stubbornness or honest disagreement, a complete separation could not be countenanced because it would question the very raison d'être of the movement as the guardian of Jewish tradition.[19] That most laymen had a different view of themselves and a very different level of observance did not alter matters. The need to avoid outright breaks with Orthodoxy, combined with the desire not to highlight splits between "elite" and "folk," fostered a disinclination to engage divisive theological issues directly.[20] Chosenness, an issue forced on the movement by forces within and without, was something of an exception, with predictable results.

On the one hand, the election tradition had to be affirmed, if only because it was there. Continuity was in and of itself a value; one aimed to conserve, not to reform. On the other hand, the movement was also committed (in the words of its Prayer Book Commission) to intellectual integrity as well as to relevance to the needs and ideals of the day.[21] Kaplan and his disciples, ever a force to be reckoned with inside the movement, frequently reminded their colleagues of the stumbling block which the idea of election posed to these commitments. The skepticism which the Reconstructionists voiced on the matter extended beyond their own ranks. Chosenness, therefore, was shorn of elements which gave offense, chiefly the outright claim that God had done the electing and, in some cases, the claim that Israel was uniquely the elect. No coherent synthesis reconciling the movement's conflicting guiding principles was achieved in the matter, and none was seriously attempted. Election was not the ideological centerpiece it constituted for Reform, nor, apparently, a matter which seriously troubled the rabbinic conscience, but rather a problem which needed to be overcome.

As in Reform, the position of consensus was arrived at early in our period. Summarizing "The Things That Unite Us" before the Rabbinical Assembly in 1927, Louis Finkelstein explained:

> We say He chose Israel in the sense that Israel was more keenly aware of his being than other peoples. In Israel's recognition of God we become aware of the Divine selection of Israel. It is therefore literally true that the inspiration of the Torah and the Prophets is the expression of God's choice of Israel as His people.[22]

The paragraph as it stands is opaque and self-contradictory, but Finkelstein's overall intention seems clear enough. In sentence one he avers that Israel's awareness of God constituted its election, in sentence two that this awareness was only the sign of that election. Only the latter is compatible with the claims, in sentence three, that the inspiration of Torah was the "expression" of God's choice, and that the election tradition was "literally true." But the "therefore" of sentence three is tendentious; moreover, once one has asserted divine inspiration for the Torah and the prophets, the qualification in sentence one is incomprehensible. Why not simply say that God chose Israel? The answer seems to be that Finkelstein wished to disavow direct divine revelation at Sinai as well as the exclusive election of Israel, but wanted to affirm that God had played a part in the creation of Torah and in the history of Israel. Finkelstein's relation to the tradition was equivocal. A further reason for his caution was expressed in the warning that attempts to ground loyalty to Israel on the belief "in its singular excellence" were doomed to fail. Such attempts resembled the "exaggerated and pretentious claims of Teutonic and Nordic superiority."[23]

The question, as in other movements, was whether an interpretation of election such as Finkelstein's could "meet the demands of the day": motivation of Jewish distinctiveness, and comfort in the face of continued Jewish suffering, which Finkelstein described in 1946 as greater than that of any other nation.[24] To achieve the former, Conservative rabbis generally appealed to the Jews' unique contribution to civilization, at times in terms reminiscent of the "native spirit" and "religious genius"[25] extolled by Reform.[26] The problem of suffering was more intractable. One rabbi conceded in the late twenties that Jewish martyrdom was "futile and gratuitous" unless it was motivated by the unshakable conviction that the Jew had a unique contribution to make and that his survival represented the "finger of God in history."[27] When survival itself seemed in danger in 1939, Simon Greenberg, rabbi at Har Zion Temple in Philadelphia and soon to be a major figure in his movement, responded with a sermon of extraordinary pathos. Why, Jewish women asked him, should they bring children into the world, if Israel's lot was one of unrelieved suffering? Many of Jacob's posterity were convinced that Esau had gotten the

> better part of the bargain: for while this birthright, with all its spiritual implications, made us an eternal people, it at the same time sets us up as the mark at which every arrow poisoned by lust for plunder and thirst for blood has been directed throughout the ages.

Greenberg responded that the Jews would not disappear, that parents of many other nations faced the same dilemma, and that only he who had been born and faced death had the right to decide if life was worthwhile. Much work remained to be done by Israel in keeping with its birthright. Its place on "the battlefield"

> has been chosen for us by God, and by the voluntary actions of our ancestors. We are to be the world's most permanent, most widespread, most articulate, most self-conscious, minority, remaining true to our birthright, and carrying high our standard with its divinely inscribed injunctions: to love the stranger, to love thy neighbor as thyself, to do justly, love mercy and walk humbly with God.[28]

The problems, then—accommodation to tradition, motivation of loyalty to Judaism, and explanation of suffering—were clearly articulated in the movement. The solutions ventured consisted, with only one exception, of attempts to reach a modus vivendi, rather than original searches for a fresh middle ground.

The one exception was offered by Professor Max Kadushin of JTS, a scholar of rabbinic Judaism, who addressed his colleagues on the subject of Israel's election in 1941. After attributing the burst of attention paid the chosen-people idea to the erroneous opinion that it had been the model for German boasts of superiority, Kadushin declared that Jews had no need to apologize for their traditional concept of election, because in Jewish tradition no such concept existed. His syllogistic argument rested on an approach to rabbinic thinking elaborated in an earlier work:[29] (1) the rabbis worked with a limited number of master-concepts, each signified by a corresponding term; (2) the term *beḥirah* does not appear in rabbinic thought; (3) hence, the rabbis had no such concept. Election was rather a combination of concepts—God's love,Torah, Israel—and to emphasize it was to distort the meaning of the contexts in which we find it. Only gratitude for God's love in giving the Torah was ever intended, never a biological superiority or any special talent. Misappropriated by the masses, the concept needed to be "cleansed" of the illegitimate connotations it had acquired.[30]

The problem presented by the chosen-people idea remained, however, and the "cleansing" proceeded apace. Morris Silverman, who edited the prayer book issued by the Rabbinical Assembly in 1946, told his colleagues in 1940 that problematic passages should be explained rather than eliminated. Chosenness, a suggested note would read, meant only that more was expected of Jews than of others, that they would be judged by higher standards. It was a "form of noblesse oblige" imposing great moral responsibility. The prayer book usually linked election with the Torah: Israel's "sacred trust" and its contribution to mankind. In keeping with this, the prayer recited when taking one's *aliyah* to the Torah would be "paraphrased" as "who hast chosen us from among the nations to give us Thy Torah," rather than the literal "and given us Thy Torah." The *atah baḥartanu* prayer (cited by Samuel Belkin above) would read "Thou hast chosen us from the nations, loving and delighting in us in that [not "and"] Thou hast sanctified us by Thy commandments."[31] Eugene Kohn, an early follower of Kaplan and himself the author of several expositions of the Reconstructionist approach, objected to the policy of paraphrase. It was too easy, he warned, to fall into the trap of using words to conceal thought rather than to express it. Translations should be literal, and the reader unable to accept certain passages would simply take them as symbolic. The note on chosen people was apologetic, and seemed "addressed neither to God nor to the congregation but to the gentile world."[32] Silverman's colleagues voted to retain his translations nonetheless, and so to support the policy of adaptation through paraphrase.

The many Conservative apologetics for election in the "second generation" stressed Judaism's unique contribution to civilization and related Israel's status as a chosen people to its possession of the Torah.[33] In several essays illustrative of the Conservative dilemma on the subject, Ben Zion Bokser employed Kaplan's pluralistic view of religious truth in order to argue on behalf of the doctrine which Kaplan had repudiated. All groups were equally chosen by God, for each was a unique vehicle of His revelation and an instrument of His purposes in history.[34] God was the source of all uniqueness, and therefore Israel as a distinct community was "divinely chosen both as to the causes that have fashioned it and as to the mission to universal service which it is obligated to perform in the world." However, in the same article Bokser asserted Israel's special uniqueness as a "providentially-ordered phenomenon" of "universal and permanent significance" by virtue of its status "as the custodian and protagonist of the Torah." Was this consistent with democracy? Not if democracy asserted the "empirical" equality of all men "in the face of all the facts" to the contrary. It rather held that every human being was distinct and irreplaceable.[35] One notes the vacillation between the claim that Israel is unique as all nations are, and the very different claim that it is distinct from all the rest. In 1948, addressing the Rabbinical Assembly, Bokser took the former position. Chosenness meant only that the highest measure of the individual Jew's life was the ethical commitment involved in being a Jew. However, to deny Israel's "distinctive vocation" was to doom the community to assimilation.[36]

In response, one rabbi wondered why Bokser had avoided the term mission, and suggested that "our Reform colleagues preempted it and we assumed that because they took it over, it must be *trafe* [non-kosher], and it isn't so at all."[37] Ira Eisenstein, on the other hand, observed that it was dangerous to claim a mandate from God, because others could do the same and there was no way to determine which claim was legitimate. To assert that Jews had a unique mission was to contradict Bokser's earlier argument that all peoples were equally chosen. Either all were elect, and the Jews more so, or all truly were equally elect, in which case why be a Jew?[38] Bokser, in response, criticized Kaplan's idea of vocation. "I have never been able to understand it. A vocation means a call. If it is a call, someone did the calling. Who did the calling? Did I call myself?" It was not for any individual or group to say in what the unique vocation of any other consisted.[39] Bokser, then, sought to combine Kaplan's pluralism with the mission of Reform. Only the greater role assigned to God, the largely implicit obligation to His Torah, and the vacillation between opposing notions of uniqueness distinguished his stance as Conservative.[40]

The best illustration of Conservatives' search for middle ground is provided by Robert Gordis (1908–), who became the spokesman for the Conservative "center" on this as on other issues and so earned Sklare's encomium as "the leading Conservative rabbi."[41] A graduate of CCNY and the Jewish Theological Seminary, Gordis served both on the JTS faculty and as rabbi of a congregation in Rockaway Park, N.Y. He sought to define an ideology for his movement in 1945 in a work entitled *Conservative Judaism: An American Philosophy*. A "seeing eye" and a "sensitive heart" were required to recognize God's presence, he wrote. Israel's genius for religion had qualified it to be the instrument of revelation for humanity. Its claim to a special role was no idle boast, for no other people had produced comparable prophets, or the legislators and sages who had carried the prophets' teachings to fulfillment. Judaism had also inspired Christianity and Islam. Genius was rare, and not every Jew could pretend to it, but a spark of the prophetic spirit

> dwells in nearly every Jewish heart, waiting to be fanned to a mighty flame. . . . In this profound sense the Jewish people is bidden both by its destiny and by its tradition to maintain a higher ethical standard, individually and collectively, and thus lead man to God and righteousness by example as well as precept.[42]

The similarity to Reform thinker Abraham Geiger pales somewhat when Gordis proceeds to link election to Torah and commandments.

Two years later, he wrote that each people had a function to perform and in that sense was chosen, but Israel's role in the world had been unique, and out of all proportion to its numbers.

> Granted that all language is inadequate to express the deepest realities, the function of Israel in the world can be described by no better phrase than that of divine election . . . In its most creative periods, the Jewish people has been the messenger of the Lord glorying in the distinction, though conscious of the burden. In other less spiritual ages such as our own, Israel has been a bearer of God's truth nevertheless, a Divine witness malgre lui.[43]

In *A Faith for Moderns* (1960) Gordis added that any concept of revelation presumes chosenness, for someone has to have been chosen to receive the revelation. Jewish suffering served to "balance the ledger" for the manifestly unequal endowments of men and peoples.[44]

The pronouncement by Gordis which had the largest readership, and which institutionalized his position as that of his movement, was his preface to the Rabbinical Assembly's Sabbath and Festival Prayer Book, prepared by a Commission of which he was the chairman. In many cases, he wrote, apparent divergences of outlook between tradition and the modern age disappeared when the true intent of the Prayer Book was grasped and its mode of expression understood. As justification for the claim to election, Gordis once more cited Christianity, Islam, "modern humanitarian ideals," and "the basic principles of democracy"—all "rooted in the Hebrew Bible." In addition, the doctrine was indispensable to Jewish survival, a psychological necessity, for if Jews were to remain loyal to Judaism despite the disabilities involved, they had to be convinced that "the Jewish people has played and yet will play a significant role in the world." Finally, the idea of election had invariably been linked in Jewish tradition to Torah and *mitzvot*.[45] In a parallel article, Gordis expanded on the second and third points. It could be that "a normal people living under normal conditions" needed no rationale for its survival; but the instinct of self-preservation would not suffice in Israel's case, because Jewish survival was hazardous and demanded "untold sacrifice." Changes in the translation of controversial passages, Gordis continued, were justified by the varying syntax of English and Hebrew. The latter employed a "coordinate" ("chose us and gave us the Torah") where modern English would use a "subordinate" ("chose us by giving us the Torah"). It was not a matter of paraphrase at all.[46]

The Reconstructionists were once more on hand to perceive the flaws in Gordis's argument. That Israel had contributed to Western civilization, Eisenstein pointed out, was no proof that it had been chosen by God to do so. What is more, God was not only the god of Western civilization. To claim that chosenness accorded with objective truth was "rather extreme," and to argue its retention on psychological grounds was "somewhat feeble," since its acceptance could only be the climax of one's self-acceptance as a Jew, not its cause.[47] Eugene Kohn, in a similar review of *Conservative Judaism*, argued cogently that in order to believe, "as most Conservative Jews do," that Israel had been chosen "in any special sense" for a unique destiny, one had to maintain either that the Jews were a supernatural people or that they had been endowed by nature with a superior capacity for religious experience. Gordis, too sophisticated for the first, had opted for the second, a belief which bordered on "racialism."[48]

In reply, Gordis made his first frontal attack on Kaplan, explaining that he had been reluctant to criticize the Reconstructionists previously because their activity had been "subjected to merciless attack on every conceivable ground" by opponents outside the Conservative movement. When Kaplan had moved from reinterpretation to reconstruction years before, Gordis said, he had been unable to follow. He criticized Kaplan's "god-concept" and his distortion (in Gordis's view) of Talmudic thought. Finally, he denied that belief in the chosen-people idea was "racialism, or close to it." The doctrine did not mean "that no other people, try as it may, can ever know as much about God as Jews can." Thomas Edison had a genius for invention, but now his knowledge about electricity was available to every college student.[49] Despite its modernity, the metaphor reminds one of the Talmudic view that Torah was there for the asking to any nation of the world, now that Israel had accepted it at Sinai. Nevertheless, Gordis's equivocations on the nature of Jewish uniqueness marked his divergence from tradition. He did not claim, as the sages did, that Israel was a "supernatural people," but rather fell back on the argument from psychological necessity so pronounced in his preface to the prayer book.

For a less ambiguous affirmation of election and a true attempt at traditional theology, one must turn to the Conservative right, represented by Simon Greenberg. He attempted at the close of our period to articulate "Some Guiding Principles for a Conservative Approach to Judaism" (1957), as Finkelstein had tried to do at its beginning. Israel was a "Torah people," originating in the divine call at Sinai. Judaism was not a religious civilization, for a civilization not rooted in Torah could not be Jewish even if those who "practiced" it were. Judaism was rather a "civilizing religion." The Torah made it possible and necessary to think of the Jews as "an *Am Segulah*, a specially favored people." Even if the events at Sinai had not taken place exactly as described in the Book of Exodus, nevertheless the Jews had experienced God's presence "with unprecedented clarity and intensity" and achieved an "ineffable awareness of the Divine Presence." Though he would strive to pattern his life on that conviction, Greenberg continued, he had to take into account the Torah's assumption that the rest of mankind had not been abandoned by God. They too must have received similar divine communications.

> I find it necessary to distinguish between my belief that the Torah is *the* perfect Divine Communication[50] and my preference to think and speak of it as a Divine Communication because that is the only way in which I can formulate in words my conviction that though the Torah is the perfect Divine Communication, I must approach all those who differ from me not only without hostility and condescension, but rather with positive, sincere regard and openmindedness.[51]

This is to face the dilemma squarely, in an unequivocal affirmation of the tradition—along with its central paradox—such as none of his colleagues had offered.

Time and again Conservative rabbis tiptoed to the edge of the "sea" of tradition, only to retreat at the last moment to a seemingly surer ground that actually had all the certainty of shifting sand. One senses in their hesitations both the strength of the tradition's pull and their inability to swim comfortably in its waters. A position on chosenness consistent with what they believed to be true about God's relationship to Israel and other nations, neither presuming too much nor promising too little, just could not be discovered. Caught in the middle, on uncertain ground, the Conservatives responded as one does in such a situation—with indecision, eclectic borrowing, and no little evasiveness. It is doubtful, given the constraints under which they moved, that much more could have been achieved. Equivocation had its logic, and it triumphed. Religious ideology would perform the task which a coherent theology—rarely formulated by the movement—could not accomplish.

The Elusive God of Torah

Like their counterparts in other movements, Conservative rabbis devoted little time to theology, and so remained without a theological context for election. Reaffirming chosenness, they left the nature of the Chooser ill-defined. Such sustained discussion on the subject of God as there was occurred in the course of debate on the issue most important to the movement's elite: how and how much one could revise *halakhah* without bursting the bounds of the tradition that Conservatives professed to continue. Even here, however, the technicalities of God's role remained unclear. We have seen the difficulty above: how could Conservatives understand God, while neither affirming Him as the literal author of Torah nor banishing Him to the status of a vague if inspiring providence? We have also noted that factors other than the sheer difficulty of the subject hampered the rabbis' attempts to deal with it. Sklare has pointed to four: the conflict between "schoolmen" and rabbis at the Seminary, the disparity between the Seminary and the congregants, the diversity of opinion within the rabbinate, and the postwar success of the movement despite (or because of) the lack of an articulate theology.[52] Whatever the reason, little was said directly about God, and what was said, on the whole, did not support the affirmation of election that all Conservative rabbis with one exception ventured. It may not be coincidental that the exception—Rabbi Jacob Agus of Baltimore—also offered the period's most lucid and elegant exposition about God. We will examine his position and three others in order to indicate the range of Conservative opinion—or lack of it—and then to explain why vagueness about the Chooser did not prove fatal to affirmation of the chosenness.

Agus (1911–   ) was educated at Yeshiva University (and Harvard), rather than at the Seminary, and was idiosyncratic in his approach to the issues; yet he is identified with the Conservative movement and, in his extensive writings on theology, has provided a Conservative philosophy of *halakhah*.[53] In a sophisticated discussion of God based upon the philosophy of Morris R. Cohen, Agus sought to demonstrate the existence of an "Infinite Personality" who represents "the ultimate pole of being . . . standing in continual opposition to and tension with the mechanistic universe."[54] Every individual has a sense of this larger whole, of which we constitute ephemeral parts, and the feeling of holiness or identification with the Whole leads us to want to share in its work. Such a response to the divine call can come only through ethics, and it is the norm by which religious experience must be judged. Only so is the subjective experience of God translated into the objective content of law.[55] The latter's revealed character, however, consists not in its substance but in the "general subconscious spiritual drive"—for integration into the "Self of selves"—which underlies it.[56]

There is no room in such a scheme for a special revelation to Israel, and indeed the Pole of Being does not seem to issue particular orders (the wearing of fringes on garments, for example) but rather inspires us in the direction of ethical conduct. Jews respond through *halakhah* because they are Jews, not because *halakhah* enjoys any unique status, although Israel had in the past heard God more clearly than the rest of humanity[57] and in the present offered insights which Christianity still could not match. Agus denounced the particularist elements of chosenness as "the shadowy underworld of Judaism" and urged that the Jewish student not be made "to feel unique and utterly set apart from humanity by virtue of his Jewishness."[58] His theology permitted no affirmation of chosenness, and he offered none.

Louis Finkelstein, by contrast, offered a far less comprehensive conception which nonetheless included a more far-reaching claim for the uniqueness of God's revelation to Israel. We recall that Finkelstein affirmed divine participation in the authorship of Torah, without claiming that the Torah had been revealed at Sinai. He also affirmed a divine role in Israel's history, without claiming that Israel had been chosen uniquely. The only hint of elaboration concerning the relationship among God, Torah, and Israel came in his presidential address to the Rabbinical Assembly in 1929. The Torah was "divine and prophetically revealed," but not in the sense in which past generations of Jews had believed.

> The underlying World-Energy out of which rose the earth and the fullness thereof is an Energy of Righteousness and not of iniquity. That is why the world which is a creation of this Energy turns toward righteousness as the sun-flower bends toward the sun. And that is also why the prophets who communed with, and were inspired by this Energy taught a law of righteousness.[59]

The key was Finkelstein's emphasis upon "communion" with God, which rendered his affirmation of revelation quite traditional, despite the naturalist-sounding description of God as the "underlying World-Energy." His explanations of Judaism for laymen stressed the need of all individuals for such communion with God: we felt a homesickness for the "universal Parent of all of us." He explained the role of the Sabbath and the festivals in providing "especially propitious times for such communion."[60] Study of the Torah offered another opportunity,[61] and immortality was in essence an "endless communion" with God.[62] Torah was inspired, in a sense unmatched by any other literature, and capable of providing a "divine guide for conduct with which we cannot dispense."[63] First the entire Jewish people at Sinai, then the prophets, and finally the sages throughout the generations had come to know the law while under the direct influence of contact with divinity. Despite the equivocations to which we pointed above, Finkelstein's position is quite traditional, and significantly closer to Orthodoxy than that of Agus.

Simon Greenberg's account of God was highly traditional: God created and sustains His creation; He endowed His creation with the capacity to approximate Him; exercising that capacity through knowledge, power, and will, we experience God's love. God is omnipotent, but has endowed humanity with freedom. We are immortal. Were death the "utter and irretrievable annihilation of the Being which has its visible presence in the Body," one could not rationally refute the attitude of "après moi le deluge." Resurrection is a possibility which one can neither deny nor confirm.[64]

Divine revelations, according to Greenberg, are of two sorts: "revelations," strictly defined: the ineffable, incommunicable moments granted to all, in which God's presence is experienced with overwhelming force; and "communications": flashes of inspiration also available to all, which enable the individual to create a thing of beauty, discover a truth of science, or find a path to God. Such "communications" are also of two sorts: primary and secondary. The latter, which convey knowledge, are "subject to verification beyond reasonable doubt by communicable knowledge, accessible to the senses."[65] The former, which convey values, are not subject to such validation. The Torah is the Primary Divine Communication. Greenberg could thus proceed to the unequivocal affirmation of chosenness which we noted earlier. For in Torah one finds "the noblest, literally the perfect, inherently the most inspiring, and intuitively the most persuasive formulations of the ultimate goals of human life." Insofar as one strives to achieve these goals, life is "crowned with nobility and endowed with a spiritual joy that no other creature can experience."[66] Resigning Torah, one resigns election— again the traditional view. The highest vocation, as the rabbis of the Talmud believed, is to be a student and teacher of Torah. For with access to the "perfect primary divine communication," one gains entrance to life's ultimate meaning.[67]

The finest rabbinical mind of his generation had little to say about Israel's chosenness. Indeed, until the end of a life devoted to the fashioning of a credible synthesis of faith and reason, Milton Steinberg did not address in his published writings the theological issues which so perplexed him as an individual and sounded from his pulpit. Born in 1903, the son of an immigrant father who had lost his faith to nineteenth-century rationalism and of an American-born mother who had not, Steinberg was educated in Jewish tradition by his grandparents and by Rabbi Jacob Kohn. He then moved on to the two institutions which represented the struggling halves of his soul: City College, where he studied with Morris R. Cohen, and the Jewish Theological Seminary.[68] In his early published works—*The Making of the Modern Jew* (1934), and *A Partisan Guide to the Jewish Problem* (1945)—Steinberg focused on the traumas of contemporary Jewish life. Finding the options all the bleaker for lack of vigorous institutional response by the Jewish community, he turned to Reconstructionism and remained its partisan all his life.

What Kaplan could not offer Steinberg was an acceptable theology. We recall his comment that Kaplan's was "really not a theology at all but an account of the psychological and ethical consequences of having one."[69] Elisha ben Abuya, the hero of Steinberg's historical novel *As A Driven Leaf* (1949), criticizes a distinctly Kaplanian Rabbi Akiba for holding that "doctrines in themselves are not important, but the consequences are."[70] Kaplan, Steinberg told his congregants in 1950, did not find it necessary to decide "whether God is an entity, a being, an aspect of reality, or a useful fiction," seeing the question as in effect "an intellectual game."[71] To Steinberg, like his hero Elisha, it meant all the difference in the world. One senses that he too would have preferred heresy to evasion or indifference. Immediately upon assuming the pulpit at Park Avenue Synagogue in 1933, he offered remarkably clear and candid answers to the question "What Can a Man Believe?" He could believe in God, Steinberg said, "because the universe as the manifestation of a creative mind is the only plausible basis for the order of the spheres." One could believe in immortality because it was inconceivable "that consciousness is no more than the reaction of material brain cells." One could believe in a moral law as real as the law of nature, and in the essential goodness of human nature. As a Jew, Steinberg believed in "the value of Judaism as a rich culture, as a way of life, as a contribution to the civilization of the world."[72]

It is the modesty of this last claim which is so striking, especially in light of the other affirmations that seem daring indeed, emerging as they do from a man of such considered judgment and intellectual integrity. In *The Modern Jew* Steinberg made it clear that Jews could no longer claim "election, divine guidance, personal immortality or an ultimate group victory," save "half-allegorically."[73] In *Basic Judaism* (1947) he wrote that the "right-wing modernist," presumably meaning an archtypical Conservative colleague, found invidious contrasts between Jews and others distasteful, but was not "so ready to forget the history of the idea of the Election or so indifferent to its potential future uses." Let Israel choose

God, and they would be chosen. Let other nations do the same.[74] Steinberg seems far from happy with this formulation. In a sermon the same year he observed only that

> if all history bespeaks God, that of Israel testifies to Him with especial eloquence and clarity. For this is the people which first discerned His true nature, earliest identified itself with Him, and has longest sought to do His will. And Israel is alive this day.[75]

This is as much as Steinberg would venture on the subject. He passes over it in silence in the addresses before the Rabbinical Assembly and his own congregation in 1949–50 upon "The Theological Issues of the Hour"[76]—surveys recognized even at the time as marking both a high point and a turning point in the intellectual life of the American rabbinate.[77] Steinberg opted for a non-absolute, self-limiting God in the tradition of the philosophers Pearce and Hartshorne, arguing for the "greater survival capacity of the good" as asserted in the Torah, but declining to provide a destiny for Israel greater than what his belief in God would allow. Israel had light to offer the nations, he concluded: a "sanity" and "spiritual realism" lacking in Christian doctrine, a refusal to make a virtue of paradox or close one's eyes to evil.[78]

Conclusion: Charting Middle Ground

Steinberg's comprehensive survey of contemporary theology, sketched barely here, marked a turning point because its call for more systematic attention to theology was soon echoed by the thinkers of the emerging third generation. It is quite telling that in this, the finest theological essay by far of the generation, chosenness is not considered an "issue of the hour." Steinberg simply could not believe enough to make it such. No matter what the "potential future uses" of election, the issue was foreclosed to a mind of such integrity feeling itself in lack of the requisite faith. In this we see the problem of his movement, that is, of rabbis who generally believed somewhat more than Steinberg in revelation and so in Israel's unique destiny, but still not enough to support either the traditional theology they wished to safeguard or the commitment to Jewish existence they wished more rationally to defend. The varieties of Conservative belief about God are marked; indeed it is doubtful that the "variance" *within* the movement is any less than that *between* it and others, or for that matter that the range of opinion within is any less than that compassed by American Judaism as a whole. Conservative thought is in reality too fragmentary to permit such an accounting, and in this too it is typical. Definitions of God were simply not the stuff of which denominational differences in American Judaism were made.

The movements' differing approaches to election turned rather on the question of greatest practical import—what are the chosen obligated to do?—though to be sure this divergence depended upon the varied understandings of revelation that had divided the movements from their beginnings in Germany. The rabbis did not disagree on the meaning of Jewish suffering. The matter was ultimately inexplicable, and few attempted to explain it. All invoked suffering as testimony to Jewish uniqueness, and counseled perseverance in the face of the latest persecutions. Jewish tradition had done little more. Exclusivity was also not the divisive issue. All but the immigrant Orthodox ran to embrace America, and all but a few (including the Orthodox) identified American values with Jewish teachings, not yet aware how fatefully the battle for the American Jewish soul had been joined. Though they disparaged the rhetoric of Reform rabbis on the subject, Conservatives and Reconstructionists joined in evocation of the Jewish mission, if not as a native "genius" for the moral or the spiritual, then certainly as a contribution to civilization and ethics unequaled in the history of the West.

It was, then, the issue of covenant that divided them. If, as Reform, Reconstructionist, and some Conservative rabbis maintained, *halakhah* constituted only one among many paths to God, and bound the Jew only insofar as it conformed to moral standards derived from outside it or served purposes defined outside it, then a renunciation of Israel's unique election was not only possible but necessary. If, on the other hand, one maintained with Orthodox and some Conservative rabbis that *halakhah* was a binding normative code derived from God, one could not escape the tautological affirmation that God had ordained a special way of life for Israel and, thus, that Israel was uniquely chosen. The pivotal question, in short, was what the chosen people had to do every day in order to "live up to its high calling." Reform counseled Jews to be ethical. Reconstructionists urged them to rebuild Judaism. Conservatives emphasized the study and practice of Torah. Orthodoxy referred Jews to the *halakhah*.

This question was in turn related to another, fundamental to the entire problem of election but rarely raised explicitly: what must the Jew do, as Jew, to give life ultimate meaning? It is a question every religion must address. How can a person be sure that between the discrete acts performed in his or her daily life, and the God who gives life and offers salvation from death, there exists the binding cord of authority? As Soloveitchik makes clear, Jewish tradition provides meaning through *mitzvah*, a regimen which enables Jews to superimpose purpose upon fate by involving them in God's creation of the world. Reform, "disenchanted" with this magic, tried another: the ascription of a mission to the life which Jews would have lived in any case. But this mission could not sanctify (that is, make holy through separation), because it demanded nothing which was not demanded of everyone, and left activity essentially undirected. Kaplan's idea of vocation bore the promise of useful work, and granted liberal politics the seal of ultimate value, as did Reform. He directed Jews into the more specific channel of reconstructing Judaism, identifying what salvation there was with that activity. Conservatives edged closer still to the tradition, offering the familiar rhythm of observance and the comfort of continuity (in place of the dislocation and discontinuity by definition involved in efforts at reform and reconstruction), but without the beliefs which had once sustained them. Only Soloveitchik's man of *halakhah* could have the ultimate satisfaction of knowing that his every act fulfilled the intention of his Creator.

Underneath the surface of the rabbis' discussions of chosenness, then, there lingered the questions which religions perennially attempt to answer for their adherents. What is the meaning of my life? How can I be saved from meaninglessness? What is the meaning of my suffering? How can I learn to endure, if not overcome, it? What is the meaning of my being who I am, and not another? What is my special place in the cosmos? That these questions were raised in the context of chosenness—and only imperfectly and indirectly—provides yet another clue to the nature of the rabbis' accomplishment. Imperfection and indirection—in other words, the avoidance of systematic theological reflection—have often been attributed in harsh judgment to the second generation's efforts, not least by the young theologians of the third.[79] As I have tried to show, the rabbis' reliance upon image and hyperbole to accomplish what conceptual rigor could not may well prove their most lasting contribution.

That is not to say, however, that they articulated a religious ideology for American Jewry as well as they might have, or that they utterly abandoned theology for such ideology. One gets a better sense of the scope and the limitations of their achievement by turning briefly to the comments of three non-rabbis—literary intellectuals whose craft involved them in the imaginative use of language—who were invited to address the (Conservative) Rabbinical Assembly in 1946 on the subject "Whither American Jewry?" Menachem Boraisha, a Yiddish essayist and poet born in 1888 and very much shaped by Eastern European origins he left in his twenties, asked the question which underlay all debate on chosenness: "Does it 'pay' for Jews to remain loyal to Judaism?" Yes, he replied, for "the Jews are a chosen people; in the acts of Hitler and Bevin there is revealed this choice. There is now going on a struggle between accepting this 'burden' of Judaism or throwing it off. If it does pay, then for what?" Boraisha's answer was that the Jews were a holy and martyred people, with a unique character and mission. Only the Jews had Sinai, the symbol (N.B.) of revelation; only they were a people of holiness. "Perhaps this sounds like an outlandish idea, but it is necessary that we possess a certain amount of madness."[80]

Ludwig Lewisohn—novelist, critic, and a Jew who had returned to Jewish faith in middle age and become one of its foremost exponents in America—echoed Boraisha's remarks, adding that the American environment betrayed a moral deterioration so dreadful that Jews must not seek to become part of it.[81] In a series of memoirs and essays in the 1920s, Lewisohn argued that the uniqueness of Jewish "character and experience," though difficult to formulate, was nonetheless real, and all too evident when anti-Semitism drove the difference home. The conviction of such difference could "be lived without being defined."[82] In 1950 Lewisohn ventured such a formulation, comparing the "soul" which the Jewish people found reflected in its Torah to those of all other peoples, reflected in their finest literature. He asserted that the uniqueness of the Jews was not a separateness from each of the other peoples, but a separateness from all, "specific and transcendent."[83] His speech before the Rabbinical Assembly in 1946 reiterated his conviction that the modern world into which emancipation had thrust the Jews was now discredited once and for all. Jews were still "escaping the Torah in America today," when they should be escaping America. Adaptation to its ways was "the unspeakable sin."[84]

Hayim Greenberg—an outstanding Labor Zionist intellectual, editor of that movement's journals in Yiddish (*Die Yiddisher Kemfer*) and English (*The Jewish Frontier*)—presented the fruits of his own systematic inquiry into the meaning of chosenness. In earlier essays[85] Greenberg had traced the history of the idea and its implications with careful scholarship and a comparative perspective unmatched by the period's rabbis. ("There exists hardly a people in this world which is entirely free of illusions of superiority and chosenness complexes.")[86] In *aggadah*, for example, he discerned an "almost pathological egocentrism and naive self-praise," coming as a result of persecution, yet combined nonetheless with a revolt against "narrow separatism." He stressed this internal tension and the resultant attitude of ambivalence toward non-Jews that had marked the tradition ever since.[87] Talk of chosenness was meaningless, Greenberg concluded, unless a standard for the measure of "spiritual stature" were provided and the Jews' allegedly high achievement shown to be more than the result of historical circumstance. Greenberg doubted this could be done, and so tended to regard the idea of election as a historical belief which could no longer be entertained seriously, except by the Orthodox.[88] This was the burden of his address to the rabbinical assembly. "I do not know what 'chosen people' means." He could understand it "historically" but not "metaphysically." "I do not know whether we are today, if we ever were, a chosen or the chosen people—and perhaps it doesn't matter." For it might be possible for Jews to live without the conviction of election, and this was the point: Jews wanted to live. They were afraid of collective death. "Though we have hidden suicidal intentions, suicidal dreams, we are afraid of them. We want to survive and we want to live a creative life. But what shall we live upon?" Greenberg was skeptical of the possibility of Jewish survival as merely an ethnic and not a religious group.[89] In an essay several years later he would write that Jewish life for two thousand years had either been "a mystery or a misunderstanding," and he believed that it had been a mystery.[90]

Although the currency of these communications is ideas, in each case the discourse is dominated by a single image borrowed from Jewish tradition. In Boraisha's address the word which echoes is "holiness," and its repetition prepares us for the concluding warning that because the "idea" of chosenness is "outlandish" (i.e., one cannot make sense of it by fitting it into the set of ideas which make up our understanding of the world) a "certain amount of madness" is required for its affirmation. Chosenness surpassed comprehension. It was as prerational as the will to be, as "numinous," we might say, as the realm of the holy to which it would always be joined. "You shall be a kingdom of priests and holy nation . . . holy unto the Lord your God." Lewisohn sounded the related call for exclusivity—a separation "specific and transcendent" from a surrounding culture marked by moral decay. His sermon echoes, rather precisely, Biblical injunctions against assimilation to the ways of Canaan, rabbinic portrayals of the Romans, medieval (especially kabbalist) contrasts between Jews and gentiles, and modern warnings that Western Christendom is but a superficial moral patina covering a deep legacy of paganism. (One thinks in this connection of Maurice Samuel's work *You Gentiles* (1924), or the somewhat more nuanced *The Gentleman and the Jew* (1950), in which it is asserted that "all differences among you Gentiles are trivialities compared with that which divides all of you from us." In a word, the Jew takes life with moral earnestness, while the gentile treats it as a "game and gallant adventure.")[91] Lewisohn does not argue these points, either with evidence or from beliefs already established. His appeal is rather to the set of images which centuries of history have associated with "separation specific and transcendent" in the minds of Jews. Greenberg reinforced his message by sounding the single most powerful trope in the Biblical arsenal. The choice for God and Judaism was the choice for life and against death. "I have set before you life and death, blessing and curse. Choose life!" Greenberg's task was to serve the collective will to live in the shadow of the collective death still haunting the dreams of American Jews today, let alone in

1946. To choose chosenness, Jews knew well, had been for their cousins in Europe a choice not of life but of death. Yet not to choose it was to opt for the less painful death which comes of disappearance and forgetting. Jews, Greenberg knew, were both "afraid of collective death" and disposed in the direction of its solace.

Such were the stark realities, and the directness with which the images of the three laymen engaged them gives us the sense, in reading their words, that here we have come to truths concerning Jews and chosenness that are absent from or concealed beneath the rabbis' more tempered deliberations. The rabbis frustrate us because they seem to turn the same issues round and round, touching the vital matter at the center but never quite grasping it. The merry-go-round turns and turns, but the gold ring remains elusive. Yet what the rabbis did, imperfectly and indirectly to be sure, was to seek and find a vocabulary and a mode of discourse which would permit safe approach to that center. The concepts of tradition in and of themselves were not "safe" because they fell short. To rely upon them was to fall from the "horse" and to lose all chance for the "ring" of meaning. To fall back on "mystery" or "madness" was inconceivable. This too meant abandonment of meaning. Instead, the rabbis filled their discourse, in itself so unsatisfactory, with the powerful images to which Jews had been holding on for centuries. The rabbis too talked of holiness, mystery, separation, life and death. Theology eluded them, because chosenness could not be reconciled in most cases with their other beliefs as Jews and Americans. Chosenness could be affirmed nonetheless because its image was more than the sum of the rabbis' ideas.

The Conservative movement, then, often chided for its lack of theology, only played out most graphically the dilemma confronting all the non-Orthodox movements. As rabbis who sought to "conserve" and continue Jewish tradition, they should in the nature of the case have engaged theological issues head-on. Their distance from the tradition prevented them from doing so, but they were not sufficiently removed from it simply to avoid theological questions altogether. They searched, as a result, for middle ground—between Orthodoxy and Reform or Reconstructionism, between the truth-claims of traditional theologies and Kaplan's view of all belief as ideology—and could find such middle ground only through symbolic affirmations which were often couched in traditional language and sometimes even took a theological form. In this way they chose to be chosen, in passive voice, and chose no further, procuring a measure of meaning and a modicum of continuity—no more, but no less. The third generation's thinkers live with the consequences of those choices, and, being above all the children of their parents, repeat them more often than they would care to recognize, as we shall now see.

PART
THREE

The "Third Generation"
(1955–1980)

VI

Ambassadors at Home

THE TENSIONS INHERENT in the second generation's marriage of Judaism with America, detailed in previous chapters, were all too apparent to the thinkers of the third. In part theirs was the criticism that one expects of any child come of age: parental failings were enlarged upon (and, often, the virtues of the grandparents exaggerated) in an effort to create space and legitimacy for the newly independent. In part the generations differed on the key issues that faced them because the times were different. Disenchantment with Marxism and the trauma of the war had lent religion new credibility among intellectuals, while Jews recently arrived in gentile suburbs in the postwar years found that their neighbors went to Church and believed in God and expected the Jews to do the same. Jewishness, to these non-Jewish eyes, was not an ethnicity to be left behind but a religion to be practiced, albeit privately. In part, too, the third generation could be so openly critical because the second had won for it a freedom to question both Judaism and America which the "parents," less secure in both identities, had never achieved for themselves. Every book or sermon that now discussed America and chosenness without regard to gentile opinion or recourse to apologetics paid silent testimony to the "at-homeness" the second generation had purchased so dearly. The third generation were, in short, very much the children of their parents, in receptivity as well as rebellion. Their own twenty-five years of debate on the issues which so vexed their "parents," couched in the very same terms of chosenness, exclusivity, covenant, and mission, have not resolved the tensions besetting American Jewry's relation to election, but only deepened them.

One could mark the emergence of the new generation with several indicators. There was, for example, the sudden appearance in the late forties and early fifties of a number of new periodicals in which theology received serious and sustained attention. *Commentary* first appeared in 1945, *Conservative Judaism* the same year, *Judaism* in 1952, *Midstream* in 1955.[1] There emerged, at the same time, a group of thinkers (some of them refugees from the Nazis, and some American-born) who identified themselves as theologians and announced the intention of providing a "new Jewish theology." The tradition needed to be confronted on its own terms, they declared, rather than surrendered to categories imposed from the outside—as had been the case in the previous generation.[2] One could also mark the start of the new period with the communal celebration and reflection occasioned by the tercentenary of Jewish settlement in American in 1954. American Jewry found itself amazed at its survival and success, and yet worried that its distinctiveness might not survive the temptations of America. Their success here had perhaps been too great, the chosen land too receptive to the chosen people.[3] There was, finally, the publication in 1955 of a now-classic work of sociology dedicated to the third generation and purporting to describe its religious situation. We shall use Will Herberg's *Protestant-Catholic-Jew*[4] to enter into the debates of the third generation, because the book expressed with special clarity the conflicting visions of American Judaism that continue to occupy the community even today.

Herberg's "Essay in American Religious Sociology" exulted in the achievement of acceptance signified in its title. The Jews had "made it": their share in America's "triple melting pot" was now ritually affirmed by the nation's leaders on ceremonial occasions, and their membership in the growing middle class was borne out by every survey of the population. Both achievements—the double legacy of the second generation—were remarkable. A national study undertaken in the late fifties showed that 17.6% of Jews were now engaged in professional or technical occupations, compared to 10% in the nation as a whole; 36% were managers of businesses or offices, compared to 12.6%. Almost 25% were clerical or sales workers, compared to just over 11%; while 1.3% were nonagricultural laborers, compared to 6.1% generally. A comparison of Jewish with general income disclosed "that while the percentages of Jews in the income categories up to $5000 are lower than those for the nation as a whole" (1.3% compared to 7.3% below $1000), "they are substantially higher in the income categories in excess of that amount" (a staggering 18.9% compared to 5.6% above $10,000).[5] A highly regarded study of the Providence Jewish community in the early sixties found that 41% of Jewish males were managers or proprietors (compared to 11% overall), 21% were professionals and another 21% sales workers (10% each overall), while only 12% were in blue collar jobs (compared to 58% overall!).[6] The discrimination in employment that had hampered Jewish achievement in earlier decades had virtually disappeared, with perhaps the most dramatic effect in universities. There the percentage of Jewish faculty and students far exceeded the proportion of Jews in the population as a whole. The gap in educational achievement between Jews and gentiles was consistently found to parallel that in income.[7] In short, the immigrant generation and its children, who had begun in the sweatshops and worked their way through small businesses and night schools and universities such as New York's City College, had now given way to a community over two-thirds of which was native born, one that was "solidly identified" in behavior and aspiration "with some part of middle-class consumption culture."[8]

Even more remarkably, the Jews had won the apparent acceptance of gentile Americans. In the words of a popular Jewish joke, the Jew who bought a yacht was now a "captain," not only in his own eyes and those of his admiring mother, but in the eyes of the "real" (i.e., gentile) captains as well.[9] "It would be an interesting study in the history of ideas," writes sociologist Nathan Glazer,

> to determine just how the United States evolved in the popular mind from a "Christian" nation into a nation made up of Catholics, Protestants and Jews . . . how the Jewish group, which through most of the history of the United States has formed an insignificant percentage of the American people, has come to be granted the status of a most favored religion.[10]

The present work, I believe, has made two contributions to that proposed study. We have noted, first of all, the conjunction of Jewish with American values regularly proclaimed (and exaggerated) by the rabbis, and, more importantly, the common guiding symbols of Jewish and American chosenness to which the rabbis made constant appeal. A second factor, pointed up by our study less directly, was the role that Jews have played—from Horace Kallen through Herberg to such intellectuals as David Riesman, Daniel Bell, Seymour Martin Lipset, and Alfred Kazin—in interpreting America to itself. We shall have further occasion to note the ways in which such thinkers refracted the American experience through a prism shaped by Jewish history, thereby imagining America's future in a light compatible with Jewish interests and sensibility. Kallen did so with his conception of "cultural pluralism," as did Kaplan to a lesser degree with his notion of civil religion, and now Herberg would help to legitimate—by describing it—an "American way of life," founded upon the "Judeo-Christian ethic" and dedicated to ideals inspired by the Hebrew Bible.

For all his satisfaction with these developments, however, Herberg doubted the compatibility of any authentic Judaism with the national religious consensus in which Jews had come to share. Far from promoting the flowering of Jewish faith or civilization anticipated (at least publicly) by the second generation, America in his view had robbed Judaism—indeed every faith—of its sense of uniqueness and universality. Each religion was permitted to see itself as but one among several variants on the national faith: "true" for itself and no one else, no better than any other, and certainly not favored by God. What is more, the very notion "of being singled out, of standing against the world"—in other words, of chosenness—was "deeply repugnant" to Jewish and Christian congregants "for whom well-being means conformity and adjustment." Herberg pointed to the ways in which weekly worship served the "other-directedness" that David Riesman had identified in the postwar middle class. His own theological commitments—wrested from his earlier devotion to Marxism through encounter with Reinhold Niebuhr and the works of the Jewish theologian Franz Rosenzweig—made him critical of religions which could never "rise above the relativities and ambiguities of national consciousness and bring to bear the judgment of God" on America and its ways. There was no sense in the tripartite American faith of man's nothingness before the seat of divine judgment, he complained. God was rather made to serve man and his purposes, including material prosperity and peace of mind.[11]

Herberg went on, in works which we shall examine in the next chapter, to offer a reinterpretation of Judaism better suited to his commitments. It was heavily indebted to his teachers Niebuhr and Rosenzweig, and centered on a radical reaffirmation of Israel as the people uniquely chosen by God for a destiny of universal and eternal significance.[12] Even the sociological work summarized above,[13] however, is expressive of the two dissatisfactions that we shall hear voiced again and again in the third generation, not only by rabbis and theologians but by intellectuals and in some cases laymen as well. Jews now a part of America would conceive their remaining alienation from it—as Jews and Americans—in vocabulary borrowed from the traditional lexicon of exile, covenant, messiah, and chosenness. However, Jews thus set apart from America would, unlike the previous generation, interpret chosenness in its traditional context of beliefs (God, revelation, messiah, exile) but prove unable, as Americans shaped by the culture of their time and place, to do more than embrace chosenness as a mystery beyond their comprehension. As Jews they could not quite be fully Americans, and as Americans they could not quite be fully Jews. This generation, then, had to come to terms with the tensions inherent in their identity, tensions which the second generation had believed could be eliminated over time.[14] Their discussion of the place of the Jews and Judaism in American shall be our concern in this chapter, while their confrontation with the demands of Jewish tradition will occupy us in the chapter that follows. Both efforts of reinterpretation continued to center on chosenness, endowing the concept with a richness of texture and a degree of learning hitherto absent from the discourse of American Judaism.

"A Parable of Alienation"

A principle cause of that richness of texture was the entry of Jewish intellectuals to debates in which they had not participated ten and twenty years earlier; the Jewish community, for its part, was now more at home in the intellectuals' culture and so more receptive to what they had to say. It was not that Jewish intellectuals had become religious in any traditional sense. Herberg's move from Marxist labor organizer to neo-Orthodox theologian was untypically extreme. Nor had literary intellectuals come to feel a part of the middle-class Jewish community. Elliot Cohen, the editor of *Commentary*, observed in 1949 that such intellectuals still found the community too parochial in its interests and too insistent on a "self-imposed censorship" which precluded honest criticism "lest the *goyim* hear and use it against us."[15] Lionel Trilling and Clement Greenberg had said precisely that in a symposium five years earlier,[16] and the new generation of intellectuals would voice its own alienation in a follow-up symposium organized by *Commentary* in 1961.[17] What had changed was that many Jewish intellectuals now identified with the Jewish people—or rather with its historical destiny, of late so overwhelming. They were able to feel a connection with the fate and ideals of Jews and Judaism—and to appropriate Jewish symbols for the understanding of their own situation—without acknowledging any relation to the middle-class community to which they belonged but which they continued, by and large, to scorn.

This change was reflected in (or perhaps provoked by) the recognition by several authors that the Jewish experience at the root of their art had deeper origins than the accident of immigration to America. Delmore Schwartz had written in 1944 that "if one is regarded as peculiar and left out of social life by Christian boys and girls, one is tempted to be impersonal and attribute it to being Jewish." Isaac Rosenfeld had argued that "the very simple state of being a Jew . . . should occupy no more of a man's attention than any ordinary fact of his history." Alfred Kazin had urged that American Jews stop "confusing the experience of being an immigrant with being Jewish." He himself was part of no "meaningful Jewish life or culture."[18] The events of the forties and fifties, however, had altered that perspective. Irving Howe observed in 1977 what Schwartz had denied in 1944: that American Jewish writers draw emotional strength from the traditional style of conduct embodied in the notion of "chosenness," as Southerners had done from their distinctive way of life embodied in the notion of "honor." The Jewish writers "seek to regain, escape, overcome" this chosenness, thereby "finding their gift of tongue." Responding to the past—and this claim of memory is itself "deeply engraved in Jewish experience"—they could not but feel

> a profound, even a mysterious sense of distinctiveness . . . [that] still affects crucial portions and moments of life. Nor can the hospitality, tolerance and generosity of American democracy quite dispel the Jewish sense of distinctiveness. There is too much history, too much pain, behind that sense of distinctiveness. What the American Jewish writers make of it in the context of their experience, how they transform, play with, and try sometimes to suppress it—this forms the major burden of their art.[19]

More than an American ghetto had sent them forth, in other words, rather a history of ghettoes and its resulting consciousness. They would now find the religious symbols which arose out of that experience compelling vehicles for their self-understanding as secular Jews and intellectuals in America.

Daniel Bell put the matter clearly in 1946 in a personal declaration of independence from and attachment to Jewish tradition entitled "A Parable of Alienation." He praised the tradition's "compulsion to community" and its ethical precepts as a "prism" with which the "codes and conduct of the world" were refracted. "The Jews *are* a chosen people, if not by God, then by the rest of the world." Yet Bell felt alienated from a community bent on assimilation to American comforts rather than the pursuit of its own values, and regarded this alienation as part of the human experience of homelessness that was our earthly portion. "Out of this fact emerges the tragic sense of life: *that we are destined to waste it.*" Unable to solve his dilemma through Zionism (the article appeared in the Labor Zionist organ *The Jewish Frontier*), Bell wrote, he could only assume in America the role which Jews had played in their wanderings for centuries: permanent critic and outsider.[20] This was not a stance unique to him: Schwartz, for example, had described the sensibility of the modern poet as that of "a stranger, an alien, an outsider," and defined "The Vocation of the Poet in the Modern World" as the radical rejection of the "seductions of mass and middlebrow culture." It was no coincidence that Joyce had chosen the Jew Bloom as protagonist of his Ulysses: the Jew, Schwartz wrote, "is an exile from his own country and an exile from himself, yet survives the annihilating fury of history."[21] In this Schwartz seemed to find his only authentic continuity with the tradition that had conceived these symbols, and to recognize its force, however attenuated, in his own life. "I am my father's father/You are your children's guilt/In history's pity and terror/The child is Aeneas again. . . . The past is inevitable."[22]

Mordecai Kaplan, responding to Bell's essay, argued that the sense of alienation and homelessness was only a concomitant of humanity's spiritual growth. It could in fact prove "functional" by challenging us to create a better world.[23] Barely a year after the Holocaust, Kaplan still refused to recognize the reality of evil, precisely the failing which Irving Kristol would denounce a year later as the principal inadequacy of American Judaism as a whole.[24] A more cogent response to Bell's appropriation of the symbol of exile came from Ben Halpern, a secular Zionist and editor of the *Jewish Frontier*. Halpern contrasted Bell's personal alienation from his community with the traditional alienation of the entire Jewish community from its surroundings. That distinctiveness "constituted us as a chosen people," and had been fortified by Jewish intellectuals who provided their community with its own culture, myths, and values.

> Nothing so clearly indicates how this integral alienation of the past has been breached and shattered as the findings of your essay-confession: that the values of Jewish life today inhere exclusively in the family. At one blow this reduces the whole ideological alienation of the Jews . . . into the mere mythological rebelliousness of an oppressed group.

Thinkers such as Kaplan, in an effort to make the community less "parochial," had repudiated the chosen-people idea and reinterpreted Jewish tradition in order to render it identical to democracy. However, estranged intellectuals such as Bell could not be won back to a community "whose value-trappings were not his own. It is precisely the derivative quality of these ideas which will most repel him as parochial." As an alternative means of identification with the Jewish people despite alienation from American Jewry, Halpern suggested Zionism.[25]

Halpern carried on his analysis of American Jewry in terms of chosenness and exile in the single most perceptive analysis of American Jewry to date, *The American Jew: A Zionist Analysis* (1956). Herberg's argument that the three American faiths now stood as equals was incorrect, Halpern wrote, because it failed to note that true freedom of religion must include the freedom to have one's own idea of what religion is. The American definition followed Protestantism, as, indeed, Protestant patterns of social organization were the prototype for the "American way of life." Jewish talk of a Judeo-Christian tradition was only a public-relations formula to hide the basic differences between the two faiths, the most basic of which was a different conception of the divine plan of world history. Anti-Jewish attitudes still discovered in America were not mere vulgar lapses but "woven into the warp and woof of all that is most precious in Western civilization," while Jews for their part continued to celebrate the festivals of Simhat Torah and Passover, "as though everyone recognized they were God's favorites." For Halpern the core of *galut* (exile) was the Jewish conviction that "the real history of the world is, after all, the history the Jews as a people have known," while the history of other peoples is "essentially irrelevant." Why should Jews who said proudly that "Americans are different" not affirm that the Jews remained

> the Chosen People, in the exact and specific connotation of that title: chosen by God to receive the revelation of His word and to live by it in the sight of all mankind.

The reason chosenness and exile were denied is that Jews had lost the literacy required to appreciate their own culture, and had therefore set about recasting the "externals" to suit the current taste. Judaism had become "the public facade that the Jews present to America" and the criterion of selection was simply what would please.[26]

The critique is both overly harsh and somewhat disingenuous. How Jews such as Halpern who did not believe that they had been chosen by God for Torah or anything else could nevertheless affirm that they were the Chosen People "in the exact and specific connotation" of tradition is never explained. Indeed, Halpern's larger (and valid) point is precisely that the Jews, having convinced America that they belonged to it by virtue of a faith that shared equally in the "American way of life," were for the most part unable to appreciate or even understand that faith let alone believe in it. Only a bare majority were affiliated with a synagogue, and attendance at services had always been much lower than was true of Protestants and Catholics. America regarded religious faith as a private matter, of no concern to the larger society, but if the Jews' true sense of self was to bear any relation to their public facade their faith would have to play a greater role in their lives. As it was, Halpern wrote, what remained for secular Jews was only an attenuated "sense of alienhood," lacking the "mythic sublimation" attained through the traditional ideas of exile and chosenness.[27] Unable to accept the exalted role of strangers for God's sake, and unwilling to overcome their comfortable "alienhood" in America through emigration to Israel, such American Jews persisted in an incomplete belonging and a distinctiveness which was by their own admission bereft of ultimate meaning. As we have seen, the weakness of that position was seized upon by intellectuals as cause for their own double alienation from America and fellow-Jews.

When *Midstream* magazine published a symposium in 1963 on "The Meaning of Galut in America Today," only Halpern found the idea at all applicable to American Jewry.[28] Most contributors joined Rabbi Jacob Agus in denying it any relevance. America, Agus wrote, made possible "as virile and creative a Jewish religious civilization as we could possibly want."[29] An editor's note observed "that many, too many, feel that for reasons of 'public relations' it is inadvisable to discuss this subject—that it is a theme to be avoided if not suppressed."[30] Perhaps so, but it seems that apologetic considerations were not the reason that exile was not taken seriously as a descriptive category for American Jewish life. Rather the symposium's participants sincerely believed that "America was different," constituting in its pluralism a unique exception to the pattern of Jewish history. Intellectuals might find the idea of *galut* meaningful as a description of their own situation, but the community as a whole—or at least its lay and rabbinic spokesmen—did not.

A degree of bad faith seems present in both viewpoints. The community, although it could not accept the open proclamation that "Jews are different" implicit in the notion of *galut*, clung, as we have seen, to the overtones of difference and even superiority implicit in the notion of chosenness. Philip Roth could have been speaking for many American Jews when he noted in 1963 that, while the Jewish culture transmitted to him by his parents was at best fragmentary, he had "received whole" a *psychology* which could be expressed in three words: Jews are better. "There were reminders constantly that one was a Jew and that there were *goyim* out there," and, being a different and better Jew who did not know what it meant to be a Jew, one had to

> begin to create a moral character for oneself. That is, one had to invent a Jew. . . . There was a sense of specialness and from then on it was up to you to invent your specialness; to invent, as it were, your betterness. . . . I think the amazing thing which sort of brought the blessing and burden of having been brought up in America—was to have been given a psychology without a content, or with only the remains of a content, and then to invent off of that.

The only remaining reasons for calling himself a Jew, Roth added later, was "in terms of my outsiderness in the general assumptions of American culture."[31]

What strikes one here is a sort of parody on the *reciprocity* which, as we have seen, is built into the traditional notion of chosenness. To the Bible, and the midrash, chosenness is a possibility into which one grows rather than a mantle which one can assume ready-made. However, where the Torah gives direction in the achievement of election (one follows the commandments), Roth is left to "invent" his specialness out of whole cloth, an American self-made man.[32] This pressure to create a self worthy of the inherited sense of betterness is if anything intensified by the Jew's inability to point to specifically Jewish activities as evidence that the betterness is being earned. It is the problem of mission magnified. From the other direction, the pull of experiences and ideas from the gentile society and culture compete with the more amorphous demands of Judaism, which have no comparable content and yet leave one guilty at their non-fulfillment. The male characters of Roth's novels are persistently pulled toward divergent ideals of manhood by their tradition, their mothers, their lovers, and their own conflicting desires. Can one resist and say no to such desires and demands, simply on the grounds that a Jew is one who must be different? Why should one? This is a chosenness hollowed-out from within, a mission conceived in such emptiness that the guilt of its nonfulfillment resounds all the more loudly.

Yet this same bad faith afflicts the self-definition (through chosenness) of the intellectuals. Leslie Fiedler asserts that one should not cease to be a Jew because of the Jew's burden of witness and suffering. Yet witness to and suffering for what? "The Jew is someone who *is* something else—always. . . .

> I've speculated all . . . my life about what it means to be a Chosen People, and I've always known in some way that I believe the Jews are a Chosen People; but I've always known that we are not chosen in the sense in which it is believed by the majority—always chosen to be better, or chosen to triumph over our enemies. I don't even think I was satisfied with the notion that we are chosen to suffer for the world. It suddenly occurred to me that there's a very simple meaning in talking about oneself as a Chosen People: if you are chosen, *you cannot choose*. The Jews are a chosen people because they have no choice. We are chosen: the choice is outside us.

All that one could do as a Jew, then, was to tell the world "the Messiah has not come: don't worship idols," and all that one could do as a Jewish intellectual is "abuse my own community" when it abandoned its values for others which were "second best."[33]

Here the entire language of chosenness—suffering, witness, mission, reciprocity, exclusivity, covenant, even repudiation of Christianity and idol worship!—has been appropriated and hollowed out in order to endow the Jewish intellectual with the role of prophet to his own community and the world. Insight into the psychology of election far greater than that achieved by most students of the idea, and even a certain call for distance from "the ways of the gentiles," have been turned to the apotheosis of the intellectual which one encounters frequently in the modern West but never in Jewish tradition, where intellectuals are teachers and not prophets. To be chosen is to be utterly other; the residual content of chosenness has been reduced to the single word "no." Yet the "no" is meaningless because it is not accompanied by a regimen of affirmations. The risk and terror involved in the centuries-old Jewish "no" have been replaced with the satisfactions of participation in an intellectual community of outsiders. Such a self-definition could not but prove inappropriate to rabbis and laymen for whom chosenness had to provide purpose. In their own degree of distance from America, however tentative and disguised, a vocation more sacred even than that of the poet was at stake. We now turn to its theological defense.

Jacob and Esau in America

"The essence of Judaism is the affirmation that the Jews are the chosen people: all else is commentary." So Arthur Hertzberg opened his contribution to the symposium on "The Condition of Jewish Belief" sponsored by *Commentary* in 1966.[34] We shall examine the symposium at length in the following chapter. Here our concern is not Hertzberg's resounding affirmation of chosenness, but his related contention, in a separate essay, that America was not different and that Jews were in exile even here. For as Halpern had argued, America had recast Judaism in a Protestant mold. The several religions of the new nation had signed an implicit "compact" with its society, in which they renounced any actions adversely affecting others, actions to which they had full divine right if their respective claims to absolute truth were valid. Private faith and public policy were sundered, even in Catholicism, and most clearly in Judaism, which embraced the compromise in part because of internal alienation from its own roots (i.e., the secularization of American Jewry), and in part because the community recognized that its freedom was best protected in a pluralist society not dominated by a single church. Hertzberg titled the essay "America is Different" with heavy irony.[35]

He spelled out the consequences for Judaism of that compromise in a second essay, unlike the first written for a Jewish audience (the readers of the *Jewish Frontier*) rather than an interfaith dialogue, and unlike it titled without irony: "America is Galut." Hertzberg noted the widespread Jewish assumption "that it is somehow wrong and undemocratic even to attempt to be a Jew today on foundations which have no analogues in the rest of society." Such was "the theory of the [Jewish] Establishment." In practice, however, the norms set for Jews—identification with Israel and the Jewish people, support for Jewish causes and charities, the provision of Jewish education for one's children, resistance to intermarriage—were "not really equivalent to the parallels supposedly to be found in the behavior of other minorities." While talking the language of being "just like everybody else," Jews in fact behaved uniquely and demanded such behavior from each other. Their apparent hope was that gentile Americans would believe that Jews were just like them but that Jewish children would not be deceived. In fact, Hertzberg claimed, the reverse was occurring. Younger Jews were abandoning the distinctiveness which their elders had hoped to perpetuate even while publicly denying it.[36]

Hertzberg's conclusion does indeed mark a departure from the "official" policy of the defense organizations and rabbis. Judaism could only survive in a free society by

> emphasizing what is unique to itself and by convincing its children that that uniqueness is worth having. . . . This, however, means something radically different than our contemporary Jewish "religion" which is itself a form of institutional assimilation to the prevailing American modes.

The problem, however, was that only a religious imperative could renew the Jewish commitment to being "a peculiar people," and endow it with more content than the intellectuals could manage. "Apartness must have content" but "for such content we can only wait."[37] The obstacles to theological affirmation which we shall analyze in the next chapter precluded, in his view, the self-distancing from America which was necessary for Jewish survival.

Theologians of all denominations joined Hertzberg in both the call for greater distance from American culture and the recognition that only a renewal of faith could accomplish it. I shall examine the views of four theologians briefly.

Will Herberg, in an essay entitled "The Chosenness of Israel and the Jew of Today" (1955),[38] wrote that totalitarian states were inevitably driven to persecution of the Jews because Jews represented the idea "of a dimension of human existence that transcends the social and political, and passes beyond the limits of society and state." Other individuals and groups were despised because of what they *did*, while Jews were intolerable because of what they *were*. "The Jew somehow has this challenge built into his being, because built into his being is a transnational, transcultural, transpolitical dimension that makes him irrevocably and irreducibly different." Such was the irrefutable historical evidence for Israel's chosenness, Herberg argued, and it could not but lead the Jew to the religious question of "chosen by whom?" and so to God.

> Jewish existence, as Dostoievsky saw, is intrinsically religious and God-oriented. Jews may be led to deny, repudiate, and reject their "chosenness" and its responsibilities, but their own Jewishness rises to confront them as refutation and condemnation.

The Jew whom America had hyphenated with Protestant and Catholic represented such an evasion. Herberg devoted the burden of his theology to shaking American Jewry's confidence in itself, America, and the modern world, hoping to provoke a crisis *(krisis)*[39] that would return American Jews to faith.

Arthur A. Cohen, a young novelist and theologian who had studied for a time at JTS, gave the terms "natural" and "supernatural Jew," respectively, to the evader and embracer of chosenness described by Herberg. The natural Jew was a member of the Jewish people and a citizen of the country where he or she lived. A moral person, a charitable person, perhaps even a believer, he was nonetheless one whose destiny remained a function of the groups to which he belonged. The supernatural Jew knew himself to be the bearer of a divinely given vocation, a "messianic being" who would of necessity remain apart from all times and all places until the Jewish mission had been fulfilled. If Judaism and general culture were not related from the perspective of that end of time, Judaism was narrow and exclusivist without cause, and so probably false. However, if the two were identified before the end-time, the vocaation of the Jew stood abandoned. The adjustment to the natural environment of America sought by thinkers such as Kaplan would deprive the Jew of his vocation, which alone conferred the ability "to survive what he must always survive." The Jew had to remain unnatural, unadjusted, unreconstructed—but in America this sense of exile had been difficult to maintain, and as a result most Jews no longer chose or were chosen. Rather they had become "doggedly and uncritically American," profoundly ambivalent towards the supernatural vocation that until now had sustained them.[40] At this Cohen despaired.

Joseph Soloveitchik, in the most important essay he published in the sixties, attempted to probe the situation of the "Lonely Man of Faith." The terms of his argument are heavily influenced by Kierkegaard. In two senses, he wrote, every person is lonely in his or her "God-relation." First, no one, even a biological brother of the same faith, can understand what I in my solitude say to God and what God says to me. Second, God has created humanity with a twofold nature expressed in Genesis' two stories of creation. We are "Adam I," commanded to rule the world and master it: creatures of "majesty" and "dignity" who can chart the heavens and speed around the earth. We are also "Adam II," in need of "covenantal community" with fellow-humans and with God. Both aspects of our identities are willed by God, and neither can be at home in the other. We must be out of place, alien, in the objective world that we as Adam I have created. However, the modern man of faith experiences a special loneliness, because the modern world (America) is so entirely a culture of "majesty," bent on denying the reality and psychologizing the needs of Adam II.[41]

In a related essay entitled "Confrontation," devoted to the question of ecumenical relations with other faiths, Soloveitchik argued that "modern man has forgotten how to master the dialectical art of being both one with and different from." As each individual's relation with God was incomprehensible to everyone else, so each "faith community" was "engaged in a singular normative gesture reflecting the numinous nature of the act of faith itself." It was therefore futile to seek common denominators and forbidden to assess the worth of any faith by standards applied from outside it. Each community could only cooperate with others in the "cultural enterprise of humanity" (Adam I), while holding fast to "its otherness as a metaphysical covenantal community" (Adam II).[42] In a marvelous midrash on Genesis 32, Soloveitchik wrote that Jews in their ambivalent approaches to the "outside world" resembled Jacob in his reconciliation with Esau. "When the process of coming nearer and nearer is almost consummated, we immediately begin to retreat quickly into seclusion."[43] Soloveitchik applauded both the advance and the retreat, in a lesson for American Jews that becomes even clearer if we bear in mind the traditional associations of the Biblical characters. Jacob and Esau are brothers, of course, but Jacob is the third of the patriarchs and the people Israel's namesake, while Esau is portrayed as the evil progenitor of Rome—identifiable in its paganism with secular America.

Our fourth and final example is Eugene Borowitz, professor of theology at the Hebrew Union College-Jewish Institute of Religion in New York and principal author of the Reform statement of principles, issued in 1976, which was intended to be for the third generation what the Columbus Platform was for the second.[44] Borowitz was one of the first to criticize his predecessors' lack of theology, and tried to lay the groundwork for its conception in discussions of the possible substance and form of a revitalized Reform theology.[45] Like other thinkers of his own generation (Emil Fackenheim, Abraham Heschel, and Jakob Petuchowski, along with those already cited), Borowitz believed that the traditional terms of Jewish theology mandated dissatisfaction with the estate of American Judaism. The logic was straightforward: God's revelation at Sinai demanded separation from the world (*galut*) at least until the Jewish mission was fulfilled with the coming of the messiah. Borowitz's trenchant criticism of American Jewry, however, failed to yield the possibility of renewal for which he and his fellow theologians called.

His argument in *The Mask Jews Wear: The Self-Deceptions of American Jewry* (1973) is elegantly simple. Where once Marranos had practiced the Jewish religion in private while in public pretending to be good Christians, Jews in America had become a "species of Marrano in reverse." That is, they had repressed an inner identity, a core of Jewishness, and had limited its expression to the externals of "kosher-style" and "ritualized observance." But "we are not who we say we are." Underneath, the Jewish core still existed, as demonstrated by the high priority given ethical behavior and a pronounced distaste for the pursuit of pleasure. "God lurks behind the chopped liver." The commitment to Him would now be exposed more and more as the American materialism which covered it unraveled.[46] "With all its greatness," Borowitz wrote elsewhere, "with all its promise, there is a stinking rot near the core of Western industrial democratic society."[47] Who could have the faith in America of his or her parents, following the nation's failure of self-confidence after the Vietnam War, and the Jews' realization of their essential aloneness at the time of Israel's Six-Day War in 1967? Jews who had once rushed to embrace America now moved cautiously toward acceptance of themselves. Now perhaps they could be shaken from their "quietly agnostic" stance and their preference for "diluted, dispassionate and disinterested" religion and won back to God, by means of the commitment to "the Good Deed" which they had never abandoned. What is more, Borowitz continued, this ability to "choose Jewishness" freely rather than simply inherit it from one's parents could prove a great blessing, for Judaism would mean all the more to people who had entered its covenant voluntarily.[48]

Borowitz proposed a renewal of the covenant that would necessarily involve a "creative alienation" from America. Its content would be ethics. "There is no group whose record of continuing devotion to ethical excellence, whose moral persistence in the face of the most inhuman treatment, and whose stamina in pursuit of the human is greater than that of the Jews."[49] Yet only pages earlier he had criticized "ethics-is-really-the-heart-of-being-Jewish" as the effective ideology of American (indeed of modern) Jewry, one which made America primary and Jewishness secondary, and led to the surrender of Jewish values.[50] What is more, making "ethics" the content of Jewish apartness is useless so long as one neither accepts the tradition's ethical demands (couched in *halakhah*) as binding nor performs the difficult labor, thus far unaccomplished, of separating out Jewish ethics from *halakhah* in such a way that the Jewish ethics are more than platitudes and applicable to contemporary circumstances. Having done that, Borowitz would still have the problem of imposing normative demands while retaining individual autonomy (on which, as a Reform theologian, he insists)[51]—all this without a workable concept of revelation. As Hertzberg well knew, apartness must have content "and for such content we can only wait." In the meantime, Borowitz had only an unselective critique of modern philosophy[52] and American culture which postulated their inferiority as moral instruments to a Judaism not yet defined, and a sentimental appeal to the superiority of Jewish ethics which, as so often occurs in sermons, unfairly compared gentile practice with Jewish ideals.

If successful, then, Borowitz would only distance Jews from America without bringing them closer to any real covenant. Like Roth and Fiedler, he would give them a "no" unaccompanied by any "yes." In a word, he would make them critics, hardly the role intended by the original covenant, but precisely the role assumed by intellectuals. This may be no coincidence. The historian Sidney Ahlstrom has noted that in Judaism, as in Protestantism and Roman Catholicism, a "vast chasm" has come to exist between "serious religious thinkers and American congregational life."[53] People professionally committed to their faith (and so, one must assume, existentially committed as well) can not but feel distant from congregants not inclined to make religion the principal force in their lives. What is true of rabbis is doubly true of theologians, for whom the "reference group" is not rabbis, let alone congregants, but university professors and intellectuals. The theologians share a world of discourse with the intellectuals, and a world of faith with the rabbis, but with the congregants share neither. Indeed, the freedom with which the theologians criticize America and its culture may in part reflect their own independence as employees of universities and seminaries dedicated to free inquiry rather than to the pursuit of community interests. This is not to impugn the integrity of their criticism but only to suggest that they are free to speak in a way that rabbis directly responsible to congregants and the community are not. Borowitz and his colleagues, then, may be urging on their congregants a distance from American culture which is tenable only to an intellectual who is part of an elite culture or to a theologian safe within the fortress of traditional institutions, but hardly tenable to congregants unskilled in maintaining faith in the absence of true community and in fending off doubt with sophisticated argument. The theologian can afford to be a critic of both popular Judaism and American culture, whereas the average American congregant cannot. A "chasm" does exist, then, between the spokesmen of the community on "religious" matters—the theologians—and the laymen, one which did not exist in the second generation when the community's spokesmen were rabbis. The failure to translate theology into terms comprehensible and acceptable to laymen is perhaps most significant in Reform, which continues to emphasize theology more than other movements do, to compensate for the lack of weight on observance.[54] One suspects that calls such as Borowitz's for a greater distance from America, with no rationale for that apartness beyond the vaguest of appeals to ethics, shall remain bootless. Jacob can hardly be expected to remain apart from Esau (even if he retains his claim to the birthright of the chosen) if Esau is ready to accept him and God no longer orders him to refuse.

"The Mask Jews Wear"

As with the second generation, we do not know how the congregants of the third generation, themselves, have envisioned the relationship to America incumbent upon them as a chosen people, though one suspects that the role of perpetual critic in a society which has given them its blessing would not be what most American Jews have had in mind. Little survey data exists, and the few published sermons of the third generation are silent on the matter, except on ritual occasions such as the Bicentennial when praise for America is obligatory. However, I believe that an argument of great relevance to our inquiry can be made from that silence, if we pay careful attention to the *gestures* of separation from gentile society apparently made by many if not most American Jews. The evidence for this argument—all of it indirect—is of three sorts: the findings of several studies which, it must be said at once, are blatantly unrepresentative of American Jewry as a whole; supporting analyses, albeit impressionistic, offered by the sociologists who made the studies, as well as other observers; and the attitudes expressed in the fictional works of leading American Jewish authors. Individually the pieces of evidence are scanty indeed. Together they suggest a hypothesis which merits consideration.

We begin with a finding that recurs in the sociological literature as recently as the sixties, although personal observation suggests that it may be less valid today. Jews choose other Jews almost exclusively as their close friends, and even wider friendship circles are composed overwhelmingly of other Jews.[55] Like the respondents questioned about this finding in one study,[56] we might think the reason obvious. Jews simply desire to be with others most like themselves, especially in gentile suburbs where they feel like outsiders. Distinctive tastes and interests have survived acculturation to America. This explanation is persuasive, but testimony provided by sociologists and respondents alike indicates that another factor is at work. Benjamin Ringer reports that half the residents of "Lakeville" admitted to feeling "apprehensive" or "ill at ease" with gentiles, revealing a degree of fear about gentile disapproval.[57] Their anxiety was not without cause: whereas almost half the Jews wanted to have more Gentiles in their neighborhood, and only 17% wanted fewer gentiles, among gentiles the figures were reversed: half wanted fewer Jews, only 13% wanted more.[58] "In the final analysis," Ringer writes,

> despite the significant contacts between Jews and Gentiles and the benign atmosphere that prevails in Lakeville an aura of uncertainty and fantasy still characterizes their relations. In part, this results from the fact that their relationships rarely go beyond acquaintanceship to acquire the warmth and

mutual trust of close friendships. As a result, few Jews and Gentiles appear to be in a position to gauge the feelings of the other with any accuracy, and thus they consult their own underlying anxiety or complacency, as the case may be.[59]

Yet these Jews seem to have gauged their situation very accurately indeed. They are welcomed as good citizens and good neighbors by people who nonetheless view them to some extent as intruders and upon whom, should "push come to shove" (i.e., should anti-Semitism become widespread), the Jews could not rely. As a result, the Jews keep their distance.

They do so, moreover, in a way calculated to maximize the security of their position. The authors of a second study of "Lakeville" conclude that "the majority of Lakeville Jews see themselves as ambassadors to the Gentile world. We also find that our alienated [from Judaism] and integration-minded respondents are even somewhat more committed to this role than other Jews."[60] The ambassador represents his people before another, and knows that if his behavior is found wanting his people as a whole will suffer. He must manipulate the opinion which others have of him, and, as the sociologists observe, such manipulation is acceptable in secondary relations but not in friendships requiring candor and trust.[61] Hence respondents who report their need to be on guard in the presence of gentiles[62] not surprisingly do not choose gentiles as close friends even when this is possible.

The image of ambassador is quite telling, especially given its exact conformity with traditional notions of the chosen people (God's ambassadors on earth) and that people's exile among other nations. What one lacks is a positive notion of what separates Jews from gentiles beyond the need of the former to beware of the latter. Here the argument from silence emerges. A small fraction of the sample studied by sociologists Kramer and Leventman ventured the opinion that Jews "were in some way nicer and more moral," though the authors seize on it as "perhaps the last trace of the 'chosen people' concept; it certainly incorporates some of the popular images held by philo-Semites, Jews and Gentiles alike,"[63] The inference would seem entirely unwarranted, except for the fact that "many informants demanded assurance of the interviewers' Jewish background before volunteering certain responses (especially those reflecting their less public attitudes about the dominant group)."[64] Could it be that the majority not admitting to feelings of moral superiority were less than candid? Charles Snyder, in a fascinating study of Jewish images that link gentiles to drunkenness, found that moderate drinking was associated in the minds of Jewish respondents with Jews, and excessive drinking with gentiles. But "while the prevailing Jewish belief is that excessive drinking is a Gentile characteristic," there are "strong competing values which make it difficult for many Jews to admit discussion of the matter in these terms." Snyder's respondents equivocated. Thirty-eight of seventy-three denied they had ever heard of the association in childhood, yet, when asked specifically about a childhood ditty called "Drunken is a Gentile," a majority admitted that they were familiar with it. Snyder writes that when respondents realized the interviewers were privy to such folk beliefs, it was "no longer necessary to conceal ethnocentric ideas behind a universalist front."[65] Lakeville residents, too, went out of their way to deny differences between Jew and gentiles, explaining their opposition to intermarriage almost exclusively on the probable difficulties which it would cause the partners. Only 14% even mentioned the need to preserve the Jewish people or faith! "Widely approving of the integration of the Jews into the general community, our respondents are under pressure to formulate a respectable alternative for their disinclination to sanction what is the ultimate in interfaith acceptance." They must avoid the "appearance of ethnocentrism."[66]

This would in turn explain another finding by several sociologists that the traditional customs which American Jews choose to observe seem to be those which are easily redefined in modern terms, do not demand social isolation or a unique lifestyle, and accord with the larger culture, providing a Jewish alternative where one is felt to be needed. Hanukkah and Passover, not surprisingly, are observed more than other rituals, satisfying the added requirements of being centered on the child and occurring but once a year.[67] If one must be ethnocentric at least one need not appear so. If this line of analysis is correct, the American Jews who assert that "America is different" have adopted precisely the famous advice of Y. L. Gordon which came to symbolize the position of Jews in modern Europe: be a human being in the streets and a Jew in your home. The division can only work, of course, if those whom one meets in the street are not visitors in one's home, and the opinions which one voices in the home are not heard outside it.

Having said all that, I must add that these findings of the late fifties and early sixties seem somewhat dated in the eighties, reflecting a time when Jews were new to their suburbs and when friendship with gentiles was new to nonintellectual Jews. Borowitz is therefore correct when he guesses that "the mask Jews wear" is gradually being removed. However, it seems plausible to conclude that these attitudes of twenty years ago have not vanished entirely and that the continuing Jewish silence on such matters reflects a lingering sense of moral superiority such as Borowitz himself expresses. The desire to maintain some distance from gentiles—even as one seeks their approval—has probably not disappeared, if only so that one might enjoy some private space in which to discuss Jewish concerns with other Jews without worrying about being overheard.

That privacy, however, is gone, and its absence (not the alleged sense of superiority to gentiles that it might have concealed) is of most concern to us here. For the resultant silence uncovered by the sociologists is the most telling indicator of the distance from America maintained by Jewish laymen, a distance which intellectuals and theologians not responsible to and for the Jewish community can articulate in other ways. Yet the problem which this silence brings to light affects the intellectuals and theologians too. How, in the absence of one's own culture and language, can one *not* speak the language of one's surroundings? The problem is present on two levels. "When Jews spoke a language of their own," observes sociologist Milton Himmelfarb, "they could criticize and admonish each other without worrying about giving ammunition to enemies."[68] The Israeli philosopher Nathan Rotenstreich writes,

> To continue to speak in the language of emancipation [i.e., America] while facing problems which emancipation did not resolve, or possibly even created, is an attitude of apology. We do that because our Jewish world became translucent. There is no wall to hide behind, not even a special vernacular, as there used to be when Yiddish was a flourishing Jewish medium of expression. Today, Jews live in glass houses and are afraid of losing their achievements by betraying the principle of emancipation, by acknowledging its lack of exclusive validity.[69]

Lacking that luxury, Jews can only be silent: eloquent testimony, in its own way, to the sense of exile so often denied, even if the American *galut* differs from previous exiles precisely in its lack of a separate language and culture. The second dimension of this silence—the lack of Jewish words for inherited Jewish ideas, and the effect which reliance upon English has upon one's relation to Jewish tradition, and to chosenness in particular—shall be discussed in the following chapter. Here my concern is the extent to which virtually all of the discourse examined in the present study (with exceptions primarily in this chapter) may be dishonest to the extent that it masks sentiments deemed too dangerous for expression. If the presentation of Judaism to Jews has, as critics such as Halpern have charged, been greatly influenced by the need for successful "public relations," nowhere would this be more true than in the case of the single subject most likely to arouse gentile indignation—Jewish chosenness. If so, however, the Zionists are correct: America is *galut*.

At any rate, the entire popular realm of thought on the subject is hidden from view. One perhaps glimpses it in the reception accorded a bestseller entitled *The Chosen* (not by chance, I would contend: the word itself has great appeal) or a mass-market paperback entitled *The Jewish Mystique* which contains chapters such as "Are Jews Smarter than Other People?"[70] Indeed, it is not clear whether the image of gentiles and the picture of Jewish-gentile relations that emerge from American Jewish fiction reflect popular sentiments or a stance peculiar to the intellectual authors. A little of both, one suspects. Thus, when Cynthia Ozick's short stories point up the contrast between the moral and religious tradition anchored in the centuries and a pleasure-seeking society with no history, one hears the voice of a Jewish religious intellectual. Ozick expresses both the convictions of her faith and a literary convention of America as the land without a past.[71] When Saul Bellow paints a picture in *Humboldt's Gift* of Amercia as a country fast asleep, unwilling to wake to the awful nightmare of existence, "uncorrected by the main history of human suffering," he too is faithful both to a Jewish conviction that life should be serious and culture a moral agent, and to the task which Humboldt (Delmore Schwartz) inherited from Romantic and Modernist forebears: raising a fallen society to Beauty.[72] When, on the other hand, the Jewish protagonist of Bellow's *The Victim* accuses the gentile protagonist of being a drunkard, and the latter responds that all Jews see all gentiles in this way;[73] or when the honest Jew of Malamud's *The Assistant* is the victim of a sexually driven gentile who despite himself cannot master his own cruel urges—[74] then, as Philip Roth has noted,[75] we confront head-on the imagery of the folk imagination. Here one finds the rabbinic view of the chosen people re-emergent. The moral Jew must separate himself from the licentious ways of the pagans, accepting responsibility for the world (as in *The Victim*) against gentiles who would lay the blame on powers beyond our control. Roth convincingly argues that the opposition to his own work in the Jewish community, and especially to *Portnoy's Complaint*, stems from his overturning of these categories. His personae are Jews who are the creatures of desire rather than the agents of moral order. In sum, then, popular literature offers fertile ground for investigating the Jewish imagination and folk images of chosenness. One must be careful, however, in assuming that such a collective imagination exists, especially at a time of such fragmentation of the Jewish community. The five million Jews involved have cultivated a careful silence on the matter.

The third generation, then, has withdrawn to an extent from the whole-hearted embrace of America accomplished by the second. Jewish intellectuals seized on the traditional vocabulary of chosenness and exile in order to articulate their distance from American middle-class culture and from the Jewish community which had adopted that culture. Theologians, conceiving chosenness once more in its traditional context of revelation, covenant, and exile, implicitly and explicitly urged Jews to stand apart from American values and to avoid the mistake of identifying Judaism with America or democracy. Laymen, if the sketchy sociological data are to be trusted, acted out such a withdrawal socially, perhaps out of the same conviction of Judaism's moral superiority asserted by theologians such as Borowitz and expressed in some American Jewish fiction. We stand much too close to these events to be certain of their configuration. However, the rabbi, scholar, and intellectual Jacob Neusner seems well justified in calling the Jews of the third generation "strangers at home" and in pointing to the fact that both "props" of American Jewish identity in the seventies—the Holocaust, which most American Jews did not experience, and the State of Israel, in which they have chosen not to live—are vicarious.[76] The apartness of American Jews remains tentative, and its meaning remains elusive.

If Jews of this generation *are* somewhat less prone than their parents to identify their chosenness with America's, the reason may lie as much in America's changed self-understanding as in their own. Sidney Ahlstrom has observed that the idea of America as a chosen nation and a beacon to the world was hardly credible after the racial disturbances and the unpopular war of the sixties.[77] Americans, in the words of sociologist Robert Bellah, were now party to a "broken covenant." We might alter that image somewhat, still retaining the Protestant terminology, and say that the Jews of the third generation, like Puritan descendants of immigrant grandparents, were committed to a *halfway* covenant. These Jews could not believe in God, as their grandparents had, nor could they trust wholeheartedly, as their parents had, in America (although we should not exaggerate the Jews' alienation from America by taking the position of their intellectuals as typical). Yet, "in spite of themselves, as it were, the still unregenerate children were the heirs of salvation. . . . By virtue of their baptism, they *already* bore the name of God upon them, through His pledge to the enterprise as a whole."[78] This account of the Puritans well suits America's Jews. The Jewish covenant with America is "halfway" because only so can Jews protect both of their identities, as they wait for the meaning to come. As we shall now see, their covenant with Judaism is also "halfway," for the very same reason.

VII

Children of the Halfway Covenant

THE "CONDITION OF JEWISH BELIEF" during the third generation received remarkable summary expression in a symposium of that title which appeared in *Commentary* magazine in 1966. Three conclusions may be drawn from the symposium that are of particular relevance in introducing the third generation's reflection upon chosenness. First, as editor Milton Himmelfarb astutely observed, the Jewish thinker most influential on those polled was not Mordecai Kaplan or any other American but "a German Jew . . . who died before Hitler took power and who came to Judaism from the very portals of the Church"—Franz Rosenzweig.[1] Second, the symposium's individual essays exhibit a degree of honesty, thoughtfulness, sophistication, and grounding in Jewish sources that testifies to the resurgence of interest in Jewish theology for which the theologians of the third generation had called. Third, all the participants except the Reconstructionists and Rabbi Jacob Agus affirmed that the Jews were God's chosen people, and did so in the traditional terms of revelation, covenant, messiah, and exile, rather than by citing the Jewish contribution to civilization or explaining that, in fact, it was the Jews who had chosen God. Much had changed in twenty-five years. The meanings of faith and chosenness now available to the contemporary American Jew were not what they had been only a generation before.

Rosenzweig's unique approach to Judaism has proven well suited to the theological temper of the times. His magnum opus, *The Star of Redemption*,[2] was composed (in part on postcards from the front)[3] amidst the destruction of life and hope in World War I. It begins with the existentialist's concern for the meaning of individual life and death, and asserts that these can have no meaning unless they find their place within an order of God's construction. To a generation which had seen its own hopes and secular-humanist ideologies challenged by yet another World War, Rosenzweig brought the word that common sense itself, if only we could free it of dogmatic "isms," would testify to the reality of God, man, and world. These three constituted the first triangle of his six-pointed *Star*. Each was independent of the others: none could be reduced to a function of the others, as for example by making God or world a mere projection of the human mind, or man an assemblage of mere matter. The second triangle was composed of the interrelations among the three elements, themselves a matter of common-sense belief to those who permitted themselves to believe. God had created the world, revealed Himself to man, and in the end of days would redeem both nature and history.

The crucial relationship was the second—revelation—for it defined the midpoint in which we pass our days. Rosenzweig's theory of revelation—his principal influence upon the symposium's participants and his chief contribution to modern Jewish thought—sought to overcome the gap between the religious liberal's demand for human autonomy and the Orthodox submission to divine authority. Only the first commandment (or perhaps only its first letter: a silent aleph) had been pronounced at Sinai, Rosenzweig wrote. The content of revelation, in other words, was a human record. Yet it transcribed a real encounter with God. Those who did not believe in the Bible's literal account of Sinai were privy to God's revealed word nonetheless.[4] Both Orthodoxy and Reform were correct, therefore, each in a different sense: the former because it insisted on the reality of the encounter, the latter because it insisted on the role of human actors in receiving it. Conservatives, in the middle all along, could also claim to be Rosenzweig's heirs.

Finally, Rosenzweig taught the third generation much through the example of his life. He taught the necessity and the means of translating Jewish faith into a contemporary idiom, both through his own translation (with Buber) of the Hebrew Bible and, more importantly, through the adult education program (the "Lehrhaus") which he founded in Frankfurt. He had endured a contest with doubt so severe that it almost led him in his youth to embrace Christianity, and he had endured the pain and paralysis of a nervous disease that never arrested his will to work. He was, in short, an existentialist when other philosophies had proven inadequate, a rationalist at a time of "armistice" in the war between religion and science, a believer in a personal God at a moment when liberal theology was in eclipse.[5] One learns much about the third generation by studying these sources of his appeal.

Above all, perhaps, Rosenzweig was a theologian, and even—thanks to the account of his life published by his student Nahum Glatzer—a theologian-as-hero. He was at home in German philosophy and, to a lesser extent, in the huge corpus of traditional Jewish texts, and his living room became a gathering place for young Jewish intellectuals. He thus could furnish a model for a new generation of theologians promising to reclaim theology for American Jewry. The key criterion was now to be authenticity: the understanding of Judaism on its own terms. Borowitz complained, for example, that Jewish theologians of the past century had acted as if they knew a truth superior to Judaism: "I don't." Theology must begin in faith, proceed with the work of reason, and end in faith.[6] Steven Schwarzschild described the theologian's task as opening himself to Jewish sources without prejudgment, while refusing to permit the sources to be defined or evaluated exclusively in terms of contemporary intellectual trends such as Hegelianism or Deweyism.[7] The new theologians believed that this enterprise was re-beginning with them. Fackenheim saw the need to provide an "Outline of a Modern Jewish Theology," and Borowitz could still call his own formulation of the agenda in 1968 *A New Jewish Theology in the Making*. The results of this new standard for theology are evident in the *Commentary* symposium. One of its unintended effects, of special relevance to our own study, is the sharply curtailed publication of pulpit sermons by members of the third generation, probably because the pulpit rabbis could not match the theologians in sophistication or audience.[8] The sermon's role as a principal vehicle of communal discussion of religious issues had been seriously eclipsed.

Finally, these developments could not but influence the substance of reflection on chosenness as well. We have noted in earlier chapters that the long history of Jewish thought on election was largely ignored by those who reinterpreted the idea during the second generation. We have observed, as well, that chosenness was generally considered in isolation from other concepts, a function of the fragmentary "ideology" that had supplanted more systematic "theology" as the principal mode of religious discourse. The finer thinkers of the third generation evinced a much closer acquaintance with the history of Jewish thought and pondered chosenness in its traditional conceptual context. They have still not produced systematic theology, but have tended to grasp whole the issues that have engaged them. Significantly, *Commentary* did not ask its respondents *whether* the Jews were the chosen people but *in what sense* they had been chosen. The battle to justify the idea of election had already been fought and did not need to be rehearsed. Now the question was how the belief in Israel's election accorded with what one could accept about God, revelation, exile, messiah, and so on. It is more difficult to study the third generation's reinterpretation of chosenness than that of the second, because we must examine the idea in its broader theological context. What makes the effort possible—and necessary—is that this generation too placed chosenness at the very center, urging the doctrine's affirmation even when they could not assist in its understanding.

"A Mystery and a Scandal"

The work of Emil Fackenheim best illustrates these generalizations about his generation. Like Rosenzweig a German Jew trained in nineteenth-century philosophy and an expert on Hegel, Fackenheim heralded the "new theology in the making" with an essay that appeared in *Commentary* in 1951, "Can There Be Judaism Without Revelation?" No, he replied, there could not: although belief in revelation entailed the difficult affirmation that the omnipresent God of eternity had stepped into time at a particular moment and at a particular place in order to reveal Himself to a particular people. Liberal attempts to avoid the issue by likening revelation to inspiration had rendered the supernatural a "natural product of man." To talk of unique Jewish values created by a Jewish religious "genius" was to "court moral and religious ruin." One simply had to recognize that the preservation of Jewish faith stood or fell with "the revelation at Sinai, [or] at least with the possibility of revelation in principle," and that neither science nor secular metaphysics could allow of such a possibility. These had to be disqualified as standards for judging Jewish faith. One addressed through a leap of faith the questions which reason asked but could not answer.[9]

This is the age-old problem of "universal and particular" in a new key. As Rosenzweig had written, creation and redemption could render general human existence meaningful, but only revelation could endow each individual person and individual events with meaning. Conversely, as existence was "inexorably particular," so was revelation. Human beings could confront God only as the particular individuals who they were, in the midst of particular circumstances, and never "in general." (This Buber had taught as well: the I meets every Thou in the fullness of what the I is, and this is no less true of meetings with the "Eternal Thou," God.) All religions of revelation, Fackenheim noted, presumed this particularity. His own concern was not to demonstrate that such a revelation in fact occurred at Sinai, but to explain why Judaism necessarily held that it had and to defend this possibility by marking the limits of reason.[10] In doing so he helped to reconstruct the conceptual framework of election.

Another aspect of the idea of chosenness—one especially congenial to existentialism—is highlighted in a rather technical essay entitled "Metaphysics and Historicity." Here the question is how the human self comes to be. How can one give full weight to the influence of historical circumstance in shaping a malleable human nature, without conceding that we are purely the creatures of history and so denying all freedom to our actions and truth to our thoughts? (For thought too would be "historicized" to a mere epiphenomenon of material circumstance.) Could one provide such a degree of freedom from history without assuming a wholly given human nature, and so denying the ability to change and be affected by history? Fackenheim argues that we are somewhat, but never entirely, free of both nature and history; the human situation is one of struggle to make a self from that which nature gives us and history demands of us. Selfhood is universal in its structure but defined in particulars by the unique situation of each individual. Human beings are neither the mere products of nature and/or history nor the free masters of their selves, but rather choose to be something already constituted to some extent when they choose it, yet unable to be unless they choose it.[11] This is the point: for while the vocabulary derives from Hegel and existentialism, it recalls the Biblical injunction to "choose life" and both illuminates and defends the Biblical understanding of Israel's election. This was, we recall, that chosen ones must choose in accordance with their election in order to constitute that election. Chosenness is not a given of nature, nor merely a creature of circumstance. Israel must choose it—and so become what it is. Fackenheim has neatly conceptualized a traditional tenet of Jewish faith in terms borrowed from Western philosophy and, in so doing, has defended the idea against the principal criticisms made of it in the previous generation.[12]

His most significant contribution, perhaps, has been the outline of a method for affirming the tradition despite irresolvable doubts about its truth. The specific issue, in *God's Presence in History*, is whether Jews who live in the shadow of the Holocaust can recite the words of the Passover Haggadah which praise God for having saved Jews whenever their enemies rose up to slay them. The purpose of a ritual such as the *seder*, Fackenheim writes, is to reenact the "abiding astonishment" felt by Jews at a moment when their everyday view of the world was shattered by the divine presence. At such moments—for example, the parting of the Red Sea—the "cause-effect nexus" by which we normally explain the world and its events becomes "transparent" and the "Sole Power" stands revealed. One knows—indeed the text of Exodus tells us—that the water parted because a wind blew. But the children of Israel at the moment of their salvation knew that the God who "makes the wind blow and the rain fall" had acted to save them. The problem comes a moment afterwards: how can the immediacy of astonishment not dissipate in reflection? "This could not have happened," one says for one reason or another. "It wasn't God at all—just a tidal wave." In particular:

how can the affirmation of God's "saving presence" not be overtaken by the specter of Auschwitz? Fackenheim's response is to use the "logic of midrashic stubbornness" as a model of affirmation. Midrash expresses contradictions that it cannot overcome (precisely our view of what the rabbis of the second generation had done in their own reflections upon chosenness). Once again, Fackenheim argues the mutual "irrefutability of faith and secularism," the point being that only "Auschwitz" (i.e., the Holocaust) can truly challenge our belief in the Saving Presence, and not a philosophical problem such as how God's power can exist without denying our freedom. Auschwitz, a unique event in the history of Jewish suffering, does not permit return to traditional explanations, but neither does it permit the granting of posthumous victories to Hitler inherent in the abandonment of faith *because* of Auschwitz. One must rather engage in radical midrashic doubt that stubbornly holds fast to Jewish faith even as it challenges God for His failure to save Jews.[13]

This line of thinking bears on our concern with chosenness in two ways. First, Fackenheim has begun to consider self-consciously what the practice of theology can mean in a time such as ours to a thinker such as himself. He cannot offer commentary to the tradition like Soloveitchik, nor will he, like Kaplan, subject it to alien categories. (He does, however, employ Hegelian and existentialist terminology as an aid to defining the theological enterprise and giving it philosophical justification.) His work is thus in the nature of a prolegomenon to the writing of Jewish theology on chosenness that has yet to come. It is, secondly, work which presumes the chosenness of Israel and attempts to defend its presuppositions. Indeed, Fackenheim's contention that Auschwitz is a unique challenge to faith and is not assimilable to the terms of any existing theodicy, is premised on the belief that Israel is a unique people whom God is uniquely bound to protect. Here the implication of belief in chosenness is graphic. A genocide in Africa would not have posed the same problem to Fackenheim's belief, nor, say, does the slaughter of Jews in Poland in 1648. It is because the near-destruction of God's chosen people took place in a society that seemed to mark a new high-point in the progress of Spirit that the Holocaust is adjudged unique. For all that one can question the Hegelian bias of the argument and the validity of its conclusion, Fackenheim has considered election *in situ:* in the context of divine revelation and Jewish suffering. The vocabulary may be alien, but this is after all the theological point: translation of the tradition, with minimum distortion, in order that modern ears can make sense of its words.[14]

One finds the same effort at translation in the works of two other thinkers who are, however, less philosophically sophisticated and less systematic in their theologies: Will Herberg and Arthur Cohen. Herberg, like Fackenheim, took the Holocaust as a major point of departure, but did so in order to argue the "self-defeating, self-destroying dynamic of human life conceived in its own terms." Only God could invest life with meaning, and only the personal God of the Hebrew Bible, whom man could encounter. This was unfortunately not the "god-idea" which most appealed to modern men. For reason denied the possibility of the personal God and could lead us only to a sort of pantheism "in which the totality of being, with which one's own being is somehow merged, is felt to be suffused with divinity and therefore identified with God." To rely on reason in matters of faith was therefore sinful, not to say irrational. For reason failed to recognize its own inadequacy in the face of ultimate questions.[15]

Herberg then proceeded, like Fackenheim, to explain why revelation must be particular and to show how election, once accepted as a "scandalous" paradox of faith, could elucidate facts of history that otherwise remained incomprehensible. "This is the tradition," he said in effect. "Reason cannot deny you the right to accept it. Do so and the rest of existence will become much less of a mystery." History would find its meaning only in the messianic fulfillment to be granted by God through Israel. Jewish history, too, could be comprehended only if one granted Israel's chosenness, to which its history pointed.[16] Israel, Herberg believed, had been called by God to stand witness against the world's idolatry, and Christianity had been called to assist in that vocation by acting as Israel's apostle to the gentiles.[17] Israel was eternal. The specific forms of Jewish existence, including statehood, were "merely relative, transient and localized: underlying and yet transcending them is Israel as covenant folk."[18] Like Rosenzweig, Herberg insisted that Israel as an eternal people needed—and could have, in this sense—no native land.[19]

This is to reassert Israel's chosenness with a vengeance: not since Rosenzweig's own apotheosis of Israel into an eternal people uniquely possessed of religious truth[20] had a Jewish thinker affirmed election so unequivocally, in terms going beyond what most traditional sources had claimed. Indeed, the apparent Orthodoxy of Herberg's theology is further belied by a theory of revelation borrowed from Rosenzweig and a terminology that is distinctly Christian. More importantly, his conception of the chosen people is not traditional, because it lacks all concern for the flesh-and-blood reality of the Jewish people. Absent, too, is the sense of partnership with God in the perfection of creation that is the principal purpose of Israel's chosenness as the tradition understands it. Herberg's God creates, yet all His creation is fallen; He redeems, yet the disjunction between the world as it is and the world as it shall be is absolute; He reveals, yet what He reveals cannot be transmitted through an utterly fallen and inadequate human reason. This is Jewish theology without the nuances imposed on ideas by their immersion in the lived life of a Jewish community. The Israel which has been chosen, according to such a vision, is truly a "supernatural folk" and not the aggregate of so many million souls and bodies scattered in such and such countries and necessarily preoccupied with strategies of survival.

Arthur Cohen's notion of Israel as a "supernatural community" charged with a "supernatural vocation" provided two contributions to the understanding of election. The first was rhetorical: the evocation through crafted prose of what chosenness might have traditionally meant to Jews.

> Israel has always been a mystery to Israel. But it is a mystery on its own terms. This mystery has yet to unfold before the world. . . . [Israel is] that isolate, uncontaminate, obstinate and unyielding people whom God in a moment of supreme and excellent capriciousness elected to be his own— much against our protest and cunning as well as with our agreement and joy.[21]

Second, this insistence upon the mystery of chosenness shifted the concept's "center of gravity," as it were, from past to future. Only at the messianic transformation of history would the Jew "come before the nations with more than passive testimony," and only then could Judaism be proven innocent of the charge that it is ultimately narrow and exclusivist. "We cannot imagine that God should have spoken at Sinai that only Israel, then and forever, should hear him."[22] Like the midrash which asserted that only the thresher's coming would tell for whose sake the field had been sown, Cohen argued that the meaning of chosenness cannot now be comprehended.

Arthur Hertzberg, too, emphasized that the idea of chosenness with which he began his introductory volume on Judaism would remain "a mystery and a scandal" until the end of history. Judaism, he wrote, was simply inconceivable without the idea, but

> no man, certainly not one of our own troubled generation, can dare assert that he knows the meaning of this mystery. Perhaps it is enough for this moment to know that that mystery exists; perhaps that is all that any other generation really knew.[23]

Why was Israel chosen? We do not know. Why should one remain Jewish if Israel were not chosen? The answer is unclear. Jewish faith is of lasting importance only if it is divinely ordained.[24] The Jew's role in the world at present was perhaps to reemphasize faith in the Messiah's eventual coming—when, in a "completely redeemed world," Judaism's "unique way will perhaps disappear." But, he adds, "the world is as yet unredeemed" and "the Messiah has not yet come."[25]

The effect of all these writers is not so much to make chosenness more comprehensible, as to render it a more plausible mystery through the renewed emphasis upon other, related mysteries. When Herberg, Fackenheim, Hertzberg, and Cohen speak of God, they have the Biblical God of encounter in mind as well as a process at work in the universe. When they speak of the Messiah, similarly, they seem to intend more than a symbol for a gradual perfecting of the world by human effort. The hope for redemption is credible, Fackenheim writes, only if one believes that God will enter into history from outside it.[26] Finally, when these theologians address the problem of Israel's uniqueness, they do not say, in effect, that "Judaism is true for Jews, and Buddhism for Buddhists," or that any nation can be chosen. Nor do they claim possession of the one true revelation. They rather take refuge, once more, in the mystery, invoking what we might term a "saving ignorance." No community could judge the relation which any other had to God. One could not deny the destiny of another or ignore one's own. This is of course the stance adopted by Soloveitchik in "The Lonely Man of Faith,"[27] and it is what Fackenheim intends when he writes that "the business of a prophet in Israel could hardly be to fathom the challenge addressed to Ethiopians and Philistines."[28] Thus the issue of ultimate pluralism—the uniqueness of Israel's chosenness—is gracefully avoided. We are "saved" for faith by what we cannot know.

The thinker who has given most sustained attention to chosenness over the course of the generation is Eugene Borowitz, perhaps because he knows the idea to be essential to his own emphasis upon renewal of the covenant and yet finds himself unable to affirm the doctrine in its traditional form. In a reflection upon the observance of Shavuot (the festival which recalls revelation at Sinai), Borowitz wrote that the relevant question was not what occurred at Sinai but what the occurrence means to us. Nonetheless, some minimum of belief was needed in order to maintain a "meaningful continuation of traditional practices." A "real and present God" was needed, as was "some sort of special relationship between Him and the People of Israel." Otherwise "we might just as well celebrate in private belief all by ourselves." What really happened at Sinai was a "metaphysical question" that Borowitz could not resolve in time for observance of the festival, yet he would observe it anyway. It was enough that "my sense of what is real in the universe is such that I can still go to meet my God as one of His Covenanted people."[29]

This is a precise statement of the liberal's dilemma, and as adequate a solution as has yet been ventured. Borowitz's is a bare minimum of affirmation, carved out with difficulty from a recalcitrant mystery. Yet his intimate relation with the congregational life of his movement pointed up the contrast between even this minimum—which was enough for himself and some of his fellow theologians—and what was enough (or too much) for ordinary Jews in Reform synagogues. He probed this gap in a perceptive essay entitled "The Chosen People Concept As It Affects Jewish Life in the Diaspora." The tradition (and the theologians) stressed the idea's "inner-directed" aspects: Torah, commandments, holiness, redemption, exclusivity, the sanctification of God's name. The idea's "outer-directed" aspects were far more attractive to secularized Jews, however, for the notion of service to humanity touched both self-interest and morality, growing "out of a realistic sense of the basis of our security." Finally, this outer-directed chosenness seemed to conform to experience. In the diaspora, "Jews do not seem so special. Our fundamental experience of our Jewishness is not that we are unique but rather that we are very much like everyone else." Finding it difficult to say that God does anything, let alone that He chooses Israel, most Jews neglected the idea's "inner-directed" aspects just as they neglected the commandments. Yet they did good deeds. Here, as in *The Mask Jews Wear*, Borowitz found "signals of transcendence" in the behavior of Jews who would deny all religious motivation to their acts. Convinced of the failure of secular humanism to undergird moral action, Borowitz would move such Jews from observance of good deeds to a renewed sense of covenant. Each generation would create law appropriate to its own situation—its own covenant with God—though not every way of life or every view of what is appropriate could be deemed suitable to such a covenant. Modest as even this idea of covenant is, Borowitz conceded that it would not prove acceptable to large numbers of American Jews.[30]

Nor, as we have argued earlier, is this idea of covenant theologically cogent. Borowtiz's persistent search for a means of acting on divine authority while nonetheless retaining full human autonomy can only end in the contradiction with which it begins. He himself recognizes as much in specifying, as the bare minimum of belief, the affirmation of God, revelation, and chosenness. One cannot remain continuous with a tradition and guarantee "complete freedom of conscience" and "dissent," hoping that "both Judaism as accepted guide and as rejected standard will call forth the mixture of person and tradition that should mark the modern Jew."[31] This is to seize on only the liberal half of Rosenzweig's compromise with tradition. While one applauds the recognition that theology at present cannot overcome the fragmentation of its culture, and the insistence that relation to God is possible despite the lack of clear concepts of Him,[32] one wonders how Jews are to "live the Covenant" if they neither encounter their Partner to it in "fear and trembling" nor formulate their obligations in some accord with His specifications. Borowitz can only leave us with the vague appeal to higher ethical standards that Reform had offered all along; in this sense the greater sophistication and learning of the theology avails not at all. Better to heed the warning of Jacob Neusner, another member of the third generation (ordained at JTS), that Jewish theology had emerged from a communal *halakhah*,[33] and that a sense of "what is normative in Jewish ethics" could only come after an answer to "what is before, above, beneath, beyond? . . . [One] needs to explain what he means by Torah—and by heaven."[34] Borowitz's liberal theology had not explained either.

In this he is typical of his generation, which, despite the return to traditional sources and vocabulary, has not yet provided the sytematic theology for which it called. Its achievement has remained fragmentary in the extreme. Soloveitchik, the thinker most qualified to provide such a theology, has decided instead to offer isolated essays and commentaries. Abraham Heschel came closer than any other thinker of his generation to the construction of a systematic theology. However, he devoted most of his work to the evocation for his audience of the wonder which he believed was prerequisite to faith. The leap which Heschel made from God and our obligations as creatures on the one hand to particularly Jewish faith and *halakhah* on the other is never clarified.[35] Both thinkers assume Israel's chosenness rather than argue it, Soloveitchik in essays examined above, and Heschel in the final paragraphs of his most systematic work, *God in Search of Man*. He concludes with the assertion that "Israel did not discover God . . . Israel was discovered by God. . . . We have not chosen God; He has chosen us."[36] Chosenness *is* the center of the mystery, and so belongs at the center of theologies which must fall back upon the mystery because they cannot penetrate it. Often, however, what is impenetrable to their theology is more a function of what they as modern men are prepared to believe than of what we as humans are able to know. *That* mystery is not new.

In sum, then, the third generation's theologians have advanced our understanding of chosenness only paradoxically: by placing the doctrine beyond human understanding. The Jew who asks what it means is referred to the Messiah; the Jew who asks what must be done in the meantime is referred to the several positions of the denominations on revelation. The generation's theological achievement has been limited, although its return to the concepts and sources of the tradition, and its demarcation of what cannot be said, have opened spaces of possibility for meaningful theological speech that may someday be explored to advantage.

The Legacy of the Second Generation

The theologians were not typical either of their movements or of congregational rabbis, who tended to affirm less of the tradition than the theologians and, while assenting to a more nuanced idea of election than that of their predecessors in the second generation, continued to discuss it in isolation from its theological context. (The Orthodox are of course excepted from these generalizations.) Reconstructionists continued to denounce the idea, Conservatives to affirm it equivocally without resolution of the problem of uniqueness, and Reform Jews to proclaim a sort of Jewish mission. The latter remained largely devoid of content, even when the word "mission" was disavowed, as in the previous generation, as an anachronism. Because Reform rabbis continued to give chosenness the most attention—and, almost alone among their colleagues, continued to favor the topic in their sermons—we shall begin with their attempt to reconceive the mission of Israel.

The movement's position on chosenness was articulated in the 1976 statement of principles. Celebrating the diversity which Reform not only "tolerated" but "engenders," the authors[37] nevertheless "perceive[d] a certain unity" and vowed not to "allow our differences in some particulars to obscure what binds us together." The result, predictably, is a creed of the lowest common denominator. God's reality and some form of human "share in God's eternality despite the mystery we call death" are affirmed in the first paragraph. The second asserts that the people of Israel is unique because of its involvement with God and its resultant perception of the human condition. The paragraph on Torah notes that its creation "has not ceased, and Jewish creativity in our time is adding to the chain of tradition." The section on "Our Obligations: Religious Practice" notes that while ethical obligations are paramount, other claims too must be recognized: study, worship, observance, and other activities which "promote the survival of the Jewish people and enhance its existence." Unable to ordain specific observances, the statement calls on Jews to "confront the claims of Jewish tradition" and choose their own practice "on the basis of commitment and knowledge." A subsequent paragraph details obligations to Israel at the same time as it insists that Reform be "unconditionally legitimized" there (Orthodoxy now enjoys an official monopoly) and avers that "a genuine Jewish life is possible in any land." Together, Israel and the diapora could "show how a people transcends nationalism even as it affirms it." This is a somewhat more Zionist position than had been enunciated in 1937.

Of most concern to us are the paragraphs on the Jewish mission, here titled "Our Obligations: Survival and Service" and "Hope: Our Jewish Obligation." They contrast Reform's emphasis on service to humanity in earlier periods with the recent realization of the virtues of pluralism and particularism, and cite a tension between obligations to the Jewish people and obligations to humanity. "We know of no simple way to resolve such tensions," but neither commitment could be abandoned. "Judaism calls us simultaneously to universal and particular obligations." The Jews, the statement concludes, "remain God's witness that history is not meaningless" and "affirm that with God's help people are not powerless to affect their destiny."[38]

In its tone—frank rather than grandiloquent—and in its stance squarely within the tension between universalism and particularism, the statement differs markedly from its predecessor. Even the purpose of Israel's service has been altered, from representing God and ethics in the world to witnessing "that history is not meaningless." The mission had evolved with the times.

Borowitz, a principal author, notes in his extended commentary to the statement that it "sidesteps" the issue of election. Israel's "unique involvement with God" could be understood as a function of history or as the result of a unique revelation.

> Its old bases having eroded, and our experience in recent history having been so negative, the doctrine of the mission of Israel has as good as disappeared from Reform Jewish thinking. . . . [Who] among us can still confidently proclaim that our group has a special message for all peoples, a unique idea they have not truly heard of, or a teaching that would solve the basic spiritual problems of humankind if it would only listen.

He urged that Jews rather offer the example of their survival; the Jews exemplified hope, and so their existence itself "says something about the human spirit."[39]

The disenchantment with mission which we saw growing in the second generation overtook the movement as a whole in the third. Jakob Petuchowski, arguing for the doctrine in *Commentary* in 1955, really called for a commitment to Jewish observance quite foreign to the doctrine as Reform had usually understood it.[40] Frederick A. Doppelt, long a defender of the notion in its traditional Reform sense, urged "A Reappraisal of the Chosen People Concept"[41] that emphasized the need for Jewish peoplehood as the "instrumentality" selected for the "realization of the God-idea" of Judaism as the church was the instrumentality of

Catholicism. This had not been the focus in apologia of the previous generation, including his own.[42] Dudley Weinberg, in a symposium on the subject published by the Reform lay organization, noted the sudden embrace of particularity by "an amazed and amazing generation of Jews." The doctrine of election, he wrote, could have meaning only after one had "already experienced and apprehended the choice in the pulsating, throbbing substance of our lives." One did not begin with philosophy but with one's experience of uniqueness as an individual and as a people.[43]

The shift in viewpoint of the generations is perhaps seen most clearly in the persistent criticism of the idea of mission by Daniel Jeremy Silver, son of the idea's foremost advocate in the second generation and his successor as rabbi at "The Temple" in Cleveland.[44] In "A Lover's Quarrel With the Mission of Israel" (1967), Silver pronounced the idea "a tone poem exalting a Jewish life suddenly full of possibilities" and labeled it "rhetoric rather than a careful statement of Jewish principles." (This is of course the interpretation which we offered above.) Even so, the idea derived more from "confident secular liberalism" than from Jewish faith, and, "whatever its eternal value," had become "a stumbling block to anyone who would seriously confront his faith in an age which has known Auschwitz and Israel." The Jews did not qualify as the righteous of mankind.[45] In a second article a year later Silver also doubted that they were indispensable. People can affirm only what they know from life to be significant, he argued, and so a "bare skeleton of theological concepts or disembodied moralisms can not survive." Jews should be concerned with the meaning of Judaism to them, not to the world. He concluded—somewhat surprisingly—that "I confess to an innocent and unshattered faith that God wills our survival."[46] Ten years later, in an essay on "Jewish Identity, Jewish Survival and Israel," he reiterated his criticism of the rhetoric of mission—"noble words but vague words"—and argued that the idea was irrelevant to his congregants, who wanted to know only how Judaism could enhance their lives.

> If we want to think seriously about the question of Jewish identity, we must put aside that favorite ego trip which relates everything Jewish to categories of ultimate significance and cosmic purpose. Let us put aside all pretensions of our being indispensable to civilization.

He also reiterated his faith in "God's election and providential care of Israel," and once more urged that the community turn from mission to an emphasis upon "social duty as the climax of a life of mitzvot."[47] Here the discomfort with mission and the belief in a chosenness that defies formulation are explicit. Little of substance has changed: rather, the clearing away of a sentimental rhetoric has made room for an honesty of discourse which might lead to substance, but has not yet done so.

The same holds true of the only extended treatment of the subject of chosenness to appear during the third generation, Guenther Plaut's *The Case for the Chosen People*. As the title's double-meaning indicates, the work argues that one must defend the idea of chosenness in some sense in order to justify Jewish peoplehood. Without chosenness the covenant is "fleshless," Plaut contends, and without a choosing God chosenness is meaningless. Yet Plaut also recognizes that the average Jew does not believe in his or her chosenness. "Even before the idea of chosenness was shattered in the Hitlerian onslaught and singed with doubt, it had retreated from the consciousness of the people into the refuge of the prayerbook and the study hall." Plaut's hope, therefore, is so to redefine chosenness that the "average Jew" will assent to it. His "case" is that the mission of Israel is "dynamic"; that is, the tasks to which it calls Jews are ever-changing. Perhaps it was the task of Abraham to bring knowledge of "the one God, supreme, demanding, omnipotent, to the children of men." Perhaps the meaning of enslavement in Egypt was to demonstrate the possibility of redemption; perhaps the role of the prophets was to help humanity to comprehend the idea of universal justice; perhaps, today, Jews were meant "to maintain the possibility of minority and diversity . . . to be acculturated yet not assimilated. . . . Or perhaps it is our task today as Jews to be the bearer of social ideals." Plaut justifies the resort to the "perhaps" by saying that while the Jew can know that "his existence is grounded in meaning," the meaning both changes and is withheld from him.[48]

This is hardly new to Reform. Indeed, for all that Plaut claims to redefine Isreal's mission, his examples, including the "perhaps" of the present day, are precisely those that had been staples of Reform rhetoric from Kaufman Kohler through the second generation. The only change is signaled by a description of God as "an awkward and awful predicament for the Jewish people."[49] This, one suspects, is the result of the singling-out of the Jews in their recent history. "Of course Israel is chosen," wrote Rabbi Herbert Weiner in the *Commentary* symposium. "Here is a belief that needs no ultrasensitive eyes to probe the darkness. The heavens light up with this fact, light up with a glow that comes both from Sinai and from the fires of Auschwitz."[50] Rabbi Arnold Jacob Wolf similarly wrote that "God chose the Jews in history. Sometimes we can even see His work," as in the persecutions of Hitler and Stalin.[51] Plaut, then, is not alone in this consciousness of singling-out and its terrors. These were, after all, the formative experiences of the third generation. In this sense chosenness was now undeniable, because history had intervened to make its "case." In all other respects, however—and especially the understanding of Israel's mission—Plaut has only reaffirmed the substance of inherited Reform ideas, while questioning the rhetoric in which they had been couched. In this he was typical of his colleagues.[52]

Conservative rabbis, having accepted chosenness to this degree in the second generation, had little to change in the third. Seymour Siegel, professor of theology at the Jewish Theological Seminary, wrote in the *Commentary* symposium that Israel is "not a 'natural' community" but one "founded by the divine in order that it be 'his people.' . . . 'Chosenness' is not for privilege but for covenant with God." Yet "other peoples have their covenants," he continued, citing Rosenzweig's view of Christianity as the "Judaism of the Gentiles."[53] Hershel Matt, a congregational rabbi in New Jersey, warned in his similar essay against the dangers of a "chauvinistic self-righteousness" and "apologetic equalitarianism [sic]." Israel was not chosen because of "greater original merit" but "it would be foolhardy and unworthy to deny that Israel's chosenness is meant to constitute supreme honor and blessing— certainly a superiority of sorts."[54] In another article Matt defined Jews as those who stand, by descent or conversion, within the "unique and supernatural Covenant People Israel."[55] Two publications by the Conservative lay organization were somewhat less straightforward about that uniqueness. Rabbi David Aronson's *The Jewish Way of Life* asserts that a people is chosen when it wills "to live in a way which would express God's spirit on earth" and measures its growth by moral and spiritual standards.[56] In *The Eternal People,* by Rabbis Elias Chary and Abraham Segal, it is argued that any people can become a "chosen" people if only it will accept the challenge of leading a "better, more moral life" than others.[57]

In short, the issues which forced Conservatism to equivocate on chosenness in the second generation were still unresolved. In fact, according to two observers of the movement, the split between "left" and "right" within the Conservative elite over the correct approach to halakhic change had widened rather than narrowed over the years, even as congregants became less and less observant and Orthodoxy damaged Conservative morale by showing new strength instead of disappearing.[58] Given this inability to confront theological issues *as a movement,* except in anthologies which highlighted the lack of unity, the Conservative elite could hardly be expected to give the still-divisive issue of chosenness sustained attention. The rabbis, for their part, have rarely published their sermons, for the same reasons that led rabbis in other movements to a similar course. Only Hertzberg gave voice to what would seem the logical Conservative stance on election (itself equivocal, but not without theological rationale), and he could do so precisely as a "theologian-outsider" of independent status, who neither spoke for nor stood accountable to his movement or its Seminary.[59]

Orthodoxy gained adherents in this period as a result of both the wartime immigration and success in retaining the allegiance of its young in a climate much more amenable to religion and particularism. It thus had no more reason than before to debate what it took utterly for granted. To modern Orthodox Jews[60] committed to the life in two worlds described by their authority, Rabbi Soloveitchik, chosenness was the *raison d'être* for the "covenantal community" which they maintained against America's (and their own) pursuit of "majesty." Hasidim living apart from America in a new-world ghetto such as Williamsburg in Brooklyn, or other "ultra-Orthodox" Jews affiliated with Agudat Israel, found chosenness as obvious a teaching as it had been to ancestors similarly separated from their gentile worlds over the centuries. One gets the flavor of such a view in the sermons of one of the three leading *"gedolim"* or authorities of the Agudat Israel faction of Orthodoxy, Rabbi Itzhak Hutner of the Chaim Berlin Yeshiva. (It is characteristic of Orthodoxy, Liebman notes, that congregational rabbis are eclipsed in importance by heads of *yeshivot*. The source of authority, after all, is mastery of the legal texts.)[61] Hutner writes that every festival reveals a different aspect of the *segulah* (uniqueness) of Israel, though now, in its long exile, this uniqueness is "hidden away in mystery" under the wraps of gentile rule, and performance of the commandments specific to the chosen Land of Israel is precluded. Passover recalls God's role as the redeemer of Israel, Shavuot that He is the "Teacher of Torah to His people Israel," Yom Kippur that he "forgives His people Israel" their transgressions, etc. The crucial *ḥesed* or loving kindness bestowed on the world through Israel is "the existence of the universe through justice" *(mishpat)*. Human existence, that is, can somehow be "earned" through the performance of commandments. It need not remain an absolute debt or gift which cannot to any degree be repaid. This rather original turn of thought is joined to the more traditional notion that ours is a world under the rule of *din* (law or decree) unmitigated by *raḥamim* or mercy. It is not surprising that in such a world Israel should be persecuted. The fact that God bore Israel to Sinai "on eagle's wings" is a sign of its true status, to be visible in the redeemed world when *din* is once more one with *raḥamim*.[62] The mode and language of discourse here are traditional, as is the understanding of Israel's unique relationship to God.[63]

Only the Reconstructionists could not accept chosenness. Kaplan wrote in *Commentary* exactly what he had written thirty years earlier.[64] Rabbi Harold Schulweis stated unequivocally that " 'chosen people' is an example of a doctrine believed to be of divine origin which can no longer be accepted in the light of our experience and ethics."[65] Rabbi Jack J.

Cohen wrote that Judaism would remain ineffective as an influence in the lives of the great majority of Jews so long as it was considered "a spiritual burden laid on the shoulders of the Jewish people by some extrahistorical force, such as is expressed in certain theories of the 'chosen people.' "[66] The other movements having officially adopted much of Kaplan's thinking long ago, and having adopted even more of it unofficially, little besides chosenness and the now-unfashionable "religious naturalism" divided Kaplan's movement from Reform, or for that matter from much of Conservatism. Chosenness had in effect become a badge by which one could discern the true Reconstructionist. The movement broke away in this period to found its own rabbinical seminary and to seek the allegiance of member congregations. Organizational growth, however, was not accompanied by theological innovation—both because of Kaplan's overwhelming presence and the fact that, in the new climate, the Reconstructionists could offer little that was not accepted elsewhere.[67]

Thus, while the third generation's theologians announced a significant departure from the ways of the second, the movements and their rabbis continued to interpret chosenness substantially as their predecessors had done. The one major change was the absence of apologetic, in which the generation had little need to engage. The legitimacy of Judaism in America, and the alleged contribution which chosenness had made to racial doctrines of superiority, were no longer issues. The writings of the third generation's rabbis, like those of its theologians, tend to accept the Biblical personal God of encounter as a mystery beyond rational understanding, rather than attempt, as did the previous generation, to arrive at a concept of God such as Kaplan's that could be rationally argued if not demonstrated. It is as if the events of the intervening years had not answered philosophy so much as rendered its questions irrelevant.

The principal event, of course, was the Holocaust. The renewed existence of Israel—a cause for pride, and hope—has had little bearing on the theological discussion of chosenness or any other issue. Only the isolation experienced before and during the Six-Day War served to reinforce the awareness of Jewish peoplehood and Jewish "apartness,"[68] but this was a function of the threat to Israel's existence and not of that existence itself, and even as such has left no theological residue. The shadow of the Holocaust, however—lengthening with distance from the event, as its implications came to dominate American Jewish thought in the late seventies—stands as a major dividing line between the two generations. Debates about the appropriate or necessary theological response to the Holocaust center on the question of whether it represents an evil for mankind and a tragedy for the Jewish people unique in the annals of history. These debates in turn revolve implicitly about the question of Israel's uniqueness. Yet the two issues remain separate; both parties to the debate on the uniqueness of the Holocaust can agree that Israel is chosen and indeed that "Auschwitz" is but one more demonstration of that election. The question "in what sense chosen?" thus cuts across that of "in what sense is the Holocaust unique?" The event itself could not but alter the self-conception of Jews and their understanding of election. The debate about the uniqueness of the event, however, has altered neither the one nor the other.[69]

The Language of Chosenness in America

Before leaving the third generation, we will consider one factor, aside from the social and intellectual forces detailed throughout the work, which may have caused the range of opinion on chosenness to have assumed and retained the contours which we have described. This is the second aspect of the loss of a "private" Jewish space, bounded by a Jewish language, discussed in chapter 6. There our concern was the loss of the opportunity for honest discussion unencumbered by the need to present a face to the outside world, a need which has not disappeared despite successful integration into America. Here I wish to focus on the loss of language, literally rather than figuratively understood. In other words: how might debate on Israel's chosenness have been affected by the fact that it took place in English?

Cynthia Ozick has perhaps dealt with this general question more explicitly than any other writer of her generation, both in stories that bemoan the loss of tradition and substance to American vacuity and in reflection about the difficulties in describing authentic Jewish life and faith in a language informed by the experience of neither. "I feel cramped by it," she writes of the English language.

> I have come to it with notions it is too parochial to recognize. A language, like a people, has a history of ideas, but not *all* ideas: only those known to its experience. Not surprisingly, English is a Christian language. When I write English, I live in Christendom.[70]

Ozick's pursuit of this theme extends to the legitimacy of writing stories in any language, for might not the surrender to imagination ("afflatus, trance, and image") constitute an offense against the second commandment?[71]Her questions provide entry to a Jewish philosophy of language and literature which may yet emerge from the third generation. Our concern here, however, is with the narrower question of whether the "light" of Jewish experience, particularly of chosenness, has emerged undistorted from the prism of the English language.

In a sense, anthropological studies have sufficiently demonstrated the mutual influence of language and experience. Language, in the well-known phrase of the philosopher Ludwig Wittgenstein, "marks the limits of [our] world," just as particular worlds determine the fund of words and concepts stored up for use in particular languages. The relevant question, then, is not whether discussion of chosenness in English might somehow have affected the substance of what was thought and said—for it did, surely—but to what specific examples of influence we can point. Two possibilities suggest themselves.

The first draws upon Ozick's claim that "when I write English, I live in Christendom." One could argue that the manner in which Jews of various sorts traditionally conceived and related to their God is not easily rendered into English, which is molded by the very different perceptions of Christianity. Thus, whereas the King James Bible impresses us with God's grandeur and awesome majesty, the Jewish folk-religion over the centuries, including the Yiddish culture in which most of the second generation had its roots, conceived of God in far more familiar terms.[72] Irving Howe's characterization, if somewhat sentimentalized, makes the point well.

> Toward Him the Jews could feel a peculiar sense of intimacy: had they not suffered enough in His behalf? In prayer His name could not be spoken, yet in or out of prayer He could always be spoken to. . . . The relation between God and man was social, intimate, critical, seeming at times to follow like a series of rationalistic deductions from the premise of the Chosen People.[73]

The premise was in turn supportable because of the intimacy of the relationship, and both were in turn grounded not only in folk-religion but in the "highest" reaches of Kabbalah, Talmud, and Torah. This was a God to whom one could say "shall not the judge of all the earth do justly," and whom one could dissuade from vengeance by citing the damage which it would cause to His reputation. This was also a God who, seeing Israel's hesitancy to plunge into the Red Sea, can say to Moses, "What are you crying to me for? Tell the children of Israel to get moving."[74] The colloquialism is not the translator's but the text's, and that is the point. This God was and is familiar, one who can be argued with, upbraided and chastised for His treatment of His people—for "had they not suffered enough in His behalf?" The wife exiled from the king's palace because of insolence defends herself, in midrash, by saying, "Have I not a right? I accepted your Torah on Sinai when others did not."[75] In English such familiarity tends to be sacrificed to decorum, and irritation with God to be sublimated into reverent praise.

There is, I believe, something to this line of argument, though the impact of English is hard to measure and would seem to pale before more immediate causes of felt distance from God such as secularization and the cluster of factors loosely grouped under the term modernity. One suspects that the fund of experience available to speakers of English *is* foreign to the history which elicited and reinforced Jewish notions of chosenness, but that it was the American Jews' own distance from this history, more than the language which they spoke, that determined their understandings of their election.

A second possible effect of conducting discussions of chosenness in English derives from the fact that the term "chosen people" possesses a character far more unambiguous than comparable terms in the original Hebrew. The phrase "the chosen people" does not appear in Jewish tradition. One has *"am segulah"*[76]—the people singled out, the people which is a "peculiar treasure"—but never *"am habehirah"* or *"am nivhar."* This is hardly by chance. Whereas "the chosen people" makes chosenness an ascriptive status, a quality inherent in the people as such, the Hebrew reliance on active verbs such as "God chose," "God loved," "God knew," or "God called" describes only what God did and indicates what Israel must do in response. A large portion of the American rabbis' apologetics, we recall, was devoted to this point exactly, and the clarification might have been less necessary had the debate proceeded in its own language. Only *am segulah* places chosenness in passive, adjectival voice comparable to "chosen people," thus making of election a status as permanent as one's very name. (This is perhaps why the medieval philosopher Yehudah Halevi, who, we recall, ascribed to Jews a unique and hereditary capacity for revelation, laid so much stress upon the term *segulah.*) I have been unable to locate the origin of the phrase "the chosen people"; the King James itself translates *segulah* as "peculiar treasure." In the First Epistle to Peter, too, we find "But you are a chosen generation, a royal priesthood and holy nation, a peculiar people" (2:9)—a precise rendering of the Hebrew Bible's understanding and indeed of Exodus 19:5–6. How the transition was made to the notion of the chosen people that we associate with Puritanism I have not yet discovered.

One suspects that this effect of the English language, like the one noted previously, had some impact, although once more such impact is difficult to measure. It could well be that when American Jews used the phrase "chosen people" to describe themselves to gentiles and to each other they had in mind a set of associations drawn more from the Puritan experience transmitted to them by America than from the treasury of their own tradition. Certainly the rabbis who debated chosenness made minimal reference to the texts of Jewish tradition, aside from key verses in Exodus and Deutero-Isaiah and *aggadot* such as the offer of the Torah to other nations besides Israel. This suggests that their idea of chosenness was one which they took for granted as a joint cultural legacy of Judaism and America, without consideration of possible distinctions (or at least variations in emphasis) between the two. This idea was then passed on to congregants anxious to identify with America in any case. There is no way of knowing how much influence should be ascribed to each of the two sources of their notion of chosenness, the Jewish and the Puritan, but one reason for the idea's usefulness in achieving the integration of Jews into America may well have been that English-speaking American Jews heard only those parts of their tradition compatible with the image of election predominant in their chosen land.[77] Judaism, then, would in part have become a faith transmitted to Jews by America, one Jews learned about only indirectly, at one remove.

I do not mean to exaggerate the determinism of language. Judaism has survived other exiles in other foreign cultures. But as one probes the ways in which America really is different, one should bear in mind that pre-modern Jews came to the struggle for a separate identity as the cultural equals of their environment. This has not been true of American Jews, who are by and large foreigners to their own tradition and members of a separate community only to a limited extent. If one learns anything from their reinterpretation of chosenness, it is the tenacity of their attachment to tradition despite the attenuation and limitation of that very attachment. The latter in a sense made the former possible; had the conflict between Jewish tradition and America been more pronounced, the Jews' integration here would have proved impossible. Because the conflict has been muted, Jews have been able to retain links to their tradition which may enable some future generation to achieve less equivocal affirmations of Jewish faith. In the meantime, to say the words "the Jews are chosen," even when one cannot explain or defend the sense of the proposition, serves to transmit the language of tradition, even if only in part and only in translation. "What we cannot speak about we must pass over in silence." Silence is the death of any tradition. If so, even as imperfect a translation as that which overtook chosenness must be reckoned a significant achievement.

PART
FOUR

Conclusion

VIII

The Lessons of
Chosenness in America

WE HAVE NOW traced two generations of American Jewry's public conversation about the meaning of its chosenness. Recalling R. W. B. Lewis's comment that "every culture seems, as it advances toward maturity, to produce its own determining debate over the ideas that preoccupy it,"[1] we have argued that chosenness preoccupied American Jewish thinkers because it was essential to their maturing definition of who and what American Jews were. They would not be mere Americans—but, as part of the chosen people, would somehow stand apart. Yet they would be Americans—and, if chosenness involved more exclusivity, a more demanding covenant, or a more avowedly elitist mission than was compatible with being Americans, then chosenness would have to be reinterpreted. So it was. After a close reading of the various reinterpretations of chosenness proposed over the past fifty years, these generalizations should carry a richness of reference which they did not have at the outset.

In conclusion, I would like to reflect on two matters: first, on what American Jewry's debate on chosenness can teach us about the ways in which Jewish—or any religious—tradition can be appropriated in America today; and, secondly, on whether the Jewish reinterpretation of election could have worked out any differently, either in its substance or its (ideological) form, given the constraints under which the Jewish thinkers labored. The debate on chosenness, we recall, occurred within a fairly narrow range of opinion defined by the idea's traditional meanings on the one hand and the situation of the community on the other; individual thinkers, moreover, generally adopted positions in keeping with the course charted by their respective movements. Fifty years of debate resulted in only four or five essentially different positions. These merit brief review before we proceed to examine what the debate as a whole can teach us.

Reform, having abrogated the authority of the *mitzvot*, found in "mission" a rhetoric of activity which mythologized and legitimated a relatively contentless Judaism. However, mission itself proved too elitist a rhetoric in egalitarian America, and so some in the movement fell back in the second generation on the original substance to which the rhetoric had been intended to move its audience—universalist ethics. Then, recoiling from the loss of meaning to Jewish identification implied by such a completely universalist commitment, the movement eventually found its way back to the symbol of chosenness and the qualified affirmation of particularity. Neither Reform's beliefs nor its level of prescribed observance were compatible with the doctrine of chosenness traditionally understood. An ideology which invoked election despite the lack of prerequisites to its affirmation was called in to fill the gap.

Mordecai Kaplan, having found chosenness incompatible with the integration of the Jews to America, and having denied the existence of a "choosing" God in his "trans-naturalist" theology, staked out his own position vis-à-vis Reform by refusing to reinterpret the idea of election or to accept it as a symbol. Instead he renounced it at every opportunity. Religion in his Durkheimian perspective had become ideology, the content of which was to be determined by functional criteria. These could be relatively more noble (e.g., advocating the "God-idea" best suited to the promotion of morality) or, as we have seen, rather less so (e.g., the identification of the contemporary Jew's only meaningful vocation with "Reconstructionism: A Program.") Having taught American Jewry to see the tenets of faith as symbols which expressed meanings inaccessible in propositional form, and having reinterpreted most of the tradition symbolically, Kaplan refused to accept chosenness in those terms. He did so in part because, as he stated clearly in *Judaism as a Civilization*, the very need for Reconstructionism vanished if Israel's chosenness was affirmed.

Conservatives, who generally avoided divisive issues of substance which might have threatened their fragile consensus of the center, had even more reason to avoid a clear stance on chosenness. For chosenness could not be interpreted unless one also clarified one's position on God, revelation, and Torah. These issues lay at the heart of the movement's raison d'être and were potentially most demonstrative of the split between the "elite" of the Jewish Theological Seminary and the congregational "folk." Conservatives meant to be the Orthodox of twentieth-century America: continuous with the tradition, obligated to obey its *halakhah*, yet adaptive to the changed environment of modernity. To say, with the Orthodox, "we are chosen, by God, at Sinai—period" would have been to deny the substance of, and even the need for, theological adaptation to modernity and America. To say "we are chosen, but only as everyone is"—a position indeed taken by some Conservative rabbis— would have been to renounce continuity with a tradition that knew better. Thus, in the second generation, Conservatives gave less attention to the matter of election than did Reform and Reconstructionism. When they did address it, Conservatives pursued what we have called a strategy of equivocation. The Jews were chosen, but perhaps not uniquely, in a way related to their possession of Torah. In the third generation Conservatives devoted even less time to the issue, except for several theologians who joined other participants in the *Commentary* symposium of 1966 in embracing chosenness as an indispensable doctrine beyond human comprehension.

Orthodox spokesmen of both generations gave short shrift to chosenness. Their affirmation of tradition entailed the clear assumption of election; moreover, they remained for much of the second generation a predominantly immigrant community untouched by the need to explain themselves to America. This continued to be true of "ultra-Orthodox" Jews living apart from America in the third generation. Those "modern Orthodox" who believed in the compatibility of Orthodoxy with America insisted, like Soloveitchik, that no commitment of faith such as chosenness could be understood or judged from the outside. *Pro forma* recognition was paid to the problems that other Jews (indeed, the rabbis of the Talmud) had with the doctrine's implications of superiority, but these were dismissed on the grounds that the Torah did not say Jews were better, but only called them to a higher responsibility. Orthodoxy blessed chosenness with silence when the other movements covered it and re-covered it with debate. This silence, while appealing in its purity of intention, also permitted evasion of the serious doubts entertained by committed Jews outside Orthodoxy—and, one suspects, by some inside it as well.

These, then, constituted the principal variations of opinion on chosenness, spelled out in and expressing the countervailing pulls of Jewish tradition and America. Religious Jews could not simply carry on a tradition of belief evolved centuries ago in far different circumstances; neither did they cling to reinterpreted ideas of chosenness solely because these provided them with an accommodation to a primary symbol of America essential to America's self-understanding. Rather, all that makes a person a believer and a member of the group to which he or she belongs—in this case, all that makes a Jew a Jew—conspired to sustain their belief in chosenness. The idea served to crystallize their definition of themselves. Chosenness and the commitments which it entailed, then, set limits to what Jews could and could not become in America, even as America had set limits to how election could and could not be reinterpreted.

The key element in the Jews' working out of these dilemmas seems to have been the shift from theology to sociology and religious ideology discussed in chapters 4 and 5. American rabbis of the second generation, we recall, for the most part avoided systematic exposition of their faith in terms of well-defined concepts and logically-interrelated arguments. Instead they turned increasingly to functionalist considerations of "what would work" for their congregants. They invoked images and symbols which continued to move American Jews, even though the beliefs which once undergirded those symbols no longer commanded their assent. Two possible explanations for this reliance upon ideology rather than theology can be dismissed at once. Judaism, contrary to an opinion still heard today, does have a theological tradition. Chosenness had been discussed for at least two millennia in relation to well-defined conceptions of God, revelation, exile, messiah, and commandment. American rabbis did not fail to write theology for want of precedents. America too has produced theology. The notion that Americans are too pragmatic and unphilosophical a people to indulge in theology cannot stand in the face of the evidence, despite the kernel of truth in the claim. Other factors were clearly at work, and two such considerations lead to a better understanding of the ideological form in which the religious thought of the American rabbis is generally couched.

First, theology is inherently particularistic. It primarily concerns a faith community and its relation to God. Theology thrives upon challenges from the outside, but it does so by drawing what is foreign into its own "hermeneutic circle." American Jews, fearing the charge of particularism, shied away from theology's essential concern with the communal self and instead emphasized what could readily be projected outwards. Lacking the strength of a live tradition, they were unable to synthesize the foreign into the traditional, and could only submit to its alien dictates. When we consider that theology is also an elitist enterprise, the reluctance of the Jews to engage in it becomes still more comprehensible—especially when the object of the elitist enterprise would have been the defense of a supremely elitist mission.

A second problem was the lack of theologians. Rabbis and their few lay counterparts in Jewish thought during the second generation were "middle-brow" at best. They simply did not have the tools to do theology, and even those equipped for theology were unequipped for Jewish theology. As Jacob Neusner has recently pointed out, modern Jewish thinkers have tended to draw on the Bible and on modern philosophy but not on the traditional form and substance of much of Jewish theology—*halakhah*.[2] One need not make the normative claim that a Jewish theology must be halakhic (i.e., regard the halakhic tradition as resting upon divine revelation) to note that any theology which ignores a chief component of its tradition courts the impoverishment which was, in this respect, the fate of American Judaism.

The point bears extension, for it has significance wider than the second generation or even Judaism. It would seem that theology is not just *halakhah* but also *aggadah:* that is, not just "life lived," as Neusner puts it, but also life reflected upon. If American Jews did not do theology it was perhaps because they lacked a *halakhah* and *aggadah* in this sense: a defined faith community within which a certain distinct life was lived, and so could be reflected upon. The community was disintegrating, and the *halakhah* had by and large been repudiated. (The generalizations made here apply, of course, to non-Orthodox thinkers and to the laymen in their congregations, although there were exceptions.) A fragmented community, unsure of its proper distinctiveness from the outer world, turned rather to ideology. Mission, as we noted, provided an invaluable sermonic theme in part because the word itself connoted activity to an audience denied the opportunity to see itself acting out its commitments in the world. If religion seeks to assure a person that the binding cord of authority ties the acts of his or her daily life to the God who gives life, the acts must be there to be sanctified. Except for Orthodoxy, and for some among the other movements, those acts had been reduced to philanthropy and pursuit of social justice. Theology, not surprisingly, was also curtailed.

The reemergence of theology among the third generation has not accomplished the objectives which its practitioners set for themselves. Neither, one suspects, has it made the impact upon congregants achieved by the alternatives to theology developed during the second generation.[3] Rabbis and theologians continue to turn to sociology and ideology, for "what works" possesses an authority unattainable through logical argument. Ideology "works" because it contains and even draws nourishment from contradictions which prove fatal to theology. Religious thinkers in America—and not only Jews—are likely to rely on it in the future as well, for the factors which caused the second generation to turn to it are still operative. Commitments to pluralism continue to pose dilemmas for particularist affirmation. Few are adequately equipped for theological work, and those who are lack a communal *halakhah* on which to reflect. Distrust of inherited answers continues to render functional criteria decisive, by default, regarding what is deemed true or at least important. Finally, ideological symbols of all sorts continue to move men when rational creeds and systems cannot. In such circumstances, theology is largely precluded by the very conditions of uncertainty and doubt which, to the faithful, render it so necessary.

The factors which influenced this transformation from theology to ideology, moreover, may have been endemic to the Jew's absorption into America, indeed inherent in America itself and so at work on groups besides the Jews as well. As a country founded, according to the national mythology explicated by Lewis and Bercovitch, as a "New Man" renewing creation through rejection of inherited answers from across the sea, and as a "nation of immigrants" pledged to the co-existence of many cultures, no matter how diverse, America is denied the easy agreements of a normative culture such as traditional Judaism. These conditions cannot but alter the formation of identity, shaping the definition to oneself and to other of what one really is (or, in Erik Erikson's words, what one is "never not").[4] The latter term seems especially apposite to the Jewish debate over chosenness, which revealed a good deal to Jews and non-Jews about what American Jews are "never not." Jews could or would not simply cast off the claim to election, even when it proved problematic in the context of American pluralism. The Jews are those who are never not the chosen people. Jewish ethnic identity similarly proved resistant to being recast in the more amorphous American mold in part because, as the "chosen people" label makes clear, that identity is not merely ethnic. It has built into it religious claims which defy those who would seek to "melt" into the future.

It could be argued that all immigrant ethnic identities in America have been tied at first, at least to some extent, to particularist religious affirmations. It is certainly true that they exhibited differences more substantive than those who defined the conditions for their acceptance into America would allow. Others than the Jews, then, have faced the same two alternatives: either assimilation to America would remain incomplete and the reigning pluralism be quite tenuous, because of substantial commitments to competing truths or ways of life; or ethnic identities would become superficial, reduced to cookery and nostalgia. To be other in America has in practice proven a combination of the two: pretending a greater sameness than exists[5] while at the same time claiming for otherness a greater substance than in fact remains to it. Imperfect religious ideologies are a far better vehicle for the compromises and contradictions of such a position than theologies in which all is worked out to the last detail. As we have observed, theology leaves too little room for the evasions in which life must sometimes be lived and commitments negotiated.

The second generation, then, may well prove more instructive in its failure to produce theology than the third in its good-intentioned attempts to do so. One tends to despondency when pondering the future of Jewish commitment amidst the many pressures to its erosion. Yet one is surprised to note how many Jewish institutions thrive nonetheless—

with or without substantive "content." Ideology and deeply rooted loyalties have filled the breach. American Jews continue to wrestle with the angel of their chosenness. Identities, fragmented to be sure, are fashioned and lent stability. An authentic link to tradition—true to it and to all else one is and believes—is often achieved, if only in part and with difficulty. Such are the terms of any covenant which only goes halfway.

Could things have turned out any differently? Probably not. The rabbis, to be sure, might have been more literate in their own tradition. The leaders of Reform and Reconstructionism might, by the 1930s, have been less naive as to the imminent redemption of humanity through progress. More American Jewish leaders might have been as perceptive as Milton Steinberg or Mordecai Kaplan in discerning the gravity of the community's situation and in realizing that mere enthusiasm for America was no solution. However, the balance of commitments which the second generation missed and the third has tried to set right is more easily located in retrospect. Given the tremendous pressures of acculturation to America, economic depression, war, and Nazism faced by the second generation, and the underlying forces of secularization only recently clarified by sociologists, American Jewish religious leaders did a credible job in "meeting the demands of the day."[6] That we may regret the consequences of their decisions—principally the continuing intellectual poverty of much American Jewish religious discourse—does not mean that more could have been accomplished.

One cannot come, with wisdom garnered through study of the various interpretations of chosenness, and propose an interpretation more satisfying than those we have examined. To do so would be to fall into the trap which has already snared too many in the past half-century. It is impossible to discuss chosenness adequately without first explaining what the Jewish people has been placed on this earth to do. And that task would entail the presentation of coherent conceptions of God, revelation, covenant, etc. What is needed, in other words, is not history or sociology but theology—the desideratum which the third generation has promised but so far failed to provide. The lessons of what not to do are legion. They delineate for us, however, only the bare outlines of what chosenness might mean given varying religious commitments. Criticism, as always, proves easier than theory. Criticism can, however, provide theory with several guidelines; in this respect, too, American Jewish thought is instructive in its failures. Many Jewish thinkers in America seemed to forget the symbolic nature of any religious discourse, including theology. "The Torah is written in human language." That is not to say that its words are arbitrary, or that any symbol would bear an equally adequate relation to the reality which we seek to capture in our language. But human predicates attached to the divine subject mean more and less than in ordinary speech. The words "God loved" can only refer me to my experience of love (with parents, siblings, lovers, friends) and to my experience of God (in nature, history, prayer, and observance). The words conjure up a set of images, framed by what the tradition has imposed upon, and how it has shaped, my experience of both God and love. "God chose" constitutes a similar appeal to experience and imagination. It cannot literally mean anything. The task of theology is to determine what it can mean, given the metaphorical quality of the language and the constraints on our knowledge and beliefs about the world. American Jewish thinkers did grapple with the latter, often with great integrity.

Yet it would seem that the principal problem in using such symbolic language is not the loss of belief per se, but the loss of sustaining experiences. Twentieth-century Jewish religious thought at its best is preoccupied with this problem. Martin Buber, for example, attended to the disappearance of "I-Thou" relationships between human beings—the decline of *Gemeinschaft*, in sociological parlance—because he believed that that development had caused our inability to enjoy dialogue with the "Eternal Thou." Heschel frustrated those who believed him potentially the greatest Jewish theologian of the century by spending much of his work in seeking to evoke the awe and wonder at things and at oneself which he believed led human reason to jump beyond itself to God. If he could not conjure up that experience, then talk of revelation and *mitzvot* would fall on deaf ears. Yet words of course cannot conjure up such experience, even as Soloveitchik's masterful portrait of the "Man of Halakhah" cannot bring someone who has not known the world of the Talmud to enter inside its "four ells." In all three cases—the experiences of encounter with God, of wonder that leads to belief, and of knowing God through study and observance of His law—the theology carries real power only to those who share the pivotal experiences described. It is not coincidental that each of the three theologians derived the experience at the root of his language from an Eastern European world of faith which no longer exists.

The inability to derive the language of chosenness from Jewish experience will likely preclude non-Orthodox Jews from ever producing such coherent theologies. There is no thriving and distinct Jewish life on which to draw, rather remnants retained in a mixture of faith, reverence, and aesthetic appreciation. Jews do not know themselves to be chosen, except perhaps in the ever-inexplicable wonders of Jewish history, and even there one can place the State of Israel in the context of modern nationalism, and dissipate the Holocaust's uniqueness through recall of the recent murders of other countless millions. Daily life, as Eugene Borowitz observed, testifies to a lack of Jewish distinctiveness rather than the reverse.[7] If American Jews have of late turned from chosenness to Israel and then the Holocaust as props of their identity, as Jacob Neusner claims, this would only confirm the predicament which we have described.[8] For if chosenness is relevant to their experience only in part, Israel offers at best a vicarious source of identity, the self-image of the Jew as pioneer, fighter, and isolated hero battling implacable foes. The imagery is inapplicable to America, and perhaps even dangerous. While identification with the victims of the Holocaust cannot be explained simply, and preoccupation with the tragedy is readily understandable, one is struck by the fact that American Jews, secure economically and in their status as Americans, should identify with the helpless victims of horrible persecutions. The centuries have left their mark on American Jews, however forgetful they have become. This attenuated sense of history, obligation, and guilt is no doubt responsible for such attachment to chosenness as persists among the nonreligious. Such is the extent of their experience of election. Chosenness will make more sense to them when its images resonate in minds which have come to know it from personal experience.

However—the final lesson which criticism can impart to theory— what enabled chosenness to resonate with meaning when other symbols could not was in part its own inherent power. In urging that we all select from tradition in accordance with the criterion of "inner power,"[9] Buber, the religious liberal, only wished to make conscious and voluntary a choice undertaken by anyone who transmits a tradition. What is selected—or, better, emphasized—in a particular time and place will be that which addresses the situation and needs of that community. Chosenness was not abandoned when other symbols were because it resisted the universalist transformation which overtook such ideas as the messiah (which became "human progress") and exile (transformed into "alienation"). Its psychological resonance was profound, witness Freud's recognition that "if one had done so much for one's father, one wanted to have a reward, or at least to be his only beloved child, his Chosen people."[10] Its sociological relevance also endured, despite the Jews' emancipation from the ghetto, precisely because they now had to choose a place in the world once taken for granted as the lot of the chosen. Its historical import was underlined by the terrible events of the day. That is why the idea's religious resonance could not be entirely "abstracted" from the traditional referents and, so, utterly neutralized.

The symbol's various elements hung together, and in turn imposed their own dynamic on interpretation and even impelled action. The idea of "vocation" has "behaved" similarly, the Puritan conception giving way to the secular connotation of the "professions." In the case of chosenness, the internal "dynamic" is visible in the arrogance to which those who believe in it were prone, or were regarded as prone by their rabbis, and in the guilt attendant on not being able to live up to its expectations. The Puritan elect too had been warned by their ministers in the seventeenth century against the shattering of faith on the "rocks of presumption" or its loss in the "gulf of desperation."[11] American Jews were thus not the first to navigate around such dangers. Like the Puritans they needed to act out their calling in useful labor and to see it enacted by a community. They too worried about the roles of ascription and achievement in attaining the status of election. The parallel is instructive because it reminds us that ideas and symbols possess an immanent logic. Indeed, the power of that logical coherence may itself be a factor in imposing a particular idea or symbol on people bereft of a clear course or sense of self. Chosenness "succeeded" when other ideas "failed" because it possessed both coherence and relevance to American Jews. In another time and place, other symbols would have achieved primacy and, in the future, no doubt they will. Good theology— enduring theology—taps the deepest needs of the community at a given moment, and so presumes the existence of a community sufficiently alike in predicament and belief to be touched deeply by the same powerful resonances.

The attempt at "imagining Jews" in America will continue. What we have witnessed in American Judaism, then, is not only a case study in the secularization of religious belief and observance, but a chapter, not unlike others, in the transmission of a living religious tradition from one generation to the next.

Notes

Abbreviations

AJYB	*American Jewish Yearbook*
CCARJ	*Central Conference of American Rabbis Journal*
CCYB	*Central Conference of American Rabbis Yearbook*
CJ	*Conservative Judaism*
CJR	*Contemporary Jewish Record*
COM	*Commentary*
JF	*Jewish Frontier*
LJ	*Liberal Judaism*
MID	*Midstream*
MJ	*Menorah Journal*
PRA	*Proceedings of the Rabbinical Assembly of America*
REC	*Reconstructionist*

1. A Part and Apart

1. Quoted in David Philipson, "The Jewish Pioneers of the Ohio Valley," *Publications of the American Jewish Historical Society* 8 (1900):45.

2. See especially the works of Marshall Sklare and Charles Liebman cited below.

3. Two recent works pose the problem trenchantly: Jacob Neusner's *Stranger at Home* (Chicago: University of Chicago Press, 1981) and Anne Roiphe's *Generation Without Memory* (New York: Linden Press/Simon and Schuster, 1981).

4. Charles Liebman, *The Ambivalent American Jew: Politics, Religion, and Family in American Jewish Life* (Philadelphia: Jewish Publication Society, 1973), pp. vii, 26–27.

5. R. W. B. Lewis, *The American Adam* (Chicago: University of Chicago Press, 1971), pp. 1–2.

6. Cf. Solomon Schechter, "Election of Israel," in *Aspects of Rabbinic Theology* (New York: Schocken Books, 1969), p. 57.

7. Quoted in *The New York Times*, September 22, 1980, p. B7.

8. Figures from Nathan Glazer, *American Judaism*, 2nd ed. (Chicago: University of Chicago Press, 1972), pp. 60, 82–83. The generalizations which follow are standard. See for example Glazer, chaps. 5–6; Marshall Sklare, *Conservative Judaism* (New York: Schocken Books, 1972), chaps. 3–4; Ben Halpern, *The American Jew: A Zionist Analysis* (New York: Theodore Herzl Foundation, 1956), chap. 1; Charles Liebman, "A Sociological Analysis of Contemporary Orthodoxy," *Judaism*, Summer 1964, p. 285. For an account of American Jewish History, see Lucy Dawidowicz, *On Equal Terms: Jews in America 1881–1981* (New York: Holt, Rinehart and Winston, 1982).

9. Charles Liebman, "Reconstructionism in American Jewish Life," AJYB, 1970, p. 4.

10. Ibid., p. 21.

11. This study examines only the English-speaking second- and third-generation communities. The Yiddish community constitutes a distinct (and largely first-generation) group with a separate set of problems and so shall remain beyond the bounds of the present essay. Sermons originally given in Yiddish by Orthodox rabbis are, however, likely represented in the published Hebrew collections of *derashot* (homilies) which have been examined.

12. Judith R. Kramer and Seymour Leventman, *Children of the Gilded Ghetto: Conflict Resolutions of Three Generations of American Jews* (New Haven: Yale University Press, 1945), p. 30.

13. On this matter see also P. I. Rose, ed., *The Ghetto and Beyond: Essays on Jewish Life in America* (New York: Random House, 1969), pp. 8, 129. The complications of using generational terminology are examined in detail by Herbert J. Gans, "The Origin and Growth of a Jewish Community in the Suburbs," in Marshall Sklare, ed., *The Jews: Patterns of an American Group* (New York: Free Press, 1958), p. 209. Finally, for a usage by a leading member and analyst of the "third generation" see Will Herberg, "Religious Trends in American Jewry," in Harold U. Ribalow, ed., *Mid-century* (New York: Beechurst Press, 1955), p. 252.

14. Cf. discussion of this phenomenon in the symposium "Under Forty," CJR, Feb. 1944, pp. 3–36.

15. The only available survey records the opinions of adolescents. Charles Rosen, "Minority Group in Transition: A Study of Adolescent Religious Convictions and Conduct," in Sklare, *The Jews*, pp. 336–46.

16. Cf. Liebman, *American Jew*, p. 115, and Jerome E. Carlin and Saul Mendlovitz, "The American Rabbi: A Religious Specialist Responds to Loss of Authority," in Sklare, *The Jews*, pp. 377–404. See also Sklare, *Conservative Judaism*, chap. 6.

17. See the survey described in the text and cited in note 19 below.

18. See the considerations advanced by Uriel Tal, *Christians and Jews in Germany*, trans. Noah J. Jacobs (Ithaca: Cornell University Press, 1975), pp. 21–22.

19. Joseph Zeitlin, *Disciples of the Wise: The Religious and Social Opinions of American Rabbis* (New York: Teachers College of Columbia University, 1945), pp. 41–90, 113–16. Because the rabbis represented in our study held views similar to those polled by Zeitlin, and comprise all of the rabbinical leadership as well as a significant number of the rank and file, we may safely conclude that they give a fair picture of the thought of the second-generation American rabbinate as a whole. We will find a rabbi's movement to be the key predictor of his views.

20. This could be an artefact of a possibly greater percentage of response by younger and native-born rabbis.

21. A similar methodology is adopted by Moshe Davis in his study, *The Emergence of Conservative Judaism: The Historical School in Nineteenth Century America* (Philadelphia: Jewish Publication Society, 1965), p. 309. All the movements published journals (although Orthodox rabbis lacked such an organ during the second generation), and these have been examined, along with such independent publications as the *Menorah Journal* and (in the third generation) *Commentary* and *Judaism*. Our most valuable source for the second generation remains the sermon, and the published sermons of the period have been exhaustively surveyed in an effort to specify the character of the rabbis' reinterpretations and gauge the needs which prompted them. Published sources have been used exclusively. Examination of the correspondence of several major figures, and conversations with several others, added little to the record of the public debate.

22. Orthodoxy, furthermore, was composed primarily of first-generation American Jews until after the Second World War. Examination of some six dozen collections of *derashot* by Orthodox rabbis turned up only one discussion of election, dating from 1963.

23. The figure includes usages of *bahur* but not *mivhar* or *bahir*. I have relied upon Solomon Mandelkern, *Concordantiae* (Jerusalem: Schocken, 1975) and Francis Brown, S. R. Driver, and Charles A. Briggs, *Hebrew and English Lexicon of the Old Testament* (Oxford: Clarendon Press, 1972). The Biblical text relies upon our awareness of *bahar's* many resonances when it juxtaposes one usage with another, for example I Chron. 6:16 or I Kings 8:6, where God's choice of Zion is linked to His choice of David. See G. E. Mendenhall, "Election" in George A. Buttrich, ed., *The Interpreter's Dictionary of the Bible*, Vol. 2 (New York: Abingdon Press, 1962), p. 76. The findings of R. G. Rogers support this view: "The Doctrine of Election in the Chronicler's Work and the Dead Sea Scrolls" (diss., Boston University, 1969), especially chaps. 1–3. Rogers reports the view of T. C. Vriezen that only the word *bahar* is adequate to the "theological-cultural" idea of election, the usage of such other possibilities as *yada'* (know), *kara'* (call) and *lakah* (take) being very limited (Rogers, p. 88). See also Klaus Koch, "Zur Geschichte der Erwahlungsvorstellung in Israel," *Zeitschrift für die Alttestamentliche Wissenschaft* 67 (1955): 205–16, notable for its careful scrutiny of individual usages. Koch finds that the *wort-feld* or scope of the concept *bahar* is broad enough to contain coherently its broad variety of meanings.

24. Thus the consensus among Biblical scholars that election is primarily the *"mise à part d'un homme ou d'un objet,"* as a rule *"à raison de leurs qualités éminentes."* See Henri Lesêtre, "Election," in F. Vigouroux, ed., *Dictionnaire de la Bible*, Vol. 2 (Paris: Letouzey et Ané, 1912), p. 1653. Itzhak Heinemann similarly stresses the call to specific service, and finds that this primary meaning obtains in the word's wider sense (the election of the people and the land) as well as in the narrower sense of appointment (kings, priests, etc.) See his "Behirat Am Yisrael Bamikra," *Sinai* 16 (1944–45):18, 22. H. H. Rowley, who stresses the call to service throughout *The Doctrine of Biblical Election* (London: Lutterworth Press, 1950), finds a theological dilemma in election. If God chose Israel arbitrarily, His justice is in question, while if God chose Israel on account of its merits, His grace is in question (p. 39). Heinemann for his part insists (p. 17) that election is by no means an honor merited by the elect.

In any event, the many selections of persons for tasks encountered in the Old Testament must be looked at in this context of service first of all, and the cognate *baḥur* in fact comes to denote a special class of elite warrior: cf. Judges 20:15–17, 34; II Sam. 6:1, 10:9; I Kings 12:21. Persons are chosen in some seventy usages, places (e.g., Jerusalem) in about fifty, and "things" such as "life," "the way" or "wisdom" in about thirty-five. Rivka Scharf Kluger notes that in ninety-two of one-hundred-sixty-four passages God is the subject of the verb *bahar*. See "The Idea of the Chosen People in the Old Testament," in *Psyche and Bible* (New York: Spring Publications, 1974), p. 8.

25. By extension, David "chooses" the stones with which to battle Goliath (I Sam. 17:40)—the exceptional usage of the term which defies the generalizations presented here.

26. Cf. II Kings 23:27, Ps. 78:67–68, and Isa. 7:15, 41:18, as well as passages cited below.

27. The Bible often takes pains to contrast divine choices with human mis-choices, for example in the story of the B'nai Elohim who saw that the daughters of men were good and so chose them (Gen. 6:2), an account followed immediately by the report that God "sees" the evil of man and his thoughts and therefore withdraws the gift of eternal life. The rebellion of Korah is a nice illustration of the point that mis-choice is the sign of non-chosenness: Num. 16:5–17:25. As Heinemann points out (p. 23), chosenness is always conditional on fulfillment of the demand for proper human choice.

28. Thus the special function of (and stress on) the word *bahar* in the book of Deuteronomy, which invokes the word sixteen times in the course of only three chapters as part of its effort to justify the centralization of the cult. Gerhard Von Rad, among others, therefore, sees election as primarily a Deuteronomic conception. See his *Old Testament Theology*, trans. D. M. G. Stalker (Edinburgh: Oliver and Boyd, 1963), p. 178.

29. On this term see the article by Benjamin Oppenheimer in *Beit Mikra* IV, 71 (1978): 427–34. He establishes that *segulah* implies a status of vassalage rather than mere possession by another.

30. As Heinemann observes (p. 23), "We have not spoken at length about the word *brit* (covenant) because it is not *brit* which instructs us about the meaning of *behirah* (chosenness) but the reverse . . ."

31. Generalizations about the rabbinic corpus do not come easily: its expositions are voluminous, span at least half a dozen centuries, and present a broad diversity of viewpoints. Yet, as the scholar Max Kadushin has observed, the rabbis do exhibit "a striking general agreement" on chosenness as on much else, a consensus which I have attempted to summarize here. Cf. Max Kadushin, "Behirat Yisrael," *PRA* 1941, pp. 20–25. Kadushin's contention that since the rabbis do not use the term *"behirat Yisrael"* they do not know the concept—there being no rabbinic concepts not signified by specific terms, in his view—has been convincingly refuted by E. E. Urbach, *The Sages: Their Concepts and Beliefs*, trans. Israel Abrahams (Jerusalem: The Magnes Press of Hebrew University, 1973), p. 923, n.5.

32. Cf. Schechter, pp. 58–62. For the former images, cf. *Mekilta de-Rabbi Ishmael*, ed. Jacob Z. Lauterbach (Philadelphia: Jewish Publication Society, 1933), "Shirata," I, pp. 12, 22–23; B. T. Ḥagiga 5b. For the latter see *Leviticus Rabba* 2:4, *Song of Songs Rabba* 5:1 and *Sifre* #345 p. 143b, ed. M. Friedmann (Vilna, 1864).

33. Many rabbinic discussions of election betray a decidedly polemical intent. See Eugene Mihaly, "A Rabbinic Defense of the Election of Israel," *Hebrew Union College Annual* 35 (1961): 103–35; Yosef Heinemann, *Aggadot and Their History* (Hebrew) (Jerusalem: Keter, 1974), pp. 118–28, and 157–58; and E. E.

Urbach, "Homilies of the Sages about Gentile Prophets and about Baalam in Light of the Jewish-Christian Polemic" (Hebrew), *Tarbiz* 25 (1956): 272–88.

34. *Mekilta de-Rabbi Ishmael*, I, pp. 198–99 *(Ha-ḥodesh)*.

35. *Sifre* #345, p. 143b. See also fantasies of revenge such as *Mekilta*, pp. 13–21, *Leviticus Rabba* 27:6 and *Song of Songs Rabba* 5:6.

36. *Mekilta*, pp. 234–35.

37. *Lamentations Rabba* 3:1. Many *aggadot* stress the special severity of God's judgment of Israel, stemming from the unique closeness of their relation. See Abraham Joshua Heschel, *Torah From Heaven* (Hebrew) (London: Soncino, 1962), pp. 93–110.

38. *Song of Songs Rabba* 7:3. I should stress that the matter of rabbinic response to catastrophe is complex and only now beginning to receive extensive treatment in scholarly literature. For one recent analysis see Jacob Neusner, *Method and Meaning in Ancient Judaism* (Missoula, Mont.: Scholars Press/Brown Judaic Studies, 1979).

39. See the thorough study of these issues by Chaim Tshernowitz, *History of Halakhah* (Hebrew) (N.Y.: Va'ad Hayovel, 1945), pp. 137–43, 225–71, 285–313. For the laws governing the Sons of Noah and the resident alien see Maimonides, *Mishneh Torah, Melakhim*, ch. 10 and *Rotseah* 5:3. Two remarkable rabbinic passages cite inequities in the treatment of Jews and non-Jews as proof of God's special love for Israel—for how else could such apparent injustice be countenanced? See *Sifre* #343 and B.T. *Baba Kamma* 38a.

40. Cf. the telling passages from *Epistle to Yemen* and *Hilkhot Issurei Bi'ah* (19:17) in Isadore Twersky, ed., *A Maimonides Reader* (New York: Behrman House, 1972), pp. 445, 122–23.

41. Yehudah Halevi, *Kuzari*, trans. Hartwig Hirschfeld (New York: Pardes, 1946). See especially I, 27, 95; II, 30, 34, 36–42; IV, 23. Halevi makes frequent references to Israel's status as *segulah*.

42. For an introduction to this material see Gershom Scholem, *On the Kabbalah and its Symbolism* (New York: Schocken Books, 1965), pp. 87–117.

43. This analysis is indebted to Jacob Katz's study *Exclusiveness and Tolerance* (New York: Schocken Books, 1973). See especially pp. 13, 21–22, 45. See also his *Tradition and Crisis* (New York, Schocken Books, 1971), p. 190. Ironically, Katz observes, the existence of the Jews' separate world—legitimated and explained by the notion of their chosenness—depended on the constant contact of its inhabitants with the outside world, even as this contact was severely restricted, to the satisfaction of both sides, by the demands of halakhic observance.

44. Cf. Katz, *Exclusiveness*, chap. 7.

45. Compare Katz's analysis of the Jews' maintenance of a set of values "both formally and substantively independent of Gentile culture," in pp. 112–20.

46. For an overview see Katz, *Tradition*, pp. 215, 225; Jacob Katz, *Out of the Ghetto: The Social Background of Jewish Emancipation, 1770–1870* (Cambridge, Harvard University Press, 1973); and Michael A. Meyer, *The Origins of the Modern Jew: Jewish Identity and European Culture in Germany, 1749–1824* (Detroit: Wayne State University Press, 1967), pp. 125–26. For the views of the key transitional figure—Spinoza—see chapter 4 below.

47. Quoted in W. Guenther Plaut, ed., *The Rise of Reform Judaism: A Sourcebook of its European Origins* (New York: World Union for Progressive Judaism, 1968), p. 59. See also Jakob J. Petuchowski, *Prayerbook Reform in Europe* (New York: World Union for Progressive Judaism, 1968), especially chapters 9, 11, 12.

48. Abraham Geiger, *Judaism and its History*, trans. Charles Newburgh

(New York: Bloch, 1911), pp. 22, 37, 43–47, 50, 68, 80. See also the citations from his work in Plaut, p. 157. See also Michael A. Meyer, "Universalism and Jewish Unity in the Thought of Abraham Geiger," in Jacob Katz, ed., *The Role of Religion in Modern Jewish History* (Cambridge: Association for Jewish Studies, 1975), pp. 91–104.

49. Nachman Krochmal, *Moreh Linevukhei Hazemen (Guide for the Perplexed of the Day)* in *The Writings of Nachman Krochmal*, ed. Simon Rawidowicz (London and Waltham, Mass.: Ararat Publishing Society, 1961).

50. See, most conveniently, Hirsch's apologetic *The Nineteen Letters on Judaism*, trans. Bernard Drachman (New York: Feldheim Publishers, 1969), and the essays collected in Heinrich Graetz, *The Structure of Jewish History and Other Essays*, trans. and ed. Ismar Schorsch (New York: The Jewish Theological Seminary of America, 1975).

51. The philosophical continuity is well summarized in Beryl Howard Levy, *Reform Judaism in America: A Study in Religious Adaptation* (New York: Bloch, 1933), preface and chapters 1–2. The extent to which American Reform was a German export or a native American product is assessed by Aryeh Rubenstein in "The Origins of the Reform Movement in American Judaism and the Controversy Surrounding It, 1840–1869" (Hebrew diss., Hebrew University of Jerusalem, 1973), pp. 78–87, 97.

52. See the citation in David Philipson, *The Reform Movement in Judaism*, 2nd ed. (New York: Macmillan, 1931), p. 175; and David Einhorn, "Inaugural Sermon," trans. C. A. Rubenstein (Baltimore: Har Sinai Congregation, 1919), pp. 12–16; and see also his *Olath Tamid: Book of Prayers for Israelitish Congregations* (New York: Congregation Adath Yeshurun, 1872), pp. 69, 84, 256–68.

53. See Isaac Mayer Wise, "To the Ministers and Other Israelites," *The Occident*, Dec. 1848, pp. 431–35; "The Messiah," *The Occident*, July 1849, pp. 181–91, and Part 2, August 1849, pp. 229–44. See also Levy, *Reform*, p. 48, and James G. Heller, *Isaac M. Wise: His Life, Work and Thought* (New York, UAHC, 1965).

54. The first conference of American Reform rabbis, held in Philadelphia in 1869 and attended by both Wise and Einhorn, declared that the destruction of the Temple had served God's purpose by dispersing the Jews "for the realization of their high priestly mission, to lead the nations to the true knowledge and worship of God." See Philipson, *Reform*, pp. 354–55.

55. Kohler's works are replete with references to Israel's mission and election, the latter doctrine constituting in his view "the central point of Jewish theology and the key to an understanding of the nature of Judaism." See especially his greatest work, *Jewish Theology, Systematically and Historically Considered* (New York: Macmillan, 1928), pp. 323–28, 367–75. The passage cited above appears on p. 323. See also *Backwards or Forwards? A Series of Discourses on Reform Judaism* (New York: Congregation Beth El, 1885), pp. 7–13, 32–38; and "Israel's Mission in the World" in *Hebrew Union College and Other Addresses* (Cincinnati: Ark Publishing Company, 1916), pp. 161–67. See also the Pittsburgh Platform of 1885, of which Kohler was the guiding spirit, quoted in Philipson, *Reform*, pp. 356–57. The platform asserted that "we recognize in the modern era of universal culture and intellect, the approaching of the realization of Israel's great messianic hope for the establishment of the kingdom of truth, justice and peace among all men."

56. For the writings of Rabbi Isaac Leeser, leader of the prestigious Mikveh Israel Congregation of Philadelphia, and editor of *The Occident*, the only national

Jewish periodical of the day, see Isaac Leeser, "The Mission of Israel," *Occident*, June 1844, p. 114, and July 1844, p. 174; "The Example of Israel," *Occident*, January 1849, pp. 1–2, 7–10. For the positions of Benjamin Szold and Marcus Jastrow of Philadelphia, two leaders of the "Historical School" seeking middle ground between Reform and Orthodoxy, see Davis, *Emergence*, pp. 305–06.

57. Kaufman Kohler, "American Judaism" in *Hebrew Union*, p. 200.

58. Schechter, *Aspects*, p. 57.

59. Cf. Arthur Hertzberg, "Varieties of Jewish Modernity" in *Being Jewish in America: The Modern Experience* (New York: Schocken Books, 1979), p. 9.

60. Philip Roth, "Imagining Jews" in *Reading Myself and Others* (New York: Farrar, Straus and Giroux, 1975), pp. 245–46.

2. "Nation, People, Religion—What Are We?"

1. Glazer, *American Judaism*, pp. 60, 82–83; Bernard D. Weinryb, "Jewish Immigration and Accommodation to America," in Sklare, *The Jews*, p. 4.

2. Glazer, *American Judaism*, p. 82.

3. Ibid., p. 81. See also his "Social Characteristics of American Jews, 1654–1954," AJYB, 1955, pp. 3–41.

4. Nathan Reich, "Economic Trends," in Oscar I. Janowsky, ed., *The American Jew: A Composite Portrait* (N.Y.: Harper, 1942), pp. 162–66. See also Arthur Ruppin, *The Jews in the Modern World* (London: Macmillan, 1934), p. 124, and Robert Gutman, "Demographic Trends and the Decline of Anti-Semitism" in Charles Herbert Stember et al., *Jews in the Mind of America* (N.Y.: Basic Books, 1966), pp. 368–69. For the position of Jews in the economic life of America see "Jews in America," *Fortune*, Feb. 1936, pp. 79–85, 128–44, discussed below.

5. Seymour Leventman, "From Shtetl to Suburb," in Rose, *Ghetto*, pp. 46–47. On the social history of the second generation see the excellent recent work on New York's Jewish community: Deborah Dash Moore, *At Home in America: Second Generation New York Jews* (New York: Columbia University Press, 1981).

6. Rose, *Ghetto*, pp. 9–10.

7. Mordecai M. Kaplan, "The Organization of American Jewry," *Jewish Education* VII, 3 (Oct–Dec 1935): 136.

8. Leventman, "From Shtetl," p. 46. For the level of Conservative observance see Sklare, *Conservative Judaism*, pp. 63, 200–212, and for Orthodoxy see Howard W. Polsky, "A Study of Orthodoxy in Milwaukee" in Sklare, *The Jews*, pp. 327–32, as well as Charles Liebman, "A Sociological Analysis of Contemporary Orthodoxy," *Judaism*, Summer 1964, pp. 285–304, and "Orthodoxy in American Jewish Life," AJYB, 1965, pp. 21–97. Membership figures of the three movements during the second generation changed from 50,000 Reform, 75,000 Conservative and 200,000 Orthodox families in 1937 to 150,000 Reform, 100,000 Conservative and 100,000 Orthodox families in 1952. See Glazer, *American Judaism*, p. 105, and AJYB, 1951, p. 87.

9. Leventman, "From Shtetl," p. 47.

10. John Higham, *Strangers in the Land: Patterns of American Nativism 1860–1925*, 2nd ed (New York: Atheneum, 1974), pp. 247–53.

11. Quoted in Stanley Cohen, "The First Years of Modern America," in William E. Leuchtenberg, ed, *The Unfinished Century: America Since 1900* (Boston: Little, Brown and Co., 1973), p. 287.

12. Higham, *Strangers*, pp. 254–64.

13. Ibid., p. 277.

14. John Higham, *Send These to Me: Jews and Other Immigrants in Urban America* (New York: Atheneum, 1975), pp. 117–30. For the ideological underpinnings of American anti-Semitism see Michael N. Dobkowski, *The Tarnished Dream: The Basis of American Anti-Semitism* (Westport, Conn.: Greenwood Press, 1979), especially chaps. 3–6 and the criticism of Higham on p. 5.

15. Higham, *Strangers*, pp. 278ff.

16. C. Bezalel Sherman, *The Jew Within American Society: A Study in Ethnic Individuality* (Detroit: Wayne State University Press, 1961), pp. 175–76. For one account of discrimination in the academic profession see Ludwig Lewisohn, *Upstream: An American Chronicle* (New York: Boni and Liveright, 1922).

17. Higham, *Strangers*, pp. 278ff, citing Heywood Broun and George Britt, *Christians Only: A Study in Prejudice* (New York: Vanguard Press, 1931), pp. 231–32.

18. Higham, *Send These*, p. 190. See also Broun and Britt, *Christians Only*, and Bruno Lasker, ed., *Jewish Experiences in America* (New York: The Inquiry, 1930), p. 3.

19. Lasker, ibid, pp. 64–71.

20. Dobkowski, *Tarnished Dream*, chaps. 3–5.

21. Higham, *Send These*, pp. 146, 166–67.

22. Walter Hart Blumenthal, "Birds of a Feather—and Ugly Words," *American Hebrew*, Feb. 21, 1930, pp. 517–18.

23. Dobkowski, *Tarnished Dream*, pp. 197ff.

24. Stember, *Mind of America*, pp. 8–9, 116–21, 134–38. Asked in 1938 if the persecution of the Jews in Europe was their own fault, 12% of those polled answered "entirely" and about half responded "partly." Asked in 1941 if any groups were doing less than their share for national defense, those surveyed named Jews twice as often as Germans or Japanese, and 25% agreed that Jews were less patriotic than other citizens. Asked in 1944 if, once in combat, any groups were more likely than others to avoid difficult assignments, 75% pointed to Jews, 26% to German Americans, 14% to Negroes. Throughout the war, 31–48% would have supported or sympathized with an anti-Semitic candidate, 24% saw Jews as a menace to America, and those polled labeled Jews the least desirable immigrants except for Germans and Japanese. In 1945, 58% held that the Jews had too much power in America. Sentiment against blacks also rose during the war years: see in the same volume Thomas F. Pettigrew, "Parallel and Distinctive Changes in Anti-Semitic and Anti-Negro Attitudes," pp. 377–403. For evidence of the growing number of anti-Semitic organizations in this period see Donald S. Strong, *Organized Anti-Semitism in America*. (Washington, D.C.: American Council on Public Affairs, 1941.).

25. Kramer and Leventman, *Gilded Ghetto*, p. 43.

26. Horace M. Kallen, "Education of Jews in Our Time," *Jewish Education* 9 (September 1939):85.

27. Mordecai M. Kaplan, "The Organization of American Jewry," p. 133.

28. Milton Steinberg, *The Making of the Modern Jew* (New York: Behrman House, 1948), pp. 246–47; see also pp. 233–35.

29. Milton Steinberg, "First Principles for American Jews," CJR, December 1941, pp. 587–96.

30. Kurt Lewin, "Self-Hatred Among Jews," CJR, June 1941, pp. 219–232.

31. Moore, *At Home*, pp. 11–14, Chaps. 2–3. For a description of one area see Jeffrey S. Gurock, *When Harlem Was Jewish, 1870–1930* (New York: Columbia University Press, 1979). Gurock cautions that we should use the terms "first and

second settlement" to refer to "differing types of settler behavior" rather than "static geographical localities," since not all Jews moved from a simple immigrant ghetto to a "second area of settlement" further removed from downtown and then on to a third.

32. Abraham G. Duker, "Structure of the Jewish Community," in Janowsky, *American Jew*, pp. 144–46.

33. Moore, *At Home*, p. 12.

34. Duker, "Structure," p. 143.

35. Ibid., pp. 150–56.

36. Ibid., pp. 142–43.

37. Moore, *At Home*, p. 135. See all of chap. 5 for a sketch of the synagogue center movement.

38. Duker, "Structure," p. 148.

39. Zeitlin, *Disciples*, pp. 41–45.

40. Ibid., p. 50.

41. Ibid., p. 46.

42. Moore, *At Home*, p. 15.

43. Ibid., pp. 11–15, 201–29.

44. "Jews in America," pp. 70, 141.

45. Ibid., pp. 79–85.

46. Ibid., pp. 128–41.

47. Ibid., pp. 130–31, 141.

48. Carl Mayer, "Religious and Political Aspects of Anti-Judaism," in Isacque Graeber and Stuart Henderson Britt, eds., *Jews in a Gentile World* (New York: Macmillan, 1942), pp. 318–19.

49. Talcott Parsons, "The Sociology of Modern Anti-Semitism," in Graeber and Britt, ibid., pp. 107, 114–15.

50. For an example of another polemical battle, see John Cournos, "An Epistle to the Jews," *Atlantic Monthly*, December 1937, pp. 723–38, and the response by Hayim Greenberg, "The Jews and Jesus," JF, January 1938, pp. 10–13. Cournos's article was advertised by *Atlantic* as "a touching plea for the union of Judaism and Christianity."

51. For a characterization of *The Christian Century*, see Martin Marty, *Righteous Empire: The Protestant Experience in America* (New York: Dial Press, 1970), p. 213.

On the Jewish side, see the editorial "Religious Totalitarianism," JF, July 1936, pp. 9–10. For the magazine's view on Hitler, see for example John Sheridan Zelie, "Why Do the Gentiles Rage," *The Christian Century*, October 7, 1931, pp. 1239–41.

52. *The Christian Century*, May, 1933, pp. 443, 582–84. The editor and probable author of all the editorials cited here was Charles Clayton Morrison.

53. "The Jewish Problem," *The Christian Century*, April 29, 1936, pp. 624–26. Kaplan stood accused of a "cultural fatalism [which] makes it impossible for one religion to understand another or for the devotee of one religion to cross over to another." See, in the same issue, another article which makes the same argument more crudely: Joseph Ernest McAfee, "An Open Letter to Rabbi Weisfeld," pp. 632–33.

54. "Jewry and Democracy," *The Christian Century*, June 9, 1937, pp. 734–35.

55. Ibid., pp. 735–36.

56. "Why is Anti-Semitism?", *The Christian Century*, July 7, 1937, pp. 862–64. A similar complaint about "Pluralism—National Menace" appeared on June

13, 1951, pp. 701–702. Yet elsewhere the magazine considered Christianity itself to be a culture, not a religion, expressing the fear that the culture of America would be other than Christian. See "A God-Centered Education," April 28, 1937, pp. 542–44.

57. Hayim Greenberg, "The Universalism of the Chosen People," JF, October 1945, p. 11.

58. Edward Israel, CCYB, 1936, p. 266

59. Philip Bernstein, "Towards a Program for American Judaism," CCYB, 1938, pp. 280–82. Rabbi Louis I. Mann noted in the same discussion that only Morrison was responsible for the editorials, for the magazine's other editors had disagreed with his position. He gave no source for this information. Reinhold Niebuhr, himself an editor of the magazine, supported the Jewish right to remain a nationality in the diaspora and even to establish a state in Palestine. See "Jews After the War," *The Nation*, February 21 and 28, 1942.

60. *The Christian Century*, July 7, 1937, pp. 878–79.

61. Mordecai M. Kaplan, "The 'Christian Century' Problem," REC, May 29, 1936, p. 34.

62. Mordecai M. Kaplan, "When Religious Liberals Are Intolerant," *Opinion*, July 1936, pp. 18–20.

63. Leo Jung, *Crumbs and Character: Sermons, Addresses, Essays* (New York: Night and Day Press, 1942), pp. 15–24.

64. Ibid.; on America as a new Adam, see Lewis, *American Adam*.

65. Leo Jung, "Ancient Heathenism and Modern Democracy," in *Harvest: Sermons, Addresses, Studies* (New York: Philipp Feldheim, 1956), pp. 84–85.

66. Leo Jung, "Crumbs and Character," in *Crumbs*, pp. 163–68.

67. See for example "The Dangers of the Pulpit" (1929), "The Blessing of Jacob and American Citizenship (A War Sermon)" (1942), and "Abraham Lincoln and Kavanah" (1939) in *Crumbs*; "Civil Liberties and the American Dream" (1937) in *Harvest*; *Living Judaism* (New York: Night and Day Press, 1927), part 4; and "A Challenge to Jewry," *Orthodox Union*, January 1936, pp. 5–6.

68. Samuel Belkin, *Essays in Traditional Jewish Thought* (New York: Philosophical Library, 1956), pp. 75–79, 94. (The essays date from 1943 onwards, but dates of individual essays are not given.)

69. Ibid., pp. 122–25.

70. For other Orthodox views see Nathan A. Barack, *Mount Moriah View* (New York: Bloch, 1956), pp. 25ff; Bernard Revel, "The Bible and American Democracy," *Orthodox Union*, July–August 1938, p. 3; and Emanuel Rackman, "Democracy's Religious Root," MJ, Autumn 1951, pp. 163–68. Almost all Orthodox thinkers in this study are "Modern Orthodox"; members of more traditional groups generally did not address themselves in English to the issues which concern us. For the substance of this distinction see the articles cited by Charles Liebman in chapter 2, note 8 above.

71. Abba Hillel Silver, *The Democratic Impulse in Jewish History* (New York: Bloch, 1928), especially pp. 1–24.

72. Jacob R. Marcus, "Democracy and Judaism," LJ, December 1945, pp. 11–19.

73. Nelson Glueck, "Come Let Us Reason Together, " CCYB, 1952, pp. 332–39.

74. Ibid.

75. See, ibid., pp. 147ff, 174ff, and Glueck's denunciation of the McCarran-Walters Bill and of McCarthyism, pp. 334–39. On Glueck and his tenure as

president of HUC see Michael A. Meyer, "A Centennial History," in Samuel E. Karff, ed., *Hebrew Union College—Jewish Institute of Religion at One Hundred Years* (Cincinnati: HUC Press, 1976), pp. 87–90, 100–101.

76. For other statements of the Reform position see Louis Witt, "Judaism and Democracy" (UAHC Tract #11, Cincinnati, n.d.); Abraham J. Feldman, "Contributions of Judaism to Modern Society" (UAHC Tract #29, Cincinnati, n.d.), pp. 10–14; "America and the Jew" in CCYB, 1954, pp. 137–47; and Ferdinand Isserman's comments in CCYB, 1940, p. 223.

77. See Finkelstein's "The Aims of the Conference" in Lyman Bryson and Louis Finkelstein, eds., *Science, Philosophy and Religion: A Symposium* (New York: The Conference on Science, Philosophy, and Religion in their Relation to the Democratic Way of Life, 1941), p. 3. (Finkelstein, born in Cincinnati in 1895, became chancellor of the Jewish Theological Seminary in 1951.)

78. Louis Finkelstein, *The Pharisees*, 3rd ed. (Philadelphia: Jewish Publication Society, 1966), especially pp. ix–xviii, xxxi, 145ff. See also Finkelstein's contribution to *The Religions of Democracy* (New York: Devin-Adair, 1945), his statement in Stanley High et al., *Five Faiths for Today* (New York: Town Hall Press, 1941), pp. 160–62, and his *Tradition in the Making* (New York: Jewish Theological Seminary, 1937), p. 12.

79. Simon Greenberg, "Democracy in Post-Biblical Judaism," CJ, June 1945, pp. 1–8. See also his later statement "Judaism and the Democratic Ideal" (1966) in *Foundations of a Faith* (New York: Burning Bush Press, 1967), pp. 113–34, and his recent reiteration in *The Ethical in the Jewish and American Heritage* (New York: Jewish Theological Seminary of America, 1977). Greenberg, born in Russia in 1901, arrived in the United States in 1905, and served the majority of his career as the rabbi of Har Zion Temple in Philadelphia.

80. Robert Gordis, "The Biblical Basis of Democracy," CJ, June 1948, pp. 1–12.

81. Robert Gordis, *The Root and the Branch* (Chicago: University of Chicago Press, 1962), pp. 82–83.

82. For an attack on Gordis's position by a Reform rabbi see the remarks of Benjamin Friedman, CCYB, 1946, pp. 249–58. For other conservative statements see Louis M. Levitsky, *A Jew Looks at America* (New York: Dial Press, 1939), pp. 4, 14, 32, 41ff, and Abraham Katsh; "Hebraic Contributions to American Life" (typescript, New York University, 1941).

83. By Melvin Kranzberg, REC, February 24, 1956, pp. 7–13.

84. See below, chapter 4.

85. Compare Nathan Rotenstreich, *The Exile of Israel in American Jewish Thought* (Hebrew) (Jerusalem: Institute for Contemporary Jewry of the Hebrew University, 1967).

86. Julian Morgenstern, "Assimilation, Isolation, or Reform," CJR, April 1942, pp. 143–44; Zacharian Shuster, "Whither American Jewry," CJR, June 1943, pp. 227–30; Philip Bernstein, "The New Israel and American Jewry," CCYB, 1948, pp. 285–86; Robert Gordis, *Judaism for the Modern Age* (New York: Farrar Straus and Cudahy, 1955), pp. 114–15; Mordecai M. Kaplan, *Future of the American Jew* (New York: Reconstructionist Press, 1955), p. 4.

87. Compare Nathan Rotenstreich, "Emancipation and its Aftermath," in Divid Sidorsky, ed., *The Future of the Jewish Community in America* (New York: Basic Books, 1973), p. 52.

88. Finkelstein, *Tradition*, p. 12. The elements common to both religions, he wrote elsewhere, were emphasis on ideals of freedom and equality, the respect

said to be due the human personality, and the goal of bettering human life. See "American Ideals and the Survival of Western Civilization," CJR, June 1941, pp. 233–42.

89. Julian Morgenstern, "Judaism's Contribution to Post-War Religion," (HUC Inaugural Address published Cincinnati, 1942), pp. 3–5, 11. See also Ferdinand Isserman, *This is Judaism* (Chicago: Willett, Clark, 1944), pp. 207–17.

90. See: Milton Steinberg, "The Common Sense of Religious Faith" (1947), in Arthur Cohen, ed., *Anatomy of Faith* (New York: Harcourt Brace and Company, 1960), pp. 96ff; Steinberg's comments in "The Theological Issues of the Hour," PRA, pp. 366, 407; Bernard Heller, "The Judeo-Christian Tradition," JF, November 1946, pp. 59–60; Paul Tillich, "Is There a Judeo-Christian Tradition?", *Judaism*, April 1952, pp. 106–109; Heller's reply to Tillich, "About the Judeo-Christian Tradition," *Judaism*, July 1952, p. 257–61; Heller's "The Judeo-Christian Tradition Concept: Aid or Deterrent to Goodwill," *Judaism*, August 1953, pp. 133–39; Henry Enoch Kagan, "The 'Judeo-Christian Heritage'—A Psychological Revaluation and a New Approach," CCYB, 1953, pp. 253–81; Robert Gordis, "The Nature of Man in the Judeo-Christian Tradition," *Judaism*, August 1953, pp. 101–104; and Gordis, *Root*, chaps. 3–4.

91. Felix Levy, "The Uniqueness of Israel," in Sefton D. Temkin, ed., *His Own Torah: Felix A. Levy Memorial Volume* (New York: Jonathan David, 1969), pp. 161–73. (Levy, born in New York, was the rabbi of Congregation Emanu-el in Chicago from 1908 until his retirement.)

92. "Conference on the Perpetuation of Judaism" (The 30th Biennial Council of the UAHC, proceedings published Cincinnati, 1927), pp. 25–27. For a similar statement see (Judge) Jerome Frank, "Red, White and Blue Herring," *The Saturday Evening Post*, December 6, 1941, pp. 9–10, 83–84.

93. "Judaism and the Modern World" (The 31st Biennial Council of the UAHC, proceedings published Cincinnati, 1929) pp. 3–10.

94. Ibid., p. 11.

95. CCYB, 1937, pp. 97–100.

96. Julian Morgenstern, "Nation, People, Religion—What Are We?" (Cincinatti: UAHC, 1943). See also "With History as our Guide," CCYB, 1947, pp. 257–87.

97. Julian Morgenstern, *As A Mighty Stream: The Progress of Judaism Through History* (Philadelphia: Jewish Publication Society, 1949), pp. 418–23.

98. CCYB, 1939, pp. 331–48. For other statements of Goldenson's views see his presidential addresses to the CCAR: CCYB, 1934, pp. 146–47 and 1935, pp. 133–53.

99. CCYB, 1939, pp. 357–61. A similar debate on the issue of particularism and universalism took place at the CCAR convention in 1947, the occasion being a discussion of whether Reform rabbis should officiate at mixed marriages: CCYB, 1947, pp. 172–83.

100. For a survey of Kallen's life and work see the tribute by Milton Konvitz, AJYB, 1974, pp. 55–72.

101. Horace M. Kallen, *Cultural Pluralism and the American Idea* (Philadelphia: University of Pennsylvania Press, 1956), p. 90. See also Kallen's "The Meaning of William James for 'Us Moderns'" in *The Philosophy of William James* (New York: Modern Library, 1925), pp. 44–45 and *What I Believe and Why—Maybe*, ed. Alfred J. Marrow (New York: Horizon Press, 1971), p. 166. A comparison with the master brings the student's departures into relief: see especially

James's *Pragmatism* (Cleveland: World, 1955), *A Pluralistic Universe* (London: Longmans, Green, 1909), and *Essays in Pragmatism* (New York: Hafner, 1951).

102. Horace M. Kallen, *Secularism is the Will of God* (New York: Twayne, 1954), pp. 80, 96; "Of Truth" in Frederick Burkhardt, ed., *The Cleavage in Our Culture* (Boston: Beacon, 1952), pp. 32, 35–39. Kallen there defends his position against Bertrand Russell's charge that such relativism permitted "arbitrament of the big battalions." For a discussion of "the real" by Kallen see Horace M. Kallen and Sidney Hook, eds., *American Philosophy Today and Tomorrow* (New York: Lee Furman, 1935), p. 255.

103. *American Philosophy*, pp. 252, 255.

104. That determination is said to motivate man's achievements in the arts and sciences, which thereby affirm human freedom, "conquer Fate and defeat God." Horace M. Kallen, *Art and Freedom*, 2 vols (New York: Duell, Sloan and Pearce, 1942), p. 963. William James cites Job's cry, "Though he slay me, yet will I trust in him"—quoted often by Kallen—as the paradigmatic expression of a religious attitude to life. See *The Varieties of Religious Experience* (London: Fontana Library, 1970) p. 59.

105. Darwin furnished added support. Overturning the accepted association between truth and permanence, he had shown, in Kallen's view, that processes of variation, multiplication, and individualization are the essential springs of movement in all history, while processes of unification are secondary, maintained only by artificial agencies. Horace M. Kallen, *Individualism—An American Way of Life* (New York: Liveright, 1933), p. 176.

106. Horace M. Kallen, *Culture and Democracy in the United States* (New York: Boni and Liveright, 1924), pp. 61, 72, 120ff.

107. Horace M. Kallen, *Cultural Pluralism*, pp. 82, 87–97. For the critics, see especially Flower (pp. 120–22), Henle (pp. 146–50), and Pfeffer (pp. 159–63). Milton Gordon notes that advocates of cultural pluralism were generally guilty of Kallen's failure; their assumption that values could sharply conflict and society nevertheless function as one unit went unexamined. Milton Gordon, *Assimilation in American Life* (New York: Oxford University Press, 1964), p. 16.

108. Horace M. Kallen, *The Education of Free Men* (New York: Farrar Straus, 1949), pp. 115–21, 202.

109. Kallen, *Secularism*, pp. 11, 15, 30, 184. For a valuable critique of this work see Harold M. Schulweis's review in *Judaism*, Fall 1955, pp. 366–71.

110. Horace M. Kallen, *The Book of Job as a Greek Tragedy* (New York: Hill and Wang, 1959), pp. 45, 68, 72–77. See also pp. 56–57.

111. Horace M. Kallen, "Hebraism and Current Tendencies in Philosophy" (1909), in *Judaism at Bay: Essays Toward the Adjustment of Judaism to Modernity* (New York: Bloch, 1932), p. 13.

112. Horace M. Kallen, "On the Impact of Universal Judaism" (1910), in *Judaism at Bay*, pp. 21–22, 25.

113. Horace M. Kallen, *Zionism and World Politics* (Garden City, N.Y.: Doubleday Page, 1921), p. vii. For further attacks on Reform and election in the work see pp. 36–38, 65–66, 132, 136. For a Reform rabbi's response see Bernard Heller's review of *Judaism at Bay*, "Dr. Kallen's Judaism," MJ, Spring 1934, pp. 73–82.

114. Horace M. Kallen, "Retrospect and Prospect" (1932), in *Judaism at Bay*, pp. 248–52.

115. On this subject see Sarah Leff Schmidt, "Horace M. Kallen and the Americanization of Zionism" (diss., University of Maryland, 1973).

116. Kallen, "Retrospect," pp. 248–49. Kallen there attributes his interest and activity in Jewish matters primarily to the influence of Solomon Schechter. For an account of religion typical of the pre-1932 Kallen see *Why Religion?* (New York: Boni and Liveright, 1927).

117. Horace M. Kallen, "The Dynamics of the Jewish Center" (1930), *Judaism at Bay*, p. 229. On this subject compare Louis Kaplan, "Judaism and Jewish Education in Horace M. Kallen's Philosophy of Cultural Pluralism" (diss., Dropsie University, 1971).

118. Horace M. Kallen, "Judaism, Hebraism and Zionism" (n.d.), *Judaism at Bay*, pp. 34–36.

119. Horace M. Kallen, "The Struggle for Jewish Unity: Two Addresses" (New York: Ad Press, 1933), pp. 19, 21; and *Frontiers of Hope* (New York: Horace Liveright, 1929), p. 451. See also "Of Them Which Say They Are Jews" (1944) and "National Solidarity and the Jewish Minority" (1942), *Of Them Which Say They Are Jews and Other Essays on the Jewish Struggle for Survival*, ed. Judah Pilch (New York: Bloch, 1954), pp. 33–39, 58–70.

120. Kallen, "Dynamics," pp. 232, 237, 245.

121. Horace M. Kallen, "Jewish Education and the Future of the American Jewish Community" (1943), in *Of Them*, pp. 191–92.

122. Horace M. Kallen, "To Educate Jews in Our Time" (1933), *Of Them*, p. 176. See also, in the same work, "Is There a Jewish View of Life" (1938), and "Judaism as Disaster" (1940), as well as Kallen's essays "Critical Problems in Jewish Education," *Jewish Education* 19 (1947):11–16, and "Jewish Education and Jewish Survival," *Jewish Education* 34 (1964):223–29.

123. Kallen, "Judaism, Hebraism and Zionism," pp. 39–40.

124. Horace M. Kallen, "Jewish Teaching and Learning in the American Scene," (1949), *Of Them*, p. 239.

125. Kallen, "What I Believe," pp. 179–82. Kallen confessed there to Ira Eisenstein that Barrett Wendell's lectures at Harvard on the role of the Old Testament in the organization of the Congregational Churches had brought him back to the faith of his father, a rabbi.

126. Ben Halpern, "Zion in the Mind of America," in Sidorsky, ed., *Future*, p. 33.

127. Kallen's correspondence with Kaplan, in the collection of the American Jewish Archives, indicated deep mutual respect: see a letter of Kaplan's dated May 1, 1951, in which he calls Kallen "one of the truly great scholars of our times."

128. Mordecai M. Kaplan, *Judaism as a Civilization: Toward a Reconstruction of American-Jewish Life* (New York: Schocken Books, 1967), chaps. 1–15. Quotation on p. 178.

129. Mordecai M. Kaplan, *The Future of the American Jew* (New York: Macmillan, 1948), pp. 94–105, 518–22, 102. (Hereafter FAJ). See also Mordecai M. Kaplan, *Questions Jews Ask: Reconstructionist Answers* (New York: Reconstructionist Press, 1956), pp. 30–31.

130. Kaplan, FAJ, p. 102.

131. For a detailed discussion of these matters see chapter 4.

132. See the formulation of this proposal by Kaplan's son-in-law and disciple Ira Eisenstein, "The New Diaspora and American Democracy," PRA, 1949, pp. 259–68, and the response which it evoked from his fellow Conservative

rabbis, pp. 269–89. See also his "Toward a Religion of Democracy in America," REC, February 23, 1945, pp. 55–61. One notes that Eisenstein's call, like Kallen's, came in the wake of the war. Perhaps the "religious" rather than "cultural" emphasis in Kaplan's thought was likewise related to a current of the time: the American "religious revival." Eisenstein, born in 1906, served as Leader of the Society for the Advancement of Judaism in New York, founded by Kaplan, and was until recently the president of the Reconstructionist Rabbinical College.

133. See Liebman, "Reconstructionism," pp. 3–99.

134. Robert Gordis, *Conservative Judaism: An American Philosophy* (New York: Behrman House, 1945), p. 22.

135. The opening of the Columbus Platform, CCYB, 1937, p. 97. For estimates of Kaplan's role in bringing Reform to this new conception, see the statement by Roland Gittelsohn in Ira Eisenstein and Eugene Kohn, eds., *Mordecai Kaplan: An Evaluation* (New York: Jewish Reconstructionist Foundation, 1952), p. 237, and see the symposium "Mordecai Kaplan's Influence Upon Reform Judaism," CCARJ, June 1956, pp. 23–26.

136. The formulation is of course that popularized by Will Herberg in his *Protestant-Catholic-Jew* (Garden City, N.Y.: Doubleday, 1955).

137. Solomon Freehof, "Reform Judaism and Zionism: A Clarification," MJ, Spring 1944, p. 37.

138. Rotenstreich, "Emancipation," pp. 47–52.

139. Ben Halpern notes this point in his masterful study *The American Jew*, p. 111.

140. Reinhold Niebuhr, *The Irony of American History* (New York: Scribners, 1962), p. 4–24. See also H. Richard Niebuhr, *The Kingdom of God in America* (New York: Harper and Row, 1959), p. 1, and compare Sidney Ahlstrom, *A Religious History of the American People* (New Haven: Yale University Press, 1972), pp. 2–7, 306, 845.

141. Sacvan Bercovitch, *The Puritan Origins of the American Self* (New Haven: Yale University Press, 1975) pp. ix, 62, 72–79, 108f. See also Bercovitch's recent study, *The American Jeremiad* (Madison: Univ. of Wisconsin Press, 1978). See also Yehoshua Arieli, *Individualism and Nationalism in American Ideology* (Cambridge: Harvard University Press, 1964), pp. 71–77, 246–56, 269–76; Lewis, *American Adam;* and Seymour Martin Lipset, *The First New Nation* (New York: Basic Books, 1963) p. vii.

142. See chapter 1, note 8.

143. Kaufman Kohler, "American Judaism," *Hebrew Union College*, pp. 196, 200.

3. Reform Judaism and the "Mission unto the Nations"

1. Israel Freidlander, "Dubnow's Theory of Jewish Nationalism," in *Past and Present: Selected Essays* (New York: The Burning Bush Press, 1961), p. 253. See also "Hezekiah's Great Passover" (1911).

2. Meyer, "Centennial History," p. 132. When Morgenstern referred in the same address quoted here to Revisionist Zionism as "practically identical with Nazist and Fascist theory," Abba Hillel Silver and Joshua Loth Liebman, both graduates of HUC, initiated a public protest. Only after the dimensions of the Holocaust became apparent did Morgenstern come to support the Jewish commonwealth.

3. Julian Morgenstern, "Unity in American Judaism: How and When?" (Cincinnati, 1945), p. 14.

4. Felix Levy, "How Judaism May Be Advanced" (1928) in Temkin, ed., p. 52.

5. CCYB, 1936, pp. 90–91. For debate on the statement see pp. 93–107.

6. The 1937 draft statement was prepared by Samuel Cohon (chairman), and, among others, Levy, Abba Hillel Silver, and David Philipson. Levy, as president of the CCAR, cast the tie-breaking vote to consider the statement.

7. CCYB, 1937, pp. 98–99; discussion, pp. 101–13.

8. Ibid., p. 107.

9. Ibid., pp. 418–20.

10. Maurice Eisendrath, "Retreat or Advance?", CCYB, 1937, pp. 202–24.

11. Felix Levy, "Four Permanent Values in Judaism," in Temkin, ed., pp. 283–84.

12. The theme of chosenness recurs in Silver's writings, always with the emphasis on Israel's choice, first of all through its prophets, of God and His way. See, for example, "Why Do the Heathen Rage" (1926) in Herbert Weiner, ed., *Therefore Choose Life: Selected Sermons, Addresses and Writings*, Vol. 1, (Cleveland: World, 1967), pp. 364–77; *The Democratic Impulse in Jewish History*, pp. 27–42; and *Where Judaism Differed: An Inquiry into the Distinctiveness of Judaism* (Philadelphia: Jewish Publication Society, 1957), especially pp. 1–5, 27–74, 82.

13. Samuel Cohon, "The Doctrine of the Chosen People," LJ, May 1946, pp. 31–38, 48.

14. Attributed to Wise by his student Louis I. Newman in *Biting on Granite: Selected Sermons and Addresses* (New York: Bloch, 1946), p. 10. Yet another usage of the "God-choosing people" occurs in Morris N. Kertzer's work *What is a Jew?* (Cleveland, World, 1953), pp. 9–11.

15. Quoted in Bernard Heller, "The Jewish Concept of the Chosen People"—Popular Studies in Judaism—#1 (Cincinnati, Tract Commission of UAHC-CCAR, n.d.). Shaw is quoted in the New York Times of July 10, 1938, as saying, according to Heller, that "the faith of the Jew is his enormous arrogance based on his claim to belong to God's chosen race. The Nordic nonsense is only an attempt to imitate the posterity of Abraham." Wells's article on "The Future of the Jews" appeared in *Liberty Magazine*, December 24, 1938. Heller's article can be dated to the period 1939–1942.

16. Leo M. Franklin, "The Saving Remnant," CCYB, 1935, pp. 159–61. For very different responses to Jewish suffering see the remarks by Bernard Heller in the CCYB, 1939, p. 353, and the lectures on the suffering-servant theme by William Fineshriber and Ferdinand M. Isserman in, respectively, ibid., pp. 257–68, and CCYB, 1940, pp. 216–35.

17. Heller, "Chosen People," pp. 3–8, 15–16, 20–23, 26–29.

18. Ibid, pp. 28–29. See also Bernard Heller, "The Jewish Mission," REC, March 3, 1944, pp. 9–14.

19. Frederic A. Doppelt, "Are the Jews a Chosen People?", LJ, February 1942, pp. 6–8; and "Has Israel a Mission?", LJ, March 1942, pp. 1–13. See also his "A Reappraisal of the Chosen People Concept," CCARJ, June 1961, pp. 11–15, 21.

20. Theodore N. Lewis, "A Creed for American Jews," *Congress Weekly*, March 26, 1943, pp. 11–12.

21. See note 19 above.

22. Louis I. Newman, "A Kingdom of Priests and a Holy Nation," in *Biting on Granite*, pp. 284–95.

23. Ibid., quoting "The Chosen" by Robert Nathan.

24. Leon I. Feuer, *On Being a Jew* (New York: Bloch, 1947), pp. 24–60, 78.

25. *Union Prayer Book, Vol. 2: Yamim Ha-noraim* (New York: CCAR, 1948), pp. 262–66.

26. Bernard J. Bamberger, "Are the Jews a Chosen People?", REC, January 1946, pp. 16–19. The polemic is explicitly directed against Mordecai M. Kaplan.

27. Bernard J. Bamberger, "The Central Task," CCYB, 1949, pp. 224–27. One notes the allusion to the New Testament, which serves to root Bamberger's defense of election in defenses made of it against Christianity by Jews in the rabbinic period.

28. Ibid., p. 228, and Levy, "Halakhah," in Temkin, ed., pp. 152–59. (Levy's essay is datable to the period after 1948). For a similar statement of the Reform dilemma, including a similar attack on Kaplan, see Theodore Lewis, "The Idea of Israel," CCYB, 1937, pp. 187–200.

29. Eugene B. Borowitz, "Theological Conference: Cincinnati 1950," COM, June 1950, p. 569. Reform statements on chosenness in the second generation were legion. See, for example, the following: Samuel S. Cohon, "Universal and Particular in Judaism," *Judaism*, April 1952, pp. 121–28; Beryl D. Cohon, *From Generation to Generation* (Boston: Bruce Humphries, 1951), pp. 21–22; Solomon B. Freehof, *Preface to Scripture* (Cincinnati: UAHC, 1950), Part One, p. 75; Jacob L. Halevi, "Clashing Concepts," LJ, March 1945, pp. 28–32; Beryl D. Cohon, *Judaism in Theory and Practice* (New York: Bloch, 1954), pp. 85–90; Abraham J. Feldman, *The Faith of a Liberal Jew* (Hartford: Congregation Beth Israel, 1931), pp. 81–85.

30. Comparisons based on prayer books issued by the CCAR in 1895, 1927, 1937, and 1953. See the debate on chosenness in the 1937 edition in CCYB, 1937, pp. 87–88.

31. Jakob J. Petuchowski, "Where Judaism Differed," COM, August 1957, pp. 153–59.

32. Silver, *Democratic Impulse*, p. 41. Silver's differentiation of ancient Israel from its neighbors stressed Israel's gift of "moral freedom" and "spiritual refinement" to a world of chaos, corruption, and sexual license.

33. Levy, "A Liberal Jew Looks at Jewish Liberalism," in Temkin, ed., pp. 174–86.

34. For comments on the lack of attention to theology, see Levi A. Olan, "Judaism and Modern Theology", CCYB, 1956, pp. 197–215; Robert Gordis, *Conservative Judaism*, p. 9; and Jacob Agus, *Guideposts in Modern Judaism: An Analysis of Current Trends in Jewish Thought* (New York: Bloch, 1954), p. 15.

35. Even Orthodox thinkers who adhered to traditional notions of God and chosenness did not share the tradition's concern with the contradictions of its position.

36. See for example CCYB, 1930, pp. 304–57; 1931, pp. 217–29; 1932, pp. 242–93; 1935, pp. 229–45; 1942, pp. 297–312; 1952, pp. 399–455; 1953, pp. 282–318, 348–430; 1956, pp. 197–215; 1957, pp. 174–86; 1959, pp. 212–23. See also David Polish, "The Forsaken God," LJ, November 1946, pp. 10–16, and the responses which it evoked, LJ, January 1947, pp. 13–17.

37. CCYB, 1937, p. 97 (paragraph #2 of the Columbus Platform).

38. CCYB, 1936, p. 90.

39. Meyer, in his "Centennial History," p. 95, writes that very few students at HUC "felt that Cohon's eclectic theology directly influenced their own convictions." However, Cohon "achieved extraordinary influence through the practical work he did for the Central Conference of American Rabbis, formulating its new platform and editing the revision of its prayerbook. A Russian Jew not seeking to escape Jewish particularity, [Cohon became] . . . a crucial figure in the transition from classical to present-day Reform Judaism." Our claim that he is representative derives not from his influence but from a reading of his own works and those of his colleagues.

40. See note 12 above.

41. CCYB, 1953, p. 375.

42. Ibid., pp. 380–81.

43. Samuel S. Cohon, "The Jewish Idea of God," (Cincinnati: HUC, n.d.), pp. 22–24, 30–32.

44. Samuel S. Cohon, *Jewish Theology: A Historical and Systematic Interpretation of Judaism and its Foundations*, ed. J. H. Prakke and H. M. G. Prakke (Assen, The Netherlands: Royal Vangorcum, 1971), pp. 133, 141.

45. Ibid., pp. 142, 130.

46. Cohon, "The Jewish Idea of God," pp. 34–37.

47. Cohon, *Theology*, p. 127.

48. Ibid.: "The idea of God cherished by any people constitutes the culmination of its highest aspirations and strivings. Within it are focused men's hopes, fears, ideals, and goals. The Jewish idea of God embodies the very substance of the Jewish spirit. With Halevi, we therefore may regard Israel as the channel of God's revelation. Our history may be viewed as our growth in God consciousness."

49. Ibid.

50. Ibid., p. 82.

51. CCYB, 1953, p. 381.

52. Abba Hillel Silver, "My Quest for God" (1926), in *Choose Life*, p. 40.

53. Abba Hillel Silver, "The Vision of the One World" (1949), ibid., pp. 91–94.

54. Compare Abba Hillel Silver, "Why I Believe and What I Believe (1923), ibid., pp. 46–47; "There is Yet Room for Vision" (1952), p. 428, and "Suffering and Death" (1952), pp. 228–48; and with Cohon, *Theology*, pp. 43–44, 345–56.

55. See note 36 above.

56. CCYB, 1931, pp. 151–52.

57. Bernard J. Heller, "The Modernists Revolt Against God," CCYB, 1930, pp. 323–57.

58. Nathan Rotenstreich, *Jewish Philosophy in Modern Times* (New York: Holt, Rinehart and Winston, 1968), pp. 2–6.

59. Ibid.

60. The phrase is of course Peter Berger's. See *The Sacred Canopy* (Garden City, N.Y.: Doubleday Anchor, 1969).

61. Given what we know about the lives of the congregants and (if their rabbis are any indication) about their beliefs.

62. The phrase is taken from Paul Tillich, "The Religious Symbol," in *Religious Experience and Truth*, ed. Sidney Hook (New York: New York University Press, 1961), pp. 308–10. See also Tillich's *Dynamics of Faith* (New York: Harper Torchbooks, 1958), pp. 50–51.

63. Alexander Altmann, "The New Style of Preaching in Nineteenth-Century German Jewry," in Altmann, *Studies*, pp. 65–116, especially pp. 83, 104–109, 115–16.

64. I have not undertaken a systematic content-analysis of the sermon literature. However, the predominance of mission- or election-related themes is striking.

65. Solomon B. Freehof, *Modern Jewish Preaching* (New York: Bloch, 1941), p. 48. On the Reform worshipper's inactivity during the service, see Freehof, "Reform Judaism and Prayer" in Abraham J. Feldman et al., eds., *Reform Judaism: Essays by Hebrew Union College Alumni* (Cincinnati: Hebrew Union College Press, 1949), pp. 81–106.

66. Compare Ann Douglas, *The Feminization of American Culture* (New York: Knopf, 1977), on the new role and rhetoric of the American Protestant clergy in the nineteenth century. Douglas points to a link between these and the new role of women in the congregations and in charity work. Two members of the HUC board who objected to the ordination of women in 1921 did so on grounds that if women became rabbis "the Reform synagogue would become even more 'an affair of the women' than it already was." See Meyer, "Centennial History," p. 98.

67. For the mission theme's classic statement, see Johann Gottlieb Fichte, *Addresses to the German Nation*, trans. R. F. Jones and G. F. Turnbull (New York: Harper & Row, 1968).

68. See the most famous example: Ahad Ha'am, "Slavery in Freedom" in *Selected Essays*, ed. Leon Simon (New York: Atheneum, 1960), pp. 171–94.

69. The information presented here, when not based on the CCAR yearbooks for the years mentioned, is from Leonard J. Mervis, "The Social Justice Movement and the American Reform Rabbi," *American Jewish Archives VIII*, 2 (1957), pp. 121–230. Compare Zeitlin, *Disciples of the Wise*, pp. 113–58.

70. See the CCYB for yearly reports by the committees on Social Justice and International Peace (merged once the Second World War began), particularly for 1932, 1934–36, 1938–39, 1942–47, 1950–52.

71. CCYB, 1936, p. 82.

72. CCYB, 1937, p. 186. Rabbi William Braude charged in 1942 that the cause of social justice had become a "surrogate religion" for many in the movement, and observed that rabbis were quite courageous in their espousal of radical causes so long as their congregants were not involved; CCYB, 1942, p. 283.

73. *The 65th Annual Report of the UAHC: Proceedings of the 36th Biennial Council*, pp. 280–87.

74. CCYB, 1935, pp. 333ff.

75. Moore, *At Home in America*, pp. 201–30. Compare Liebman, *American Jew*, pp. 135–39.

76. Emil Fackenheim, "Liberalism and Reform Judaism," CCARJ, April 1958, p. 2.

77. See notes 16, 24, 25 above.

78. Joshua Loth Liebman, "New Trends in Reform Jewish Thought," in Feldman, ed., *Reform Judaism*, p. 68.

79. John Preston, "The New Covenant, whereunto are adjoyned Four Sermons Upon Ecclesiastes" (London, 1630), pp. 206–207.

80. See Marshall Sklare and Joseph Greenblum, *Jewish Identity on the Suburban Frontier: A Study of Group Survival in the Open Society* (New York: Basic Books, 1967), p. 324. "Lakeville" residents defined being a good Jew as, first of all,

taking pride in one's heritage and not seeking to hide it, and, second, leading an ethical life, promoting civic betterment, and supporting humanitarian causes.

4. Mordecai Kaplan and the New Jewish "Vocation"

1. Biographical details from Liebman, "Reconstructionism," pp. 25–39.

2. See Liebman, ibid. He notes (p. 4) that "an understanding of the sociological problematics of Reconstructionism leads us to the core problematic of American Judaism—the nature of Jewish identity." For more on Kaplan and his movement, see the dissertation by Richard L. Libowitz, "Mordecai M. Kaplan as Redactor: The Development of Reconstructionism" (Temple University, 1979).

3. Mordecai Kaplan, *Judaism as a Civilization*, p. 15 (JC hereafter).

4. Ibid., p. 7.

5. Ibid., pp. 22–24.

6. Ibid., pp. 36–43. For further discussions of the outmoded world-view, see pp. 342, 379.

7. Ibid., pp. 253–55.

8. Mordecai Kaplan, *Judaism in Transition* (New York: Behrman, 1941), p. 102 (hereafter JT).

9. Ibid., pp. 123, 272–73.

10. Ibid., p. 281. See Kaplan's Durkheimian discussion of "folk religion" in JC, pp. 333, 337.

11. JT, pp. 123, 159.

12. JC, p. 307.

13. JC, p. 182. Emphasis added.

14. See especially the text on which Kaplan relied: Emile Durkheim, *Elementary Forms of the Religious Life*, trans. Joseph Ward Swain (New York: Free Press, 1965).

15. For other Durkheimian influence see: JC, pp. 85, 307, 333; JT, p. 259; Mordecai Kaplan, *The Meaning of God in Modern Jewish Religion* (New York: Reconstructionist Press, 1962), p. 249 (hereafter MOG); FAJ, p. 47.

16. JC, p. 205.

17. JC, p. 84.

18. In this connection see Durkheim's *The Division of Labor*, trans. George Simpson (New York: Free Press, 1964) and *Suicide*, trans. John A. Spaulding and George Simpson (New York: Free Press, 1951).

19. JT, p. 135.

20. JC, p. 308.

21. Ibid., p. 309.

22. MOG, pp. 40–43.

23. Ibid., pp. 94–103.

24. FAJ, p. 47. See also p. 79.

25. Ibid., p. 55.

26. Ibid., p. 57.

27. Ibid., pp. 214–16, 221.

28. Ibid., pp. 226–30.

29. Ibid., p. 229.

30. Franklin H. Littell, "Thoughts About the Future of Christianity and Judaism: A Christian View of Reconstructionism," REC, April 4 and 18, 1947,

pp. 10–16, 16–22. See Kaplan's response, "We Still Think We Are Right," May 2, 1947, pp. 14–19.

31. Mordecai M. Kaplan, "The Way I Have Come" in Eisenstein and Kohn, *Mordecai M. Kaplan*, pp. 318–19. For other comments by Kaplan on election in these years, see his *Questions*, pp. 42, 57, 204–06, 452, 478–507.

32. Mordecai M. Kaplan, *Judaism Without Supernaturalism: The Only Alternative to Orthodoxy and Secularism* (New York: Reconstructionist Press, 1958), p. 25 (hereafter JWS).

33. Ibid., p. 68.

34. Ibid., p. 94.

35. Ibid., pp. 28–33.

36. Ibid., pp. 102–105.

37. Ibid., p. 157. See also p. 22.

38. See, for example, his more balanced treatment of the rabbis of the Mishnaic and Talmudic periods in *The Greater Judaism in the Making: A Study of the Modern Evolution of Judaism* (New York: Reconstructionist Press, 1960), e.g., pp. 40, 67–75.

39. See William Perkins, "A Treatise of the Vocations," in *Works* (Cambridge, 1603), pp. 903–39. The classic modern treatment is of course Max Weber, *The Protestant Ethic and the Spirit of Capitalism*, trans. Talcott Parsons (New York: Scribner's, 1958).

40. JT, p. 34; FAJ, pp. xvi, 229, 236. Reconstructionism is that which enables Judaism to save the Jew. The X which enables Y to save Z can itself be said to save Z.

41. See below.

42. MOG, pp. 25–26. The following discussion is indebted to an unpublished dissertation by Charles Vernoff, "Supernatural and Transnatural: An Encounter of Religious Perspectives—The Theological Problematic in the Modern Judaic World-View of Mordecai M. Kaplan" (Univ. of Cal. Santa Barbara, 1979).

43. Ibid., p. 133.

44. Ibid., p. 160.

45. Ibid., pp. 165–328; *Questions*, p. 94.

46. MOG, p. 324.

47. Ibid., the Table of Contents.

48. Ibid., pp. 72–76, 82; FAJ, pp. 183–84, 236.

49. JWS, p. 201.

50. Ibid., pp. 102–105.

51. MOG, pp. 188–94, 303.

52. JWS, pp. 28–33.

53. Alfred North Whitehead, *Religion in the Making* (New York. Macmillan, 1926), p. 16.

54. JC, pp. 324, 336.

55. FAJ, pp. 516–22.

56. Ira Eisenstein, "The New Diaspora and American Democracy," PRA, 1949, pp. 259–68, and discussion, pp. 269–89. See also Eisenstein's "Toward a Religion of Democracy in America," REC, February 23, 1945, pp. 55–61.

57. Mordecai M. Kaplan, J. Paul Williams, and Eugene Kohn, eds., *The Faith of America* (New York: Henry Schuman, 1951). For the characterization of America, see p. 9. Williams, a methodist minister, lectured at Mt. Holyoke College.

58. Robert N. Bellah, "Civil Religion in America," in Donald R. Cutler, ed., *The Religious Situation: 1968* (Boston: Beacon Press, 1968), pp. 331–56.

59. FAJ, p. 437; "The Way I Have Come," p. 318.

60. "The Way I Have Come," pp. 296–98.

61. Matthew Arnold, *Literature and Dogma: An Essay Towards a Better Apprehension of the Bible* (New York: AMS Press, 1970), especially pp. x, 10–35, 175–81, 209–15. See also the sequel, *God and the Bible: A Review of Objections to Literature and Dogma* (New York: AMS Press, 1970).

62. Matthew Arnold, *Culture and Anarchy* (Cambridge: Cambridge University Press, 1971), especially pp. 14–20, 47–48. On p. 166 Arnold puts the matter of national sancta most succinctly: "The State is the religion of all its citizens without the fanaticism of any of them."

63. Arnold, *Literature and Dogma*, p. 28.

64. John Dewey, *A Common Faith* (New Haven: Yale University Press, 1934), especially pp. 1–28, 43–54. The criticism of Arnold is on p. 54.

65. See Ahad Ha'am, *Selected Essays*, especially "Priest and Prophet" (1894), "Flesh and Spirit" (1904), "Many Inventions" (1890), "Slavery in Freedom" (1891), and, on the Jewish "genius" for morality, "The Transalvation of Values" (1898). See also "The National Morality" in his *Complete Writings* (Jerusalem: Hotza'ah Ivrit, 1947), pp. 159–64.

66. Benedict de Spinoza, *A Theologico-Political Treatise*, trans. R. H. M. Elwes (New York: Dover Publications, 1951), pp. 3–56.

67. Ibid., pp. 6, 10.

68. Ibid., pp. 182–89, 245–56.

69. For an assessment of the various sorts of "civil religion" see John Wilson, *Public Religion in American Culture* (Philadelphia: Temple University Press, 1979), especially pp. 145–58. Certainly Machiavelli in *The Prince* and *The Discourses*, Hobbes in *Leviathan*, Spinoza in the *Tractatus*, and even More in *Utopia* see religion primarily in terms of its function in promoting the public peace, even if their assessments of the truth or falsity of the beliefs in question may vary.

70. MOG, p. 244.

71. The summary is Liebman's. See "Reconstructionism," p. 15.

72. Julian Morgenstern, "Unity," pp. 14–15.

73. Mordecai M. Kaplan, "Reform and Reconstructionism: Where They Part Company," REC, May 27, 1960, p. 8. See Meyer, "A Centennial History," p. 148 for Kaplan's consideration of the presidency of the Jewish Institute of Religion. In terms of ethnicity and observance, Kaplan would have been far more at home at JIR than at HUC.

74. See the Zeitlin survey noted above.

75. See the symposium, "Mordecai Kaplan's Influence Upon Reform Judaism," CCARJ, June 1956, pp. 23–26.

76. Milton Steinberg, "The Theological Issues of the Hour," PRA, 1949, p. 378.

77. For such criticism see Agus, *Guideposts*, pp. 405–409; Eliezer Berkovits, "Reconstructionist Theology: A Critical Evaluation" in *Major Themes in Modern Philosophies of Judaism* (New York: Ktav, 1974) pp. 150–90, especially, pp. 162–72; and Eugene Borowitz, "The Idea of God," CCYB, 1957, pp. 183–86.

78. JWS, p. 10.

79. Liebman, "Reconstructionism," pp. 46–68.

80. Robert Lowry Calhoun, *God and the Common Life* (Hamden, Conn: The

Shoe String Press, 1954), especially pp. 207–37. The work was originally published by Scribners in 1935, and Kaplan cites it in FAJ, p. 229, fn. 27.

81. Ibid., p. 229.

82. Ibid.

83. See Talcott Parsons, "Professions," in *International Encyclopedia of the Social Sciences*, ed. David L. Sills (New York: Macmillan/Free Press, 1968), vol. 12, pp. 536–47, and "The Professions and Social Structure," in *Essays in Sociological Theory, Pure and Applied* (Glencoe: Free Press, 1949), pp. 185–196.

84. On these matters see the suggestive essay by Thorstein Veblen, "On the Intellectual Pre-eminence of the Jews," in *Essays in Our Changing Order*, ed. Leon Ardzrooni (New York: Viking Press, 1939), pp. 219–31.

85. Liebman, "Reconstructionism," pp. 68–97.

5. Conservatism, Orthodoxy, and the Affirmation of Election

1. Quoted from a public lecture in Jerusalem in 1976 at which the author was present.

2. Orthodoxy, too, must be viewed as such a response, rather than as the simple continuation of that which has always been. On this general issue see Moshe Samet, "Orthodox Jewry in the Modern Period" (Hebrew), *Mehalkhim* 1 (1969): 29–40.

3. Quoted in Kenneth Burke, *A Rhetoric of Motives* (Berkeley: University of California Press, 1969), p. 49.

4. "Identification," Burke argues (ibid., pp. 19–29), is the principal weapon in the rhetorician's armory. By linking the audience's "you" to his own "I" the speaker persuades them that his cause and interest are theirs.

5. Burke refers (ibid., pp. 57–58) to that kind of elation wherein the audience feels as though it were not merely receiving, but were itself creatively participating in the poet's or speaker's assertion. Could we not say that, in such cases, the audience is exalted by the assertion because it has the sense of collaborating in the assertion? So it was with mission.

6. Burke's paraphrase of Karl Mannheim, ibid., p. 104.

7. Clifford Geertz, "Ideology as a Cultural System" in *The Interpretation of Cultures* (New York: Basic Books, 1973), pp. 207, 210, 220.

8. Samuel Belkin, *Essays in Traditional Jewish Thought* (New York: Philosophical Library, 1956), pp. 36, 123, 164.

9. Ibid., p. 164.

10. Joseph B. Soloveitchik, "The Lonely Man of Faith," *Tradition*, Summer 1965, p. 10.

11. Joseph B. Soloveitchik, *"Ish Ha-halakhah"* in *In the Secret of Aloneness and Togetherness*, ed. Pinchas Peli (Jerusalem: Orot, 1979) (Hebrew), pp. 39–55, 60–70, 75–87, 91n, 139–87. The "Man of *halakhah*" is explicitly identified with the religious Jew and the "man of religion" with the Christian on pp. 76 and 155.

12. Joseph B. Soloveitchik, "The Voice of My Beloved Knocking," in Peli, ed., pp. 368–78.

13. Ibid., pp. 333–52.

14. Liebman, "Contemporary Orthodoxy," p. 285, and Charles Liebman, "Orthodoxy in American Jewish Life." AJYB 1965, pp. 71–72. Liebman even suggests that Orthodoxy before the Second World War might be been characterized as "lower-class Conservative Judaism."

15. The problem of suffering, addressed in other movements through

chosenness, might have been even more acute in Orthodoxy due to its dispro-portionate population of immigrants and refugees. Indeed a letter to the Or-thodox publication *Jewish Life* (April 1948, p. 66) complains of the author's inability to celebrate the statehood of Israel, because "who knows how much blood will still flow on and after May 15. Thus I cannot see why we should rejoice for we were chosen by God to suffer. I would advise *Jewish Life*, which is based upon the Torah, to explain more fully why we Jews should carry the sins of the nations, and as innocent bystanders to [*sic*] give to God ten victims to their one?" A powerful question indeed.

16. See Samson R. Weiss, "The '*Am Segulah*' Concept," *Jewish Life*, May–June 1957, pp. 17–18. The author was at the time Executive Vice-President of the Union of Orthodox Jewish Congregations. Another development marking the change in Orthodoxy's relation to its environment was the launching of *Tradi-tion*, a journal of Orthodox thought first published in 1958.

17. For other Orthodox comment on election see: the collection of essays by Belkin cited above; Emanuel Rackman, *One Man's Judaism* (New York: Philosophical Library, 1970); and the one Hebrew *derashah* (homily) on election discovered in a survey of such *derashot* from the period, likely to have been given in Yiddish: Shmuel Unger, *Na'ot Deshe al ha-Torah* (Mount Kisco, N.Y.: The Naitra Yeshiva, 1963), p. 240. One notes that Orthodox comment on the ques-tion comes a generation later than that of other movements.

18. Marshall Sklare, *Conservative Judaism*, chaps. 1–4. (The book was origi-nally published in 1955.)

19. More contemporary evidence for this problem is contained in the report of the Commission charged by the Seminary with investigating the possible ordination of women—and in the fate of that report. Ordination was recom-mended by the commission and tabled by the faculty, lest the decision rend the institution in two. See the report and the preface to it by Chancellor Gerson D. Cohen in CJ, Summer 1979, pp. 56–80.

20. Sklare, *Conservative Judaism*, pp. 180–90, 221–40. On all of this section, compare Sklare, chaps 6–7.

21. Robert Gordis, "A Jewish Prayer Book for the Modern Age," CJ, Octo-ber 1945, pp. 10–11.

22. Louis Finkelstein, PRA 1927, p. 43. By contrast, see the transcribed account of Louis Ginzberg's unequivocal defense of chosenness, made in re-sponse to Kaplan: PRA 1932, p. 306.

23. Finkelstein, p. 51.

24. Louis Finkelstein, "Modern Man's Anxiety: Its Remedy," COM, De-cember 1946, p. 544.

25. See for example Abraham Hershman, "The Election of Israel," in *Israel's Fate and Faith* (New York: Bloch, 1952), pp. 36–42, from which the phrases quoted here are taken.

26. For another example see Israel Goldstein, "Are People More Religious Than They Admit" and "The Definition of a Good Jew," (New York: Congrega-tion B'nai Jeshurun, 1927), p. 14.

27. Ibid., p. 13.

28. Simon Greenberg, "The Birthright," in *Living as a Jew Today* (New York: Behrman, 1940), pp. 3–4, 21–22.

29. Max Kadushin, *Organic Thinking: A Study in Rabbinic Thought* (New York: JTS, 1938). See also *The Rabbinic Mind* (New York: Blaisdell, 1965) and the critique by Urbach cited in chapter 1, note 31.

30. Max Kadushin, "The Election of Israel in Rabbinic Thought" (Hebrew), PRA, 1941, pp. 20–25.

31. Morris Silverman, "Vitalizing Public Worship," PRA, 1940, pp. 162–64, 171.

32. Ibid., pp. 180–88.

33. See for example: Julius H. Greenstone, "The Election of Israel," CJ, June 1945; the wartime presidential message of Louis Levitsky to the Rabbinical Assembly, PRA, 1944, pp. 288–89; and David Aronson, *The Jewish Way of Life* (New York: The National Academy for Adult Jewish Studies of the Jewish Theological Seminary of America, 1946), pp. 137–43.

34. Ben Zion Bokser, "Doctrine of the Chosen People," CJR, June 1941, pp. 243–52. The article was the only theological piece ever published in the magazine, a fact of some significance.

35. Ben Zion Bokser, "The Election of Israel," CJ, July 1947, pp. 17–25.

36. Ben Zion Bokser, "The Future of the American Jewish Community," PRA, 1948, pp. 194–99.

37. Ibid., pp. 212ff.

38. Ibid.

39. Ibid., pp. 226–27.

40. See also Ben Zion Bokser, "Religion and Secularism," *Judaism*, Spring 1952, pp. 152–53.

41. Sklare, *Conservative Judaism*, p. 230.

42. Gordis, *Conservative Judaism*, pp. 53–54.

43. Robert Gordis, "The Faith I Live By," MJ, 1947, pp. 195–98.

44. Robert Gordis, *A Faith for Moderns* (New York: Bloch, 1961), pp. 139–40, 146. See also his *Judaism for the Modern Age*, pp. 16, 77–78.

45. Robert Gordis, "Preface," *The Sabbath and Festival Prayer Book* (New York: The United Synagogue of America, 1946), pp. vi–ix.

46. Gordis, "A Jewish Prayer Book," pp. 12–13.

47. Ira Eisenstein, "Further Comment on *Conservative Judaism*," CJ, November 1946, pp. 21–25.

48. CJ, June 1946, pp. 10–14.

49. Ibid., pp. 17–28.

50. An explanation of the distinction between "primary" and "secondary" communications is provided in the following section of the study.

51. I quote from the slightly revised version of the address, entitled "God, Man, Torah and Israel," in Simon Greenberg, *Foundations of a Faith* (New York, Burning Bush Press, 1957), pp. 31–89. The extended quotation is on pp. 88–89. The address originally appeared in PRA 1957, pp. 69–124.

52. Sklare, pp. 225–28.

53. Agus's essay, "Law as Standards—The Way of Takkanot," is reprinted in the movement's own collection *Conservative Judaism and Jewish Law*, edited by Seymore Siegel, a professor at the Seminary, and published by the Rabbinical Assembly (New York, 1977). For Agus's other work see *Guideposts; The Meaning of Jewish History* (London: Abelard-Schulman, 1963); and *Modern Philosophies of Judaism* (New York: Behrman, 1941).

54. Agus, *Guideposts*, p. 248. See discussion, pp. 231–57.

55. Ibid., pp. 257–89.

56. Ibid., pp. 262, 298.

57. Ibid., pp. 289–304.

58. Jacob Agus, "Assimilation, Integration, Segregation—The Road to the

Future," *Judaism*, Fall 1954, pp. 498–510; and "Toward a Conservative Philosophy of Jewish Education," in Judah Pilch, ed., *Judaism and the Jewish School* (New York: Bloch, 1966), pp. 238–39. For his insistence that Judaism be defined as a religion see "Building Our Future in America: Towards a Philosophy of American Judaism," MJ, Spring 1953, pp. 1–21.

59. PRA 1929, p. 27. In his 1927 address, "The Things That Unite Us," Finkelstein called upon Jews to abandon the anthropomorphic conceptions of God to which Israel's faith had in his view deteriorated in the last three to four centuries. PRA, 1927, p. 44.

60. Louis Finkelstein, *The Beliefs and Practices of Judaism* (New York: Devin-Adair, 1952), p. 50.

61. Louis Finkelstein, *Tradition in the Making*, p. 19.

62. Finkelstein, *Beliefs and Practices*, p. 22.

63. Finkelstein, *Tradition*, p. 10. Oral Torah still in the process of creation was included by Finkelstein in the concept of Torah, and so derived from communion with God.

64. Greenberg, "God, Man, Torah and Israel," pp. 31–45

65. Ibid., p. 49. See discussion pp. 45–49.

66. Ibid., p. 58. See discussion, pp. 49–58.

67. Ibid.

68. For the biographical details see Simon Noveck, *Milton Steinberg: Portrait of a Rabbi* (New York: Ktav, 1978).

69. Steinberg, "Theological Issues," p. 378.

70. Milton Steinberg, *As A Driven Leaf* (Indianapolis: Bobbs-Merrill, 1939), p. 242.

71. Milton Steinberg, *Anatomy of Faith*, p. 248.

72. Noveck, p. 65.

73. Steinberg, *The Making of the Modern Jew*, p. 179.

74. Milton Steinberg, *Basic Judaism* (New York: Harcourt, Brace, 1947), pp. 95–96.

75. Steinberg, *Anatomy*, p. 100.

76. The lectures, given at Park Avenue Synagogue two months before his death, were retitled "New Currents in Religious Thought."

77. See the comments by Will Herberg in PRA, 1946, p. 411.

78. The address is found in PRA, 1946, pp. 356–408. For more of Steinberg's work see *A Believing Jew: The Selected Writings of Milton Steinberg* (New York: Harcourt, Brace, 1951). The finest assessment of his work is that of Arthur Cohen in *Anatomy of Faith*, pp. 11–60, and *The Natural and the Supernatural Jew* (New York: McGraw-Hill, 1964), pp. 219–34.

79. These theologians are examined in chapter 7.

80. PRA 1946, pp. 256–57.

81. Ibid., p. 265.

82. Ludwig Lewisohn, *Up Stream*, pp. 120–23; *Mid-channel: An American Chronicle* (New York: Harper and Brothers, 1929), p. 102. See also *Israel* (New York: Boni and Liveright, 1925), pp. 23, 107. The quotation is from *Mid-channel*, p. 102.

83. Ludwig Lewisohn, *The American Jew: Character and Destiny* (New York: Farrar Straus, 1950), p. 1–11, 25–34, 45–47, 70. The phrase "specific and transcendent" is found on p. 26.

84. PRA 1946, pp. 265–67.

85. Hayim Greenberg, "Chosen Peoples," JF, September 1941, pp. 8–11;

"The Universalism of the Chosen People," JF, October 1945, pp. 10–18, November 1945, pp. 26–35, and December 1945, pp. 29–37.

86. Greenberg, "Chosen Peoples," p. 9.

87. Greenberg, "Universalism," October 1945, pp. 14–15.

88. Greenberg, "Chosen Peoples," pp. 10–12.

89. PRA 1946, pp. 269–70.

90. Hayim Greenberg, "Jewish Culture in the Diaspora," JF, December 1951, p. 18.

91. Maurice Samuel, *You Gentiles* (New York: Harcourt, Brace, 1924); *The Gentleman and the Jew* (New York: Alfred A. Knopf, 1950). The quotations are from *You Gentiles*, pp. 12, 31.

6. Ambassadors at Home

1. *Tradition* appeared in 1958, a lag perhaps reflecting the general lag of Orthodoxy in feeling the impact of America. (See chapter 5.)

2. The most salient examples are Eugene Borowitz, *A New Jewish Theology in the Making* (Philadelphia: Westminster Press, 1968) and Emil Fackenheim, "Outline of a Modern Jewish Theology" in *Quest for Past and Future* (Boston: Beacon Press, 1968), pp. 96–111. See also Lou M. Silberman, "Concerning Jewish Theology in North America: Some Notes on a Decade," AJYB 1969, pp. 37–58.

3. See, for example, the special issue of *Judaism*, Autumn 1954.

4. Will Herberg, *Protestant-Catholic-Jew* (Garden City, N.Y.: Doubleday, 1955).

5. Nathan Reich, "Economic Status," in Oscar I. Janowsky, ed., *The American Jew: A Reappraisal* (Philadelphia, JPS, 1965), pp. 56–63.

6. Sidney Goldstein and Calvin Goldscheider, *Jewish Americans: Three Generations in a Jewish Community* (Englewood Cliffs: Prentice Hall, 1968), p. 79.

7. See Seymour Martin Lipset and Everett C. Ladd, Jr., "Jewish Academics in the United States: Their Achievements, Culture and Politics," AJYB 1971, pp. 89–128. For the gap in educational achievement see the data cited above and the recent report by David E. Drew, "Profile of the Jewish Freshman," *American Council on Education Research Reports*, vol. 5, #4, 1970.

8. Herbert J. Gans, "The Origin and Growth of a Jewish Community in the Suburbs: A Study of the Jews of Park Forest," p. 231.

9. The joke appears in Seymour Leventman, "From Shtetl to Suburb" in Rose, ed., *The Ghetto*, p. 33.

10. Glazer, *American Judaism*, p. 1.

11. Herberg, *Protestant-Catholic-Jew*, pp. 70–76, 87, 277–84.

12. See Will Herberg, *Judaism and Modern Man: An Interpretation of Jewish Religion* (New York: Harper, 1965). Originally published 1951.

13. For a summary by Herberg himself see "Religious Trends in American Jewry" in Harold U. Rabalow, *Mid-century* (New York: The Beechhurst Press, 1955), pp. 250–66.

14. Glazer (*American Judaism*, p. 9) put the matter succinctly when he wrote in 1957 that "there comes a time—and it is just about upon us—when American Jews become aware of a contradiction between the kind of society America wants to become—and indeed the kind of society most Jews want it to be—and the demands of the Jewish religion."

15. Elliot E. Cohen, "The Intellectuals and the Jewish Community," COM, July 1949, pp. 26–30.

16. "Under Forty: A Symposium on American Literature and the Younger Generation of American Jews," CJR, February 1944, pp. 3–36.

17. "Judaism and the Younger Intellectuals," COM, April 1961, pp. 306–59.

18. "Under Forty," pp. 9–14, 34–36.

19. Irving Howe, "Introduction" to *Jewish-American Stories* (New York: New American Library, 1977), pp. 3–4.

20. Daniel Bell, "A Parable of Alienation," JF, November 1946, pp. 12–19.

21. Cited in James Atlas, *Delmore Schwartz: The Life of an American Poet* (New York: Farrar Straus Giroux, 1977), pp. 96, 302.

22. Verses from "The Ballad of the Children of the Czar," in *Selected Poems* (New York: New Directions, 1967), pp. 22–23.

23. Mordecai M. Kaplan, "Comments on 'A Parable of Alienation'," JF, December 1946, pp. 10–13.

24. Irving Kristol, "How Basic is *Basic Judaism?*", COM, January 1948, pp. 27–34.

25. Ben Halpern, "Letter to an Intellectual," JF, December 1946, pp. 14–17.

26. Ben Halpern, *American Jew*, pp. 38–46, 64–67, 112–13.

27. Ibid., p. 88.

28. *Midstream*, Winter 1963, pp. 3–45. Halpern's essay appears on pp. 20–23.

29. Ibid., p. 5.

30. Ibid.

31. Philip Roth, comments in a symposium on "The Jewish Intellectual and Jewish Identity" sponsored by the American Jewish Congress, in *Congress Bi-Weekly*, September 16, 1963, pp. 21, 39.

32. I owe the insight that Roth's outlook must be connected to American adulation of the "self-made man" to Deborah Dash Moore.

33. Leslie Fiedler, ibid., pp. 25, 33.

34. Reprinted as *The Condition of Jewish Belief* (New York: Macmillan, 1966), p. 90. Hertzberg, a Zionist, a historian of Judaism, and an active participant in Jewish political life, also serves as the rabbi of a Conservative congregation in Englewood, New Jersey.

35. Arthur Hertzberg, "America Is Different" in Arthur Hertzberg, Martin E. Marty, and Joseph N. Moody, *The Outbursts That Await Us: Three Essays on Religion and Culture in the United States* (New York: Macmillan, 1963), pp. 129–54. For a similar analysis—and a critique of Hertzberg—see John Murray Cuddihy, *No Offense: Civil Religion and Protestant Taste* (New York: Seabury Press, 1978).

36. Arthur Hertzberg, "America is Galut," JF, July 1964, pp. 7–9.

37. Ibid., p. 9.

38. *Midstream*, Autumn 1955, pp. 83–91.

39. Herberg's theology owes much to the Protestant neo-Orthodoxy of Karl Barth, who of course coined the term *krisis* in this usage.

40. Arthur A. Cohen, *Supernatural Jew*, pp. 6–8, 52–53, 72, 188–91, 217–19. See also Cohen's *The Myth of the Judeo-Christian Tradition* (New York: Schocken, 1971) and his review of Eugene Kohn's *Religion and Humanity* in *Judaism*, Summer 1954, pp. 276–82.

41. Joseph B. Soloveitchik, "Lonely Man of Faith," p. 5–67. The special dilemma of the modern man of faith is discussed on p. 8.

42. Joseph B. Soloveitchik, "Confrontation," *Tradition*, Winter 1964, pp. 18–23.

43. Ibid., pp. 26–27, 10–13.

44. See the statement and Borowitz's extensive commentary in the four volumes *Reform Judaism Today* (New York: Behrman House, 1978). The statement appears in vol. I, pp. xix–xxv.

45. See for example "Faith and Method in Modern Jewish Theology," CCYB 1963, pp. 215–28, and "The Problem of the Form of a Jewish Theology," *Hebrew Union College Annual*, vols. 40–41, 1969–70, pp. 391–408.

46. Eugene Borowitz, *The Mask Jews Wear* (New York: Simon and Schuster, 1973), pp. 10–15, 36, 48–60, 125.

47. Borowitz, *New Jewish Theology*, p. 206. The description of American Jewry in this paragraph of the text is found on p. 42.

48. Borowitz, *Mask*, p. 48.

49. Ibid., pp. 86–96, 210. The quotation is found on p. 96.

50. Ibid., pp. 74–76.

51. See for example *New Jewish Theology*, p. 213.

52. See the critique by Michael Morgan to Borowitz's "Liberal Jewish Theology in a Time of Uncertainty, a Holistic Approach," CCYB, 1977, pp. 178–89. Morgan's valid criticisms notwithstanding, the essay is a fine analysis of the dilemmas facing liberal Jewish theology.

53. Ahlstrom, p. 983.

54. See, for example, Borowitz's active effort to expound the new Reform credo—*Reform Judaism Today*.

55. Kramer and Leventman write (p. 175) that 82% of the (second-generation) fathers sampled had only Jewish friends and were not on visiting terms with any gentiles, while 80% of the (third-generation) sons counted only Jews among their four closest friends and 70% included gentiles in their wider social circles. Sklare and Greenblum, in *Jewish Identity*, pp. 275, 286, found that 80% of those sampled had mostly Jewish close friends, while 50% said that over 90% of their friends were Jewish.

56. Sklare and Greenblum, p. 280.

57. Benjamin Ringer, *The Edge of Friendliness: A Study of Jewish-Gentile Relations* (New York: Basic Books, 1967), p. 138.

58. Ibid., p. 156.

59. Ibid., p. 267.

60. Sklare and Greenblum, p. 287.

61. Ibid., pp. 287–88.

62. Ibid., p. 282.

63. Kramer and Leventman, p. 194. Sixty-two percent denied that there were any differences between Jews and gentiles.

64. Ibid., p. xvii.

65. Charles R. Snyder, "Culture and Jewish Sobriety: The Ingroup-Outgroup Factor," in Sklare, *The Jews*, pp. 574–77. Snyder speculates that Jews are unwilling to drink in gentile company because of their "instrumental roles"; that is, they are anxious about the "loss of cognitive orientation, itself a means to other ends." Compare Sklare and Greenblum in the text above.

66. Sklare and Greenblum, pp. 309, 313.

67. Ibid., p. 57.

68. Milton Himmelfarb, *The Jews of Modernity* (New York: Basic Books, 1973), p. 79.

69. Nathan Rotenstreich, "Emancipation and its Aftermath," in David Sidorsky, *The Future of the Jewish Community in America* (New York: Basic Books, 1973), p. 61.

70. *The Chosen* by Chaim Potok appeared in 1967; *The Jewish Mystique* by Ernest van den Haag appeared in 1969.

71. See, in particular, "The Pagan Rabbi" and "Envy, or, Yiddish in America."

72. Saul Bellow, *Humboldt's Gift* (Baltimore: Penguin Books, 1976), p. 292.

73. Saul Bellow, *The Victim* (New York: Avon Books, 1975), pp. 37–38; see also pp. 41, 219.

74. Bernard Malamud, *The Assistant* (New York: New American Library, 1957).

75. Roth, "Imagining Jews," p. 25.

76. Jacob Neusner, *Stranger at Home* (Chicago: University of Chicago Press, 1981).

77. Ahlstrom, p. 967.

78. Bercovitch, *American Self*, p. 94.

7. Children of the Halfway Covenant

1. Milton Himmelfarb, "Introduction" to *Jewish Belief*, p. 2. The interesting question is why Buber's influence is not greater, and this may be a function of the questions asked. To a Jew concerned with the nature of religiosity and with the situation of the Jew in the modern world, Buber is of immense assistance. But his antinomianism and inattention to the Jewish people as a people perhaps made him less relevant to the symposium. Had *Commentary* asked the participants how they read the Bible, for example, evidence of Buber's influence would have been enormous. His impact upon Fackenheim will be noted below; Borowitz testifies to it in *New Jewish Theology*, pp. 118–48, "The Form," pp. 403–408, and *How Can a Jew Speak of Faith Today?* (Philadelphia: Westminster Press, 1969), p. 137.

2. Originally published in 1921 and available in English translation published by Beacon Press (Boston, 1972). For key excerpts see Nahum N. Glatzer, ed., *Franz Rosenzweig: His Life and Thought* (New York: Schocken, 1961), and see also "The New Thinking," pp. 190–208.

3. See Glatzer's account of his life, ibid., pp. 1–176.

4. See Glatzer, ibid., pp. 234–42, and Rosenzweig's exchange with Buber in *On Jewish Learning* (New York: Schocken, 1955).

5. These generalizations about the generation are drawn from Harold Weisberg, "Ideologies of American Jews," in Janowsky, *American Jew: A Reappraisal*, pp. 339–59.

6. Borowitz, *New Jewish Theology*, p. 188. See also pp. 42, 73, 192.

7. Steven Schwarzschild, "The Role and Limits of Reason in Contemporary Jewish Theology," CCYB, 1963, pp. 199–201.

8. It could be that members of the third generation will collect their sermons upon retirement. I have no precise figures about the number published in each generation, but an exhaustive search for sermons by those who participated in debates at their respective rabbinical conventions or were featured or mentioned in the periodicals of the period has turned up only several dozen collections of sermons by the third generation—and these mostly by rabbis prominent in the second. Examples are cited in the discussions of the various movements in part two of this chapter, below.

9. Reprinted in *Quest*, pp. 66–82. Fackenheim is a Canadian, yet, as the contribution to *Commentary* indicates, a party to the American debate.

10. A more sustained effort in this direction is Emil Fackenheim, *Encounters Between Judaism and Modern Philosophy* (New York: Basic Books, 1973).

11. Emil Fackenheim, *Metaphysics and Historicity* (Milwaukee: Marquette University, 1961). I have neither reproduced the complexity of the argument nor attempted to evaluate it, but instead focused on the issue most relevant to our inquiry.

12. I.e., that it is racist or encourages arrogance.

13. Emil Fackenheim, *God's Presence in History* (New York: Harper Torchbooks, 1972). The "midrashic framework" is discussed in part one, the "irrefutability of faith and secularism" in part two, and the mandated response to "Auschwitz" in part three. See also note 13 on page 32. The work is heavily indebted to Martin Buber's reading of the Biblical description of the parting of the Red Sea in *Moses* (New York: Harper Torchbooks, 1958).

14. Borowitz writes that "if Jewish theology must always be an 'answering' theology, then the risk of falsifying Judaism will always have to be run." *New Jewish Theology*, p. 51.

15. Herberg, *Judaism and Modern Man*, pp. 3–41, 58–66, 254–57.

16. Herberg, "The 'Chosenness' of Israel and the Jew of Today" in *Arguments and Doctrines*, ed. Arthur A. Cohen (Philadelphia: Jewish Publication Society, 1970), pp. 270–83.

17. On Christianity see *Judaism and Modern Man*, pp. 272–73.

18. Ibid., pp. 271–75.

19. Will Herberg, "Jewish Existence and Survival: A Theological View," *Judaism*, January 1952, p. 22.

20. See Rosenzweig, *Star*, pp. 298–305.

21. Cohen, *Judeo-Christian Tradition*, pp. 84, 176.

22. Cohen, *Natural and Supernatural Jew*, pp. 52–54.

23. Arthur Hertzberg, ed., *Judaism: The Unity of the Jewish Spirit Throughout the Ages* . . . (New York: George Braziller, 1962), pp. 12–13.

24. *Condition of Jewish Belief*, pp. 92–93.

25. Ibid., p. 95.

26. Emil Fackenheim, "Does Reform Need a New God Concept?," *American Judaism*, November 1953, pp. 4–5.

27. See chapter 6, note 41.

28. Fackenheim, *Quest*, p. 117.

29. Eugene Borowitz, "On Celebrating Sinai," CCARJ, June 1966, pp. 12, 16.

30. Eugene Borowitz, "The Chosen People Concept As It Affects Jewish Life in the Diaspora," *Journal of Ecumenical Studies*, Fall 1974, pp. 553–68.

31. Borowitz, *New Jewish Theology*, p. 194.

32. Borowitz, "Liberal Jewish Theology," pp. 162–69.

33. Jacob Neusner, "The Tasks of Theology in Judaism," in *Method and Meaning in Ancient Judaism* (Missoula, Montana: Scholars Press for Brown Judaic Studies, 1980), pp. 189–99.

34. Jacob Neusner, "What is Normative in Jewish Ethics?," *Judaism*, Winter 1967, pp. 19–20.

35. See especially Abraham Heschel, *Man is Not Alone* (New York: Harper Torchbooks, 1966) and *God in Search of Man* (New York: Harper Torchbooks, 1966).

36. Heschel, *God in Search*, pp. 420–26.

37. Borowitz was joined on the committee by rabbis Robert Kahn, Daniel Polish, Jack Stern, and Alfred Wolf.

38. The statement appears in *Reform Judiasm Today*, pp. xix–xxv.

39. Ibid., *Vol. II: What We Believe*, pp. 90, 109–10.

40. Jakob J. Petuchowski, "The Jewish Mission to the Nations," COM, July 1955, pp. 310–20.

41. CCARJ, June 1961, pp. 11–14.

42. See chapter 3, note 19.

43. Martin A. Cohen et al., *Dimensions Symposium: Are Jews the Chosen People?* (New York: UAHC, 1968), pp. 14–16.

44. For Abba Hillel Silver's position see chapter 4, note 11.

45. Daniel Jeremey Silver, "A Lover's Quarrel With the Mission of Israel," CCARJ, June 1967, pp. 8–18.

46. Daniel Jeremy Silver, "Beyond the Apologetics of Mission," CCARJ, October 1968, pp. 55–62.

47. Daniel Jeremy Silver, "Jewish Identity, Jewish Survival and Israel," CCYB, 1977, pp. 192–210.

48. Guenther Plaut, *The Case for the Chosen People* (Garden City, N.Y.: Doubleday, 1965), pp. 99–101, 111–23, 196.

49. Ibid., p. 126.

50. *Condition of Jewish Belief*, p. 258.

51. Ibid., p. 269.

52. For a sampling of Reform sermons on chosenness see: Nathan A. Barack, *The Jewish Way to Life* (Middle Village, N.Y.: Jonathan David Publishers, 1975), p. 129; Maurice Eisendrath, "Universalism and Particularism in Judaism" in Walter Jacob et al., eds., *Essays in Honor of Solomon B. Freehof* (Pittsburgh: Rodef Shalom Congregation, 1964) pp. 174–94; Arthur Gilbert, "The Mission of the Jewish People in History and in the Modern World," (Denmark: Lutheran World Federation Consultation on the Church and the Jewish People, 1969); Richard C. Hertz, *The American Jew in Search of Himself* (New York: Bloch, 1962), chap. 7; Theodore N. Lewis, *My Faith and People* (New York: Behrman House, 1961), p. 247.

53. *Condition of Jewish Belief*, pp. 225–26.

54. Ibid., pp. 149–50.

55. Hershel J. Matt, "Synagogue and Covenant People," CJ, Fall 1968, pp. 1–2.

56. David Aronson, *Jewish Way of Life*, pp. 154–68.

57. Elias Chary and Abraham Segal, *The Eternal People* (New York: United Synagogue Commission on Jewish Education, 1967), p. 86.

58. See Marshall Sklare's reassessment of the movement in the 1972 edition of his work *Conservative Judaism*, pp. 253–82, and Lawrence J. Kaplan, "The Dilemma of Conservative Judaism," COM, November 1976, pp. 44–47.

59. For other Conservative treatments: Morris Adler, "On the 'Chosen People'," *Congress Bi-Weekly*, October 7, 1963, pp. 97–101; Samuel Dresner and Byron Sherwin, *Judaism: The Way of Sanctification* (New York: United Synagogue of America, 1978), pp. 104, 166; and Louis and Rebecca Barish, *Varieties of Jewish Belief* (Middle Village, N.Y.: Jonathan David Publishers, 1979), pp. 140–48.

60. For the varieties of Orthodoxy see Charles Liebman's essays, "A Sociological Analysis of Contemporary Orthodoxy" and "Orthodoxy in American Jewish Life."

61. Liebman, "Orthodoxy in American Jewish Life," p. 49. The same holds true, to a degree, of all rabbis now eclipsed by scholars at the movements' seminaries.

62. Itzhak Hutner, *Paḥad Itzḥak* (Brooklyn: Gur Aryeh Institute for Advanced Jewish Scholarship, 1974), pp. 45–54.

63. For other Orthodox views see, in *The Condition of Jewish Belief:* Marvin Fox, pp. 59–69; Norman Lamm, 123–31; Aharon Lichtenstein, pp. 132–39; Emanuel Rackman, pp. 179–84; Moshe Tendler, pp. 235–44.

64. *Condition of Jewish Belief*, pp. 117–23.

65. Ibid., p. 218.

66. Jack J. Cohen, *The Case for Religious Naturalism: A Philosophy for the Modern Jew* (New York: The Reconstructionist Press, 1958), p. xviii.

67. On this see Liebman, "Reconstructionism in American Jewish Life," pp. 36–45.

68. This has become a commonplace in discussions of American Judaism, one based upon the shared experience of many Jewish spokesmen.

69. These generalizations are based upon a reading of the now extensive theological literature on the Holocaust. For the key positions see Eliezer Berkovits, *Faith after the Holocaust* (New York: Ktav, 1973); Emil Fackenheim, *The Jewish Return into History* (New York: Schocken, 1978); Irving Greenberg, "Cloud of Smoke, Pillar of Fire," in Eva Fleischner, ed., *Auschwitz: Beginning of a New Era?* (New York: Ktav, 1977), pp. 7–55; and Richard Rubenstein, *After Auschwitz* (Indianapolis: Bobbs-Merrill, 1976).

70. Cynthia Ozick, "Preface" to *Bloodshed and Three Novellas* (New York: Knopf, 1976), pp. 9–10.

71. Ibid.

72. Maimonides—hardly typical, even among philosophers—of course had other ideas on this subject, and was concerned to prevent the imagination from wandering into divine territory beyond the bounds of human knowledge.

73. Irving Howe, *World of Our Fathers* (New York: Harcourt Brace Jovanovich, 1976), pp. 11–12.

74. These passages are: Genesis 18:25; Exodus 14:15.

75. Cited in chapter 1, note 37.

76. On the term *segulah* see chapter 1, note 29.

77. One recent usage by a non-Jew is quite telling. The Rev. Dan C. Fore, a Brooklyn pastor associated with the Moral Majority movement, is quoted in the *New York Times*, February 5, 1981, p. B1 as follows: "I love the Jewish people deeply. God has given them talents He has not given others. They are His chosen people. Jews have a God-given ability to make money, almost a supernatural ability to make money." Although such a stereotype corresponds to some degree to the Biblical portraits of Joseph and Jacob described in chapter 1, the emphases upon hereditary talent and upon this particular talent hardly accord with Jewish tradition. In such a case the talent attributed to Jews is not one of which they would boast, and so the distinction of "native" and "imported" ideas of chosenness is easy. In cases where more attractive traits are ascribed to Jews the distinction is not so easy and not so readily made.

8. The Lessons of Chosenness in America

1. Lewis, *American Adam*, pp. 1–2. See chapter 1.

2. Neusner, "The Tasks of Theology in Judaism," pp. 189–95.

3. Theological reflection upon the significance of the Holocaust is the salient exception to this generalization.

4. Erik Erikson, *Gandhi's Truth* (New York: W. W. Norton, 1969), p. 266.

5. As indeed Americans do when it comes to class.

6. Max Weber, "Science as a Vocation," in Hans Gerth and C. Wright Mills, eds., *From Max Weber: Essays in Sociology* (New York: Oxford University Press, 1969), p. 156.

7. See chapter 7, note 30.

8. On this issue see Neusner, *Stranger at Home*.

9. See Martin Buber, "Herut: On Youth and Religion" in *On Judaism* (New York: Schocken, 1972), pp. 149–74, and Rosenzweig's comments in "Teaching and Law," *Franz Rosenzweig: His Life and Thought*, pp. 234–47.

10. Sigmund Freud, *The Future of an Illusion*, trans. James Strachey (New York: W. W. Norton, 1969), p. 19.

11. Bercovitch writes of American Puritanism that "the relationship between psychic uncertainty and rhetorical self-assertion is transparent in the tone of crisis that characterizes much of the literature. With every setback, the assertion of American selfhood rose to a higher pitch." *Puritan Origins*, 103. See also p. 26. I have dealt with the Puritan literature and its influence upon Weber's theory of rationalization in earlier research summarized in part in "Called to Order: The Role of the Puritan Berufsmensch in Weberian Sociology," *Sociology* (May 1979), pp. 203–18.

Bibliography of Sources Cited

1. Periodicals

American Jewish Yearbook, 1924–
American Judaism, 1951–
Central Conference of American Rabbis Journal, 1953–
Central Conference of American Rabbis Yearbook, 1929–
Commentary, 1946–
Contemporary Jewish Record, 1938–45
Jewish Frontier, 1934–
Jewish Life, 1947–61.
Judaism, 1952–
Liberal Judaism, 1933–51
Menorah Journal, 1927–
Midstream, 1955–
Orthodox Union, 1933–46.
Proceedings of the Rabbinical Assembly of America, 1927–
Reconstructionist, 1935–
Society for the Advancement of Judaism Review, 1927–29
Tradition, 1958–

2. Primary Sources, 1930–80

Adler, Morris. "On the 'Chosen People.' " *Congress Bi-Weekly*, Oct. 7, 1963.
Agus, Jacob. "Assimilation, Integration, Segregation—The Road to the Future." *Judaism*, August 1954, pp. 498–510.
———. "Building Our Future in America: Towards a Philosophy of American Judaism." MJ, Spring 1953, pp. 1–21.
———. "Goals for Jewish Living." MJ, Spring 1948, pp. 1–25.
———. *Guideposts in Modern Judaism: An Analysis of Current Trends in Jewish Thought*. New York: Bloch, 1954.
———. *The Meaning of Jewish History*. London: Abelard-Schuman, 1963.
———. *Modern Philosophies of Judaism*. New York: Behrman, 1941.

———. "The Status of American Israel—A Conservative View." CJ, Winter 1946, pp. 1–14.

———. "Toward a Conservative Philosophy of Jewish Education." In *Judaism and the Jewish School*, edited by Judah Pilch. New York: Bloch, 1966, pp. 228–41.

Aronson, David. *The Jewish Way of Life*. New York: National Academy for Adult Jewish Studies of the Jewish Theological Seminary of America, 1946.

Bamberger, Bernard. "Are the Jews a Chosen People?" REC, December 28, 1945, pp. 16–19.

———. "The Central Task," CCYB, 1949, pp. 224–29.

Barack, Nathan A. *Faith for Fallibles*. New York: Bloch, 1952.

———. *The Jewish Way to Life*. Middle Village, N.Y.: Jonathan David, 1975.

———. *Mount Moriah View*. New York: Bloch, 1956.

Barish, Louis and Rebecca. *Varieties of Jewish Belief*. Middle Village, N.Y.: Jonathan David, 1971.

Belkin, Samuel. *Essays in Traditional Jewish Thought*. New York: Philosophical Library, 1956.

Bell, Daniel. "A Parable of Alienation." JF, November 1946, pp. 12–19.

Bellow, Saul. *Humboldt's Gift*. Baltimore: Penguin, 1976

———. *The Victim*. New York: Avon, 1975.

Berkovits, Eliezer. *Faith After the Holocaust*. New York: Ktav, 1973.

———. "Jewish Living in America." *Judaism*, January 1953, pp. 68–74.

———. *Major Themes in Modern Philosophies of Judaism*. New York: Ktav, 1974.

Bernstein, Philip. "The New Israel and American Jewry." CCYB, 1948, pp. 285–96.

Bokser, Ben Zion. "The Doctrine of the Chosen People." CJR, June 1941, pp. 243–52.

———. "The Election of Israel." CJ, July 1947, pp. 17–25.

———. "The Future of the American Jewish Community." PRA, 1948, pp. 193–206.

———. "Religion and Secularism." *Judaism*, April 1952, pp. 150–57.

Borowitz, Eugene B. "The Chosen People Concept as it Affects Jewish Life in the Diaspora." *Journal of Ecumenical Studies* 12 (1975): 553–68.

———. "The Dialectic of Jewish Particularity." *Journal of Ecumenical Studies* 8 (1971): 560–74.

———. "Faith and Method in Modern Jewish Theology." CCYB, 1963, pp. 215–28.

———. *How Can a Jew Speak of Faith Today?* Philadelphia: Westminster Press, 1969.

———. "The Idea of God." CCYB, 1957, pp. 174–86.

———. "Liberal Jewish Theology in a Time of Uncertainty: A Holistic Approach." CCYB, 1977, pp. 178–89.

———. *The Mask Jews W̲ c̲.*. New York: Simon and Schuster, 1973.

———. *A New Jewish Theology in the Making*. Philadelphia: Westminster Press, 1968.

———. "On Celebrating Sinai," CCARJ, June 1966, pp. 12, 16.

———. "The Problem of the Form of a Jewish Theology." *Hebrew Union College Annual*, vols. 40–41 (1969–70): 391–408.

———. "Theological Conference: Cincinnati 1950." COM, June 1950, pp. 567–72.

Calhoun, Robert L. *God and the Common Life*. Hamden, Conn.: Shoe String Press, 1954.

Chary, Elias and Abraham Segal. *The Eternal People.* New York: United Synagogue Commission on Jewish Education, 1967.

Chertoff, Mordecai. "Understanding Judaism." JF, July 1955, pp. 23–27.

The Christian Century. "A God-Centered Education." April 28, 1937, pp. 542–44.

———. "The Jewish Problem." April 29, 1936, pp. 624–26.

———. "Jewry and Democracy." June 9, 1937, pp. 734–36.

———. "Pluralism-National Menace." June 13, 1951, pp. 701–702.

———. "Why is Anti-Semitism?" July 7, 1937, pp. 862–64.

Cohen, Arthur. *The Myth of the Judeo-Christian Tradition.* New York: Schocken, 1971.

———. *The Natural and the Supernatural Jew: A Historical and Theological Introduction.* New York: McGraw Hill, 1964.

———. "Why I Choose to be a Jew." In *The Judaic Tradition,* edited by Nahum N. Glatzer. Boston: Beacon, 1969, pp. 744–55.

Cohen, Jack J. *The Case for Religious Naturalism.* New York: Reconstructionist Press, 1958.

Cohen, Martin A. et al. *Dimensions Symposium: Are Jews the Chosen People?* New York: UAHC, 1968.

Cohon, Beryl D. *From Generation to Generation.* Boston: Bruce Humphries, 1951.

———. *Judaism in Theory and Practice.* New York: Bloch, 1954.

Cohon, Samuel S. "The Doctrine of the Chosen People." LJ, May 1945, pp. 31–38, 48.

———. *The Jewish Idea of God.* Cincinnati: Hebrew Union College, n.d.

———. *Jewish Theology: A Historical and Systematic Interpretation of Judaism and its Foundations.* Edited by J. H. Prakke and H. C.M. Prakke. Assen, the Netherlands: Royal Vangorcum, 1971.

———. "Universal and Particular in Judaism." *Judaism,* April 1952, pp. 121–128.

Commentary. "The State of Jewish Belief: A Symposium." August 1966, pp. 71–160.

Contemporary Jewish Record. "Under Forty." February 1944, pp.3–36.

Cournos, John. "An Epistle to the Jews." *Atlantic Monthly,* December 1937, pp. 723–28.

Dewey, John. *A Common Faith.* New Haven: Yale University Press, 1934.

Doppelt, Frederic A. "Are the Jews a Chosen People?" LJ, February 1942, pp. 6–9.

———. "Has Israel a Mission?" LJ, March 1942, pp. 10–13.

———. "A Re-appraisal of the Chosen People Concept." CCARJ, June 1961, pp. 11–15, 21.

Dresner, Samuel and Sherwin, Byron. *Judaism: The Way of Sanctification.* New York: United Synagogue of America, 1971.

Eisendrath, Maurice. "Retreat or Advance?" CCYB, 1937, pp. 202–24.

Eisenstein, Ira. "Further Comment on Conservative Judaism." CJ, November 1946, pp. 21–25.

———. "The New Diaspora and American Democracy." PRA, 1949, pp. 258–77.

Eisenstein, Ira and Eugene Kohn, eds. *Mordecai M. Kaplan: An Evaluation.* New York: Reconstructionist Press, 1952.

Fackenheim, Emil. "A Critique of Reconstructionism." CCARJ, June 1960, pp. 51–56, 69.

———. "Does Reform Need a New God-Concept?" *American Judaism,* November 1953, pp. 4–5.

———. *Encounters between Judaism and Modern Philosophy.* New York: Basic Books, 1973.

————. *God's Presence in History*. New York: Harper Torchbooks, 1972.

————. *The Jewish Return into History*. New York: Schocken, 1978.

————. "Judaism, Christianity, and Reinhold Niebuhr: A Reply to Levi Olan." *Judaism*, Fall 1956, pp. 316–24.

————. *Metaphysics and Historicity*. Milwaukee: Marquette University, 1961.

————. "More on Reconstructionist Theology." CCARJ, January 1961, pp. 39–43.

————. *Quest for Past and Future: Essays in Jewish Theology*. Boston: Beacon, 1968.

Feldman, Abraham J. "American and the Jew." CCYB, 1954, pp. 137–47.

————. *Contributions of Judaism to Modern Society*. Cincinnati: UAHC, n.d.

————. *The Faith of a Liberal Jew*. Hartford: Congregation Beth Israel, 1931.

Feldman, Abraham J. et al. *Reform Judaism: Essays by Hebrew Union College Alumni*. Cincinnati: HUC, 1949.

Feuer, Leon I. "Beyond Zionism." CCYB, 1957, pp. 129–38.

————. *On Being a Jew*. New York: Bloch, 1947.

Feuer, Leon I.; Roland B. Gittelsohn; and Levi A. Olan. "Mordecai Kaplan's Influence Upon Reform Judaism." CCARJ, June 1956, pp. 22–28.

Fineshriber, William H. "The Suffering Servant." CCYB, 1939, pp. 257–68.

Finkelstein, Louis. "The Aims of the Conference." In *Science, Philosophy and Religion: A Symposium*, edited by Lyman Bryson and Louis Finkelstein. New York: The Conference on Science . . . 1941.

————. "American Ideals and the Survival of Western Civilization." CJR, June 1941, pp. 233–42.

————. *The Beliefs and Practices of Judaism*. New York: Devin-Adair, 1952.

————. "Faith for Today: A Jewish Viewpoint." In *Five Faiths for Today*, by Stanley High et al. New York: Town Hall Press, 1941, pp. 158–81

————. "Modern Man's Anxiety: Its Remedy." COM, December 1946, pp. 537–46.

————. *The Pharisees*. Philadelphia: Jewish Publication Society, 1966.

————. "The Things That Unite Us." PRA, 1927, pp. 42–53.

————. *Tradition in the Making: The Seminary's Interpretation of Judaism*. New York: JTS, 1937.

————. "Tribute to Rabbi Mordecai M. Kaplan." PRA, 1951, pp. 205–10.

Fram, Leon. "What is Judaism's Mission in the Contemporary World?" CCYB, 1962, pp. 201–17.

Frank, Jerome. "Red White and Blue Herring." *Saturday Evening Post*, December 6, 1941, pp. 9ff, 83ff.

Frank, Waldo. *The Jew in Our Day*. New York: Duell, Sloan and Pearce, 1944.

Franklin, Leo. "The Saving Remnant." CCYB, 1935, pp. 154–64.

Freehof, Solomon B. *Modern Jewish Preaching*. New York: Bloch, 1941.

————. *Preface to Scripture*. Cincinnati: UAHC, 1950.

————. "Reform Judaism and Zionism: A Clarification." MJ, Spring 1944, pp. 26–41.

Gilbert, Arthur. *The Mission of the Jewish People in History and the Modern World*. Denmark: Lutheran World Federation Consultation on the Church and the Jewish People, 1969.

Gittelsohn, Roland. "Where Reform and Reconstructionism Meet." CCARJ, June 1960, pp. 6–11.

Glueck, Nelson. "Come Let us Reason Together." CCYB, 1952, pp. 332–39.

Goldenson, Samuel. "The Democratic Implications of Jewish Moral and Spiritual Thinking." CCYB, 1939, pp. 338–52.

Gordis, Robert. "The Biblical Basis of Democracy." CJ, June 1948, pp. 1–12.

————. *Conservative Judaism: An American Philosophy*. New York: Behrman, 1945.

————. *A Faith for Moderns*. New York: Bloch, 1960.

————. "The Faith I Live By." MJ, Spring 1947, pp. 184–202.

————. "A Jewish Prayer Book for the Modern Age." CJ, October 1945, pp. 1–20.

————. *Judaism for the Modern Age*. New York: Farrar Straus and Cudahy, 1955.

————. "The Nature of Man in the Judeo-Christian Tradition." *Judaism*, August 1953, pp. 101–109.

————. *The Root and the Branch*. Chicago: University of Chicago Press, 1962.

Greenberg, Hayim. "Chosen Peoples." JF, September 1941, pp. 8–12.

————. "Jewish Culture in the Diaspora." JF, December 1951, pp. 12–19.

————. "The Jews and Jesus." JF, January 1938, pp. 10–13.

————. "The Universalism of the Chosen People." JF, October, November, and December 1945, pp. 10–15, 26–35, 29–37.

Greenberg, Irving. "Cloud of Smoke, Pillar of Fire." In *Auschwitz: Beginning of a New Era*, edited by Eva A. Fleischner. New York: Ktav, 1977.

Greenberg, Simon. "Democracy in Post-Biblical Judaism." CJ, June 1945, pp. 1–8.

————. *The Ethical in the Jewish and American Heritage*. New York: JTS, 1977.

————. *Foundations of a Faith*. New York: Burning Bush Press of JTS, 1967.

————. *Living as a Jew Today*. New York: Behrman, 1940.

Greenstone, Julius. "The Election of Israel." CJ, June 1945, pp. 27–30.

Gup, Samuel M. "Currents in Jewish Religious Thought and Life in America in the Twentieth Century." CCYB, 1931, pp. 296–337.

Halevi, Jacob I.. "Clashing Concepts." LJ, March 1945, pp. 28–32.

————. "The Lord's Elect and Peculiar Treasure." *Judaism*, Winter 1956, pp. 22–30.

Halpern, Ben. *The American Jew: A Zionist Analysis*. New York: Theodore Herzl Foundation, 1956.

————. "Letter to an Intellectual." JF, December 1946, pp. 13–18.

————. "Zion in the Mind of American Jews". In *The Future of the Jewish Community in America*, edited by David Sidorsky. New York: Basic Books, 1973, pp. 22–45.

Heller, Bernard. "About the Judeo-Christian Tradition." *Judaism*, July 1953, pp. 257–61.

————. "Dr. Kallen's Judaism." MJ, Spring 1934, pp. 73–82.

————. *The Jewish Concept of the Chosen People*. Cincinnati: UAHC and CCAR, n.d.

————. "The Jewish Mission." REC, February 18, 1944, pp. 9–14.

————. "The Judeo-Christian Tradition Concept: Aid or Deterrent to Goodwill." *Judaism*, August 1953, pp. 133–39.

Herberg, Will. "The 'Chosenness' of Israel and the Jew of Today." In *Arguments and Doctrines*, edited by Arthur A. Cohen. Philadelphia: Jewish Publication Society, 1970, pp. 270–83.

————. "Historicism as Touchstone." *The Christian Century*, March 16, 1960, pp. 311–13.

————. "Jewish Existence and Survival: A Theological View." *Judaism*. January 1952, pp. 19–26.

————. *Judaism and Modern Man*. New York: Harper Torchbooks, 1965.

————. "What is Jewish Religion? Reflections on Rabbi Philip Bernstein's Article in *Life*." JF, October 1950, pp. 8–13.

Hershman, Abraham. *Israel's Fate and Faith*. New York: Bloch, 1952.

Hertz, Richard C. *The American Jew in Search of Himself*. New York: Bloch, 1962.
Hertzberg, Arthur. "America is Different." In *The Outbursts That Await Us: Three Essays on Religion and Culture in the United States*, by Arthur Hertzberg, Martin E. Marty, and Joseph N. Moody. New York: Macmillan, 1963, pp. 129–59.

——. "America is Galut." JF, July 1964, pp. 7–9.

——. *Being Jewish in America*. New York: Schocken Books, 1979.

——. *Judaism: The Unity of the Jewish Spirit Through the Ages*. New York: George Braziller, 1962.

Heschel, Abraham. *God in Search of Man*. New York: Harper Torchbooks, 1968.

——. *Man is Not Alone*. New York: Harper Torchbooks, 1968.

Jacob, Walter et al. *Essays in Honor of Solomon B. Freehof*. Pittsburgh: Rodef Shalom Congregation, 1964.

The Jewish Frontier. "Religious Totalitarianism." July 1936, pp. 9–10.

Jung, Leo. "A Challenge to Jewry." *Orthodox Union*, January 1936, pp. 5–6.

——. *Crumbs and Character: Sermons, Addresses, Essays*. New York: Night and Day Press, 1942.

——. *Harvest: Sermons, Addresses, Studies*. New York: Philipp Feldheim, 1956.

——. *Living Judaism*. New York: Night and Day Press, 1927.

Kadushin, Max. "The Chosenness of Israel in Rabbinic Thought." PRA, 1941, pp. 20–25.

——. *Organic Thinking: A Study in Rabbinic Thought*. New York: JTS, 1938.

——. *The Rabbinic Mind*. New York: Blaisdell, 1965.

Kagan, Henry E. "The 'Judeo-Christian Heritage'—A Psychological Evaluation and a New Approach." CCYB, 1953, pp. 253–81.

Kallen, Horace M. "American Jews: What Now?" *Jewish Social Service Quarterly* 26(1955): 12–29.

——. *Art and Freedom*. New York: Duell, Sloan and Pearce, 1942.

——. *The Book of Job as a Greek Tragedy*. New York: Hill and Wang, 1959.

——. *Cultural Pluralism and the American Idea: An Essay in Social Philosophy*. Philadelphia: University of Pennsylvania Press, 1956.

——. *Culture and Democracy in the United States*. New York: Arno Press, 1970.

——. *The Education of Free Men*. New York: Farrar, Straus, 1949.

——. "The Education of Jews in Our Time." *Jewish Education* 9 (Sept 1939): 85ff.

——. *Frontiers of Hope*. New York: Horace Liveright, 1929.

——. *Individualism—An American Way of Life*. New York: Liveright, 1933.

——. "Jewish Education and Jewish Survival." *Jewish Education* 34 (1964): 223–29.

——. *Judaism at Bay: Essays Toward the Adjustment of Judaism to Modernity*. New York: Bloch, 1932.

——. *Of Them Which Say They are Jews and Other Essays in the Jewish Struggle for Survival*. New York: Bloch, 1954.

——. "Of Truth." In *The Cleavage in Our Culture*, edited by Frederick Burkhardt. Boston: Beacon, 1952, pp. 30–50.

——. "Introduction" to *The Philosophy of William James*. New York: Modern Library, 1925.

——. "Philosophy Today and Tomorrow." In *American Philosophy Today and Tomorrow*, edited by Sidney Hook and Horace M. Kallen. New York: Lee Furman, 1935.

——. *Secularism is the Will of God: An Essay in the Social Philosophy of Democracy and Religion*. New York: Twayne, 1954.

————. *The Struggle for Jewish Unity: Two Addresses.* New York: Ad Press, 1933.

————. *What I Believe and Why—Maybe.* Edited by Alfred J. Marrow. New York: Horizon, 1971.

————. *Why Religion?* New York: Boni and Liveright, 1927.

————. *Zionism and World Politics: A Study in History and Social Psychology.* Garden City, N.Y.: Doubleday Page, 1921.

Kaplan, Mordecai M. "The Chosen People Idea An Anachronism." REC, January 11, 1946, pp. 13–20.

————. "Comments on 'A Parable of Alienation.'" JF, December 1946, pp. 1–13.

————. *The Future of the American Jew.* New York: Macmillan, 1948.

————. *The Greater Judaism in the Making: A Study of the Modern Evolution of Judaism.* New York: Reconstructionist Press, 1960.

————. *Judaism as a Civilization: Toward a Reconstruction of American Jewish Life.* New York: Schocken, 1967.

————. *Judaism in Transition.* New York: Behrman, 1941.

————. *Judaism Without Supernaturalism: The Only Alternative to Orthodoxy and Secularism.* New York: Reconstructionist Press, 1958.

————. *The Meaning of God in Modern Jewish Religion.* New York: Reconstructionist Press, 1962.

————. "The Meaning of the Tercentenary for Diaspora Judaism." In *American Jewry: The Tercentenary and After, 1654–1954,* edited by Eugene Kohn. New York: Reconstructionist Press, 1955.

————. "Milton Steinberg's Contribution to Reconstructionism." REC, May 19, 1950, pp. 9–16.

————. *A New Zionism.* New York: Reconstructionist Press, 1959.

————. "On Creeds and Wants: A Study in the Evolution of Judaism." MJ, Spring 1933, pp. 33–52.

————. "The Organization of American Jewry." Jewish Education 8 (1935): 36.

————. *Questions Jews Ask: Reconstructionist Answers.* New York: Reconstructionist Press, 1956.

————. *The Religion of Ethical Nationhood.* New York: Macmillan, 1970.

————. "Salute to John Dewey." REC, November 4, 1949, pp. 3–4.

————. "The Way I Have Come." In *Mordecai Kaplan: An Evaluation,* edited by Ira Eisenstein and Eugene Kohn, pp. 283–321.

————. "We Still Think We Are right." REC, May 2, 1947, pp. 14–19.

————. "When Religious Liberals are Intolerant." *Opinion,* July 1936, pp. 18–20.

————. "Where Reform and Reconstructionism Part Company." CCARJ, April 1960, pp. 3–10.

Kaplan, Mordecai, and Arthur Cohen. *If Not Now, When? Toward a Reconstruction of the Jewish People.* New York: Schocken, 1973.

Kaplan, Mordecai M.; Williams J. Paul; and Eugene Kohn. *The Faith of America.* New York: Henry Schuman, 1951.

Katsh, Abraham. *Hebraic Contributions to American Life* (Unpublished typescript, New York University, 1941).

Kertzer, Morris. *What is a Jew?* Cleveland: World Press, 1953.

Kohn, Eugene. "The Attributes of God Reinterpreted." REC, November 29, 1940, pp. 7–19.

————. *The Future of Judaism in America.* New Rochelle, N.Y.: Liberal Press, 1934.

————. *Religion and Humanity.* New York: Reconstructionist Press, 1953.

Kohn, Eugene, ed. *American Jewry: The Tercentenary and After, 1654–1954.* New York: Reconstructionist Press, 1955.

Konvitz, Milton. "Many are Called and Many are Chosen." *Judaism*, Winter 1955, pp. 58–64.

Kranzberg, Melvin, "Judaism and Democracy: 'Any Resemblance is Purely Coincidental.'" REC, October 5, 1956, pp. 7–13.

Kristol, Irving, "How Basic is Basic Judaism?" COM, January 1948, pp. 27–34.

Lazaron, Morris S. *Common Ground: A Plea for Intelligent Americanism*. New York: Liveright, 1938.

———. Letter to *The Christian Century*. July 9, 1937, pp. 878–79.

Levitsky, Louis J. *A Jew Looks at America*. New York: Dial, 1939.

Lewis, Theodore. "The Idea of Israel." CCYB, 1957, pp. 187–200.

———. *My Faith and People*. New York: Behrman House, 1961.

Lewisohn, Ludwig. *The American Jew: Character and Destiny*. New York: Farrar, Straus, 1950.

———. *Israel*. New York: Boni and Liveright, 1925.

———. *Mid-channel: An American Chronicle*. New York: Harper and Brothers, 1929.

———. *Up-Stream: An American Chronicle*. New York: Boni and Liveright, 1922.

Levy, Felix A. *His Own Torah: Felix A. Levy Memorial Volume*. Edited by Sefton D. Temkin. New York: Jonathan David, 1969.

Liebman, Joshua L. "New Trends in Reform Jewish Thought." In *Reform Judaism*, by Feldman, et al., pp. 57–80.

Littell, Franklin. "Thoughts About the Future of Christianity and Judaism: A Christian View of Reconstructionism." REC, April 4, 1967, pp. 10–16; April 18, pp. 16–22.

Malamud, Bernard. *The Assistant*. New York: New American Library, 1957.

Marcus, Jacob R. "Democracy and Judaism." LJ, December 1945, pp. 11–19.

Markowitz, Samuel. *Leading a Jewish Life in the Modern World*. Cincinnati: UAHC, 1942.

McAfee, Joseph E. "An Open Letter to Rabbi Weisfeld." *Christian Century*, April 29, 1936, pp. 632–33.

Midstream. "The Meaning of Galut in America Today: A Symposium." March 1963, pp. 3–45.

Morgenstern, Julian. *As a Mighty Stream: The Progress of Judaism Through History*. Philadelphia: Jewish Publication Society, 1949.

———. "Assimilation, Isolation, or Reform." CJR, April 1942, pp. 131–44.

———. *Judaism's Contribution to Post-War Religion*. Cincinnati, UAHC, n.d.

———. *Nation, People, Religion—What are We?* Cincinnati: UAHC, 1943.

———. *Unity in American Judaism: How and When?* Cincinnati: UAHC, n.d.

———. "With History as Our Guide." CCYB, 1947, pp. 257–87.

Nathan, Robert. "The Chosen" in Newman, *Biting on Granite*, p. 285.

Neusner, Jacob. *Stranger at Home*. Chicago: University of Chicago Press, 1981.

———. "The Tasks of Theology in Judaism." In *Method and Meaning in Ancient Judaism*. Missoula, Montana: Scholars Press, 1980, pp. 185–200.

———. "What is Normative in Jewish Ethics?" *Judaism*, Winter 1967, pp. 3–20.

Newman, Louis I. *Biting on Granite: Selected Sermons and Addresses*. New York: Bloch, 1946.

Niebuhr, Reinhold. *The Irony of American History*. New York: Charles Scribners Sons, 1962.

———. "Jews After the War." *The Nation*, February 21 and 28, 1942.

Olan, Levi A. "Judaism and Modern Theology." CCYB, 1956, pp. 197–215.

————. "Over-Anxious Jewish Theologians." *American Judaism*, November 1953, pp. 5, 19.
Ozick, Cynthia, *Bloodshed and Three Novellas*. New York: Knopf, 1970.
Petuchowski, Jakob. "Questions Jews Ask." *American Jewish Archives* 9 (1957): 54–58.
————. "Where Judaism Differed." COM, August 1957, pp. 153–59.
Plaut, W. Guenther. *The Case for the Chosen People*. Garden City, N.Y: Doubleday, 1965.
Polish, David. "The Forsaken God." LJ, November 1946, pp. 10–16.
Rackman, Emanuel. "Democracy's Religious Root," MJ, Autumn 1951, pp. 163–168.
————. *Jewish Values for Modern Man*. New York: Jewish Education Committee, 1962.
————. *One Man's Judaism*. New York: Philosophical Library, 1970.
The Reconstructionist. "The 'Christian Century' Problem." May 29, 1936, p. 34.
Revel, Bernard. "The Bible and American Democracy." *Orthodox Union*, July–August 1938, p. 3.
Roth, Philip. *Reading Myself and Others*. New York: Farrar, Straus and Giroux, 1975.
Rubenstein, Richard. *After Auschwitz*. Indianapolis: Bobbs-Merrill, 1976.
Samuel, Maurice. *The Gentleman and the Jew*. New York: Knopf, 1950.
————. *You Gentiles*. New York: Harcourt Brace, 1924.
Schulman, Samuel. "Israel." CCYB, 1935, pp. 260–311.
Schwartz, Delmore. *Selected Poems*. New York: New Directions, 1967.
Schwarzschild, Steven S. "Judaism and Modern Man." MJ, Spring 1952, pp. 102–111.
————. "The Role and Limits of Reason in Contemporary Jewish Theology." CCYB, 1963, pp. 197–214.
Shapiro, Karl. *Poems of a Jew*. New York: Random House, 1959.
Shuster, Zachariah, "Whither American Jewry?" CJR, June 1943, pp. 227–30.
Siegel, Seymour, ed. *Conservative Judaism and Jewish Law*. New York: Rabbinical Assembly of America, 1977.
Silver, Abba Hillel. *The Democratic Impulse in Jewish History*. New York: Bloch, 1928.
————. "The Future of the American Jewish Community." CCYB, 1950, pp. 358–73.
————. *Religion in a Changing World*. New York: Richard R. Smith, 1931.
————. *Therefore Choose Life: Selected Sermons, Addresses and Writings*, vol. 1. Edited by Herbert Weiner. Cleveland: World, 1967.
————. *Where Judaism Differed: An Inquiry into the Distinctiveness of Judaism*. Philadelphia: Jewish Publication Society, 1957.
————. *A Word in Its Season: Selected Sermons, Addresses and Writings*, vol. 2. Edited by Herbert Weiner. Cleveland: World, 1972.
————. *The World Crisis and Jewish Survival*. New York: Richard R. Smith, 1941.
Silver, Daniel Jeremy. "Beyond the Apologetics of Mission." CCARJ, October 1968, pp. 55–62.
————. "Jewish Identity, Jewish Survival and Israel." CCYB, 1977, pp. 192–210.
————. "A Lover's Quarrel with the Mission of Israel." CCARJ, June 1967, pp. 8–18.
Silverman, Morris. "Vitalizing Public Worship." PRA, 1940, pp. 159–79.

Soloveitchik, Joseph Ber. "Confrontation." *Tradition*, Winter 1964, pp. 5–28.
———. "The Lonely Man of Faith." *Tradition*, Summer 1965, pp. 5–67.
———. "The Man of Halakhah" (Hebrew). In *In the Secret of Aloneness of Togetherness*, (Hebrew). Edited by Pinchas Peli. Jerusalem: Hotza'at Orot, 1979, pp. 39–188.
———. "The Voice of My Beloved Knocking." in *The Secret*, pp. 333–400.
Steinberg, Milton. *Anatomy of Faith*, edited by Arthur Cohen. New York: Harcourt Brace, 1960.
———. *As a Driven Leaf*. Indianapolis: Bobbs-Merrill, 1935.
———. *Basic Judaism*. New York: Harcourt Brace, 1947.
———. *A Believing Jew: The Selected Writings of Milton Steinberg*. New York: Harcourt Brace, 1951.
———. "A Critique of 'The Attributes of God Reinterpreted.'" REC, March 7, 1941, pp. 7–9.
———. "First Principles for American Jews." CJR, December 1941, pp. 587–96.
———. *The Making of the Modern Jew*. New York: Behrman, 1949.
———. *A Partisan Guide to the Jewish Problem*. Indianapolis: Bobbs-Merrill, 1945.
———. "The Theological Issues of the Hour." PRA, 1949, pp. 356–408.
Tillich, Paul. "Is There a Judeo-Christian Tradition?" *Judaism*, April 1952, pp. 106–109.
Ungar, Shmuel. *Ne'ot Deshe al Ha-Torah*. Mount Kisco: Yeshiva of Naitra, 1963.
Union of American Hebrew Congregations. *Annual Report*. New York: 1937.
———. *Conference on the Perpetuation of Judaism*. Cincinnati, 1927.
———. *Judaism and the Modern World*. Cincinnati, 1929.
Waldman, Morris D. "America and the Jewish Community." CJR, June 1941, pp. 253–59.
Wallace, Henry A. "Judaism and Americanism." MJ, Summer 1940, pp. 127–37.
Weiss, Samson R. "The 'Am Segulah' Concept," *Jewish Life*, May–June 1957, pp. 127–37.
Whitehead, Alfred N. *Religion in the Making*. Cleveland: World, 1969.
Witt, Louis. "Judaism and Democracy." Cincinnati: UAHC, n.d.
Zelie, John S. "Why do the Gentiles Rage?" *Christian Century*, October 7, 1931, pp. 1239–41.

3. Other Primary Sources

Ahad Ha-am. *Complete Writings* (Hebrew). Jerusalem: Hotza'ah Ivrit, 1947.
———. *Selected Essays*. Edited and translated by Leon Simon. New York: Atheneum, 1960.
Arnold, Matthew. *Culture and Anarchy*. Cambridge: Cambridge University Press, 1971.
———. *God and the Bible: A Review of Objections to Literature and Dogma*. New York: AMS Press, 1970.
———. *Literature and Dogma: An Essay Towards a Better Apprehension of the Bible*. New York: AMS Press, 1970.
Buber, Martin. *On Judaism*. Edited by Nahum Glatzer. New York: Schocken Books, 1972.
Durkheim, Emile. *The Division of Labor*. Translated by George Simpson. New York: Free Press, 1964.

————. *The Elementary Forms of the Religious Life.* Translated by Joseph Ward Swain. New York: Free Press, 1965.

————. *Suicide: A Study in Sociology.* Translated by John A. Spaulding and George Simpson. New York: Free Press, 1951.

Einhorn, David. *Inaugural Sermon Delivered in the Temple of the Har Sinai Verein.* Translated by C. A. Rubenstein. Baltimore: Har Sinai Congregation, 1909.

————. *Olath Tamid: Book of Prayers for Israelitish Congregations.* New York: Congregation Adath Yeshurun, 1872.

Fichte, Johann Gottlieb. *Addresses to the German Nation.* Translated by R. F. Jones and C. F. Turnbull. New York: Harper and Row, 1968.

Friedlander, Israel. *Past and Present: Selected Essays.* New York: Burning Bush Press of JTS, 1961.

Geiger, Abraham. *Judaism and its History.* Translated by Charles Newburgh. New York: Bloch, 1911.

Glatzer, Naham, ed. *Franz Rosenzweig: His Life and Thought.* New York: Schocken Books, 1961.

Graetz, Heinrich. *The Structure of Jewish History and Other Essays.* Edited by Ismar Schorsch. New York: JTS, 1975.

Hirsch, Samson R. *Nineteen Letters.* Translated by Bernard Drachman. New York: Philipp Feldheim, 1969.

James, William. *Essays in Pragmatism.* New York: Hefner, 1951.

————. *A Pluralistic Universe.* London: Longmans, Green, 1909.

————. *Pragmatism.* Cleveland: World, 1955.

Kohler, Kaufman. *Backwards or Forwards? A Series of Discourses on Reform Judaism.* New York: Congregation Beth-El, 1885.

————. *Hebrew Union College and Other Addresses.* Cincinnati: Ark Publishing Company, 1916.

————. *Jewish Theology: Systematically and Historically Considered.* New York: Macmillan, 1928.

————. *Studies, Addresses and Personal Papers.* New York: Bloch, 1931.

Krochmal, Nachman. *Guide for the Perplexed of the Day* (Hebrew). Edited by Simon Rawidowicz. Waltham: Ararat, 1961.

Leeser, Isaac. "The Destiny of Israel." *Occident,* February 1845, p. 528.

————. "The Example of Israel." *Occident,* January 1849, pp. 479–84.

————. "The Mission of Israel." *Occident,* June 1844, pp. 109–14; July 1844, pp. 169–74.

————. "The Mission of Israel." *Occident,* April 1849, pp. 1–10.

Moses ben Maimon. *A Maimonides Reader.* Edited by Isadore Twersky. New York: Behrman, 1972.

Perkins, William. "A Treatise on the Vocations." *Works,* Cambridge, 1603, pp. 903–39.

Preston, John. "The New Covenant, Whereunto are adjoyned Four Sermons Upon Ecclesiastes." London, 1630.

Rosenzweig, Franz. *On Jewish Learning.* New York: Schocken, 1955.

Spinoza, Benedict. *Theologico-Political Treatise,* in *Chief Works,* vol. 1. Edited by R. H. M. Elwes. New York: Dover, 1955.

Wise, Isaac Mayer. "The Messiah." *Occident,* July 1849, pp. 181–91; August 1849, pp. 229–44.

————. "To the Ministers and Other Israelites." *Occident.* December 1848, pp. 431–35.

Yehudah Halevi. *Kuzari.* Translated by Hartwig Hirschfeld. New York: Pardes, 1946; Hebrew translation by Yehud dah Eben Shmuel. Tel Aviv: Dvir, 1973.

4. Secondary Sources Dealing with the Period 1930–1980

Atlas, James. *Delmore Schwartz: The Life of an American Poet.* New York: Farrar, Straus & Giroux, 1977.

Broun, Heywood, and George Britt. *Christians Only: A Study in Prejudice.* New York: Vanguard Press, 1931.

Carlin, Jerome E., and Saul Mendlovitz. "The American Rabbi: A Religious Specialist Responds to Loss of Authority." In *The Jews,* edited by Marshall Sklare. New York: Free Press, 1958, pp. 377–414.

Cohen, Elliot E. "The Intellectuals and the Jewish Community." COM, July 1949, pp. 20–30.

Cowley, Malcolm. "1930: The Year That Was New Year's Eve." COM, June 1951, pp. 567–71.

Davis, Moshe. "Mordecai Kaplan: An Interpretation." PRA, 1956, pp. 252–66.

Drew, David E. "A Profile of the Jewish Freshman." American Council on Education Research Reports, vol. 5, No. 4, 1970.

Fiedler, Leslie A. "The Breakthrough: The American Jewish Novelist and the Fictional Image of the Jew." *Judaism,* Winter 1958, pp. 15–35.

Fortune Magazine. "Jews in America." February 1936, pp. 79–85, 128–44.

Gans, Herbert J. "The Origin and Growth of a Jewish Community in the Suburbs." Sklare, *The Jews,* pp. 205–48.

Gilkey, Langdon. "Social and Intellectual Sources of Contemporary Protestant Theology in America." In *Religion in America,* edited by William G. McLoughlin and Robert N. Bellah. Boston: Beacon, 1968, pp. 69–98.

Glazer, Nathan. *American Judaism.* Chicago: University of Chicago Press, 1972.

———. "Social Characteristics of American Jews, 1654–1954." AJYB, 1955, pp. 3–41.

Goldstein, Sidney, and Calvin Goldscheider. *Jewish Americans: Three Generations in a Jewish Community.* Englewood Cliffs, N.J.: Prentice-Hall, 1968.

Gordon, Albert I. *Jews in Suburbia.* Westport, Conn: Greenwood Press, 1973.

Gordon, Milton M. *Assimilation in American Life.* New York: Oxford University Press, 1964.

Graeber, Isacque, and Britt, Stuart Henderson, eds. *Jews in a Gentile World.* New York: Macmillan, 1942.

Gutman, Robert. "Demographic Trends and the Decline of Anti-Semitism." In *Jews in the Mind of America,* by Charles H. Stember et al. New York: Basic Books, 1966.

Handlin, Oscar and Mary F. "A Century of Jewish Immigration to the United States." AJYB, 1949, pp. 1–84.

Herberg, Will. *Protestant-Catholic-Jew: An Essay in American Religious Sociology.* Garden City, N.Y.: Doubleday, 1955.

———. "Religious Trends in American Jewry." In *Mid-century,* edited by Harold U. Ribalow. New York: Beechhurst Press, 1955, pp. 250–66.

Himmelfarb, Milton. *The Jews of Modernity.* New York: Basic Books, 1973.

Howe, Irving. "Introduction" to *Jewish-American Stories.* New York: New American Library, 1977, pp. 1–17.

———. *World of our Fathers.* New York: Harcourt Brace Jovanovich, 1976.

Janowsky, Oscar, ed. *The American Jew: A Composite Portrait.* New York: Harper and Brothers, 1942.

——. *The American Jew: A Reappraisal.* Philadelphia: Jewish Publication Society, 1965.

Kaplan, Lawrence J. "The Dilemma of Conservative Judaism." COM, November 1976, pp. 44–47.

Kaplan, Louis. "Judaism and Jewish Education in Horace M. Kallen's Philosophy of Cultural Pluralism." Dissertation, Dropsie University, 1971.

Konvitz, Milton. "Horace Meyer Kallen (1882–1974): Philosopher of the Hebraic-American Idea." AJYB, 1974, pp. 55–80.

Kramer, Judith R., and Leventman, Seymour. *Children of the Gilded Ghetto: Conflict Resolutions of Three Generations of American Jews.* New Haven: Yale University Press, 1961.

Lasker, Bruno, ed. *Jewish Experiences in America.* New York: The Inquiry, 1931.

Leventman, Seymour. "From Shtetl to Suburb." In *The Ghetto and Beyond,* edited by P. I. Rose. New York: Random House, 1969, pp. 33–56.

Levy, Beryl H. *Reform Judaism in America: A Study in Religious Adaptation.* New York: Bloch, 1933.

Lewin, Kurt. "Self-Hatred Among Jews." CJR, June 1941, pp. 219–32.

Libowitz, Richard. "Mordecai M. Kaplan as Redactor: The Development of Reconstructionism." Dissertation, Temple University, 1979.

Liebman, Charles. *The Ambivalent American Jew.* Philadelphia: Jewish Publication Society, 1973.

——. "Orthodoxy in American Jewish Life." AJYB, 1965, pp. 21–97.

——. "Reconstructionism in American Jewish Life." AJYB, 1970, pp. 3–99.

——. "A Sociological Analysis of Contemporary Orthodoxy." *Judaism.* Summer 1964, pp. 285–304.

Lipset, Seymour Martin, and Ladd, Everett C., Jr. "Jewish Academics in the United States: Their Achievements, Culture and Politics." AJYB, 1971, pp. 84–128.

Manson, Harold P. "Abba Hillel Silver—An Appreciation." In *In the Time of Harvest: Essays in Honor of Abba Hillel Silver,* edited by Daniel Jeremy Silver. New York: Macmillan, 1963., pp. 1–27.

Mervis, Leonard J. "The Social Justice Movement and the American Reform Rabbi." *American Jewish Archives* 8: 2 (1957), pp. 121–230.

Meyer, Michael A. "A Centennial History." In *Hebrew Union College—Jewish Institute of Religion at One Hundred Years,* edited by Samuel E. Karff. Cincinnati: Hebrew Union College Press, 1976, pp. 3–283.

Moore, Deborah Dash. *At Home in America: Second Generation New York Jews.* New York: Columbia University Press, 1981.

Noveck, Simon. *Milton Steinberg: Portrait of a Rabbi.* New York: Ktav, 1978.

Polsky, Howard W. "A Study of Orthodoxy in Milwaukee." In Sklare, ed. *The Jews,* pp. 325–35.

Reich, Nathan. "Economic Trends." In Janowsky, ed., *Composite Portrait,* pp. 161–82.

Ringer, Benjamin B. *The Edge of Friendliness: A Study of Jewish-Gentile Relations.* New York: Basic Books, 1967.

Rose, Peter I., ed. *The Ghetto and Beyond: Essays on Jewish Life in America.* New York: Random House, 1969.

Rosen, Charles. "Minority Group in Transition: A Study of Adolescent Religious Convictions and Conduct." In Sklare, *The Jews,* pp. 336–46.

Rosenak, Michael. "The Function of Contemporary Jewish Philosophy in the Construction of Religious Educational Theory in the Diaspora" (Hebrew). Disseration, Hebrew University of Jerusalem, 1976.

Rosenberg, Stuart E. *America is Different: The Search for Jewish Identity.* New York: Burning Bush Press, 1964.

Rotenstreich, Nathan. "Emancipation and its Aftermath." In Sidorsky, ed., *Jewish Community*, pp. 46–61.

————. *The Exile of Israel in American Jewish Thought* (Hebrew). Jerusalem: Institute for Contemporary Jewry of the Hebrew University, 1967.

Schmidt, Sarah Leff. "Horace M. Kallen and the Americanization of Zionism." Dissertation, University of Maryland, 1973.

Sherman, C. Bezalel. *The Jew Within American Society: A Study in Ethnic Individuality.* Detroit: Wayne State University Press, 1961.

Sidorsky, David, ed. *The Future of the Jewish Community in America.* New York: Basic Books. 1973.

Silberman, Lou H. "Concerning Jewish Theology: Some Notes on a Decade." AJYB, 1969, pp. 37–58.

Sklare, Marshall. *Conservative Judaism: An American Religious Movement.* New York: Schocken Books, 1972.

Sklare, Marshall, ed. *The Jews: Social Patterns of an American Group.* New York: Free Press, 1958.

Sklare, Marshall, and Joseph Greenblum. *Jewish Identity on the Suburban Frontier: A Study of Group Survival in the Open Society.* New York: Basic Books, 1967.

Snyder, Charles R. "Culture and Jewish Sobriety: The Ingroup-Outgroup Factor." In Sklare, *The Jews*, pp. 570–87.

Stember, Charles H. et al. *Jews in the Mind of America.* New York: Basic Books, 1966.

Strong, Donald S. *Organized Anti-Semitism in America: The Rise of Group Prejudice During the Decade 1930–1940.* Washington, D.C.: American Council on Public Affairs, 1941.

Swyhart, Barbara. "Value Ontology: An Evaluation of Mordecai M. Kaplan's Philosophy of 'Wisdom.'" Dissertation, Temple University, 1972.

Tumin, Melvin. "The Cult of Gratitude." In Rose, *Ghetto and Beyond*, pp. 69–72.

Vernoff, Charles. "Supernatural and Transnatural: An Encounter of Religious Perspectives—The Theological Problematic in the Modern Judaic World-View of Mordecai M. Kaplan." Dissertation, University of California at Santa Barbara, 1979.

Weinryb, Bernard. "Jewish Immigration and Accommodation to America." In Sklare, *The Jews*, pp. 4–22.

Weisberg, Harold. "Ideologies of American Jews." In Janowsky, *Reappraisal*, pp. 339–57.

Zeitlin, Joseph. *Disciples of the Wise: The Religious and Social Opinions of American Rabbis.* New York: Teachers College of Columbia University, 1945.

5. Other Secondary Sources

Ahlstrom, Sidney E. *A Religious History of the American People.* New Haven: Yale University Press, 1972.

Altmann, Alexander. "The New Style of Preaching in Nineteenth-Century German Jewry." In *Studies in Nineteenth-Century Jewish Intellectual History.* Cambridge: Harvard University Press, 1964, pp. 27–45.

Arieli, Yehoshua. *Individualism and Nationalism in American Ideology.* Cambridge: Harvard University Press, 1964.

Bellah, Robert. "Civil Religion in America." In *The Religious Situation: 1968,* edited by Donald R. Cutler. Boston, Beacon Press, 1968, pp. 331–56.

Bercovitch, Sacvan. *The Puritan Origins of the American Self.* New Haven: Yale University Press, 1975.

Berger, Peter. *The Sacred Canopy.* Garden City, N.Y.: Doubleday Anchor, 1969.

Brown, Francis; S. R. Driver; and Charles A. Briggs. *Hebrew and English Lexicon of the Old Testament.* Oxford: Clarendon Press, 1972.

Burke, Kenneth. *A Rhetoric of Motives.* Berkeley: University of California Press, 1969.

Davis, Moshe. *The Emergence of Conservative Judaism.* Philadelphia: Jewish Publication Society, 1965 (and earlier Hebrew version: New York, JTS, 1951).

————. "Jewish Religious Life and Institutions in America: A Historical Study." In *The Jews: Their History, Culture and Religion.* vol 1., edited by Louis Finkelstein. New York: Harper and Brothers, 1949, pp. 354–453.

Dobkowski, Michael. *The Tarnished Dream: The Basis of American Anti-Semitism.* Westport, Conn: Greenwood Press, 1979.

Douglas, Ann. *The Feminization of American Culture.* New York: Knopf, 1977.

Geertz, Clifford. *The Interpretation of Cultures.* New York: Basic Books, 1973.

Glatzer, Nahum N. "The Beginnings of Modern Jewish Studies." In Altmann, ed., *Studies,* pp. 27–45.

Gurock, Jeffrey. *When Harlem Was Jewish.* New York: Columbia University Press, 1979.

Heinemann, Itzhak. "The Chosenness of Israel in the Bible" (Hebrew). *Sinai* 16 (1945): 17–30.

Heinemann, Yosef. *Aggadot and Their History* (Hebrew). Jerusalem: Keter, 1974.

Helfgott, Benjamin. *The Doctrine of Election in Tannaitic Literature.* New York: Kings Crown Press of Columbia University, 1954.

Heller, James G. *Isaac Mayer Wise: His Life and Thought.* New York: UAHC, 1955.

Heschel, Abraham, *Torah from Heaven* (Hebrew). London: Soncino, 1962.

Higham, John. *Send These to Me: Jews and Other Immigrants in Urban America.* New York: Atheneum, 1975.

————. *Strangers in the Land: Patterns of American Nativism, 1860–1925.* 2nd ed. New York: Atheneum, 1974.

Katz, Jacob. *Exclusiveness and Tolerance.* New York: Schocken Books, 1973.

————. *Out of the Ghetto: The Social Background of Jewish Emancipation, 1770–1870.* Cambridge: Harvard University Press, 1973.

————. *Tradition and Crisis: Jewish Society at the End of the Middle Ages.* New York: Schocken Books, 1971 (and Hebrew original: Jerusalem: Mosad Bialik, 1958).

Kaufmann, Yehezkel. *Exile and Estrangement* (Hebrew). Tel Aviv: Dvir, 1962.

Kluger, Rivka S. *Psyche and Bible.* New York: Spring Publications, 1974.

Koch, Klaus, "Zur Geschichte der Erwahlungsvorstellung in Israel." *Zeitschrift für die Alttestamentliche Wissenschaft* 67 (1955): 205–16.

Lesêtre, H. "Election." In *Dictionnaire de la Bible,* edited by F. Vigouroux. Paris: Letouzey et Ané, 1912, pp. 1653–54.

Leuchtenberg, William E., ed. *The Unfinished Century: America Since 1900.* Boston: Little, Brown and Company, 1973.

Lewis, R. W. B. *The American Adam: Innocence, Tragedy and Tradition in the Nineteenth Century.* Chicago: University of Chicago Press, 1968.

Lipset, Seymour Martin. *The First New Nation.* New York: Basic Books, 1963.

232 • Bibliography

Mandelkern, Solomon. *Concordantiae* (Hebrew). Jerusalem: Schocken, 1975.

Mannheim, Karl. *Ideology and Utopia*. Translated by Louis Wirth and Edward Shils. New York: Harcourt Brace, 1952.

Marty, Martin. *Righteous Empire: The Protestant Experience in America*. New York: Dial Press, 1970.

Mendenhall, G. E. "Election." In *The Interpreter's Dictionary of the Bible*, vol. 2, edited by George A. Buttrich. New York: Abingdon Press, 1962, pp. 76-82.

Meyer, Michael A. *The Origins of the Modern Jew: Jewish Identity and European Culture in Germany, 1749–1824*. Detroit: Wayne State University Press, 1967.

————. "Universalism and Jewish Unity in the Thought of Abraham Geiger." In *The Role of Religion in Modern Jewish History*, edited by Jacob Katz. Cambridge: Association for Jewish Studies, 1975, pp. 91–104.

Mihaly, Eugene. "A Rabbinic Defense of the Election of Israel." *Hebrew Union College Annual* 35(1961): 103–35.

Niebuhr, H. Richard. *The Kingdom of God in America*. New York: Harper and Row, 1951.

Oppenheimer, Benjamin. "*Segulah*" (Hebrew). *Beit Ha-mikra*. 4 (1978): 427–34.

Parsons, Talcott, "Professions." In *International Encyclopedia of the Social Sciences*, edited by David L. Sills. New York: Macmillan/Free Press, 1968, vol. 12, pp. 536–47.

————. "The Professions and Social Structure." In *Essays in Sociological Theory, Pure and Applied*. Glencoe, Illinois: Free Press, 1949, pp. 85–196.

Parzen, Herbert. "East European Immigrants and Jewish Secularism in America: 1882–1915." *Judaism*, Spring 1954, pp. 154–64.

Petuchowski, Jakob. *Prayerbook Reform in Europe*. New York: World Union for Progressive Judaism, 1968.

Philipson, David. "The Jewish Pioneers of the Ohio Valley." *Publications of the American Jewish Historical Society* 8 (1900): 43–57.

————. *The Reform Movement in Judaism*. New York: Macmillan, 1931.

Plaut, W. Guenther, ed. *The Growth of Reform Judaism*. New York: World Union for Progressive Judaism, 1965.

————. *The Rise of Reform Judaism*. New York: World Union for Progressive Judaism, 1963.

Rad, Gerhard von. *Old Testament Theology*. Translated by D. M. G. Stalker. Edinburgh: Oliver and Boyd, 1963.

Rogers, R. G. "The Doctrine of Election in the Chronicler's Work and the Dead Sea Scrolls." Dissertation, Boston University, 1969.

Rotenstreich, Nathan. *Jewish Philosophy in Modern Times*. London: Macmillan, 1934.

Ryback, Martin B. "The East-West Conflict in American Reform Judaism." *American Jewish Archives* 4 (1952): 3–25.

Samet, Moshe. "Orthodox Jewry in the Modern Period" (Hebrew). *Mehalkhim* 1(1969): 29–40.

Schechter, Solomon. "Election of Israel." In *Aspects of Rabbinic Theology*. New York: Schocken Books, 1969, pp. 57–64.

Scholem, Gershom. *On the Kabbalah and its Symbolism*. New York: Schocken Books, 1965.

Tal, Uriel. *Christians and Jews in Germany: Religion, Politics and Ideology in the Second Reich 1870–1914*. Translated by Noah J. Jacobs. Ithaca: Cornell University Press, 1975.

Tshernowitz, Chaim. *The History of Halakhah* (Hebrew). New York: Va'ad Ha-yovel, 1945.

Urbach, E. E. "Homilies of the Sages about Gentile Prophets and Baalam in Light of the Jewish-Christian Polemic" (Hebrew). *Tarbiz* 25 (1956): 272–88.

———. *The Sages—Their Concepts and Beliefs*. Translated by Israel Abrahams. , Jerusalem: Magnes Press of Hebrew University, 1973.

Veblen, Thorstein. "On the Intellectual Pre-eminence of the Jews." In *Essays in our Changing Order*, edited by Leon Ardzrooni. New York: Viking Press, 1939.

Warner, W. Lloyd, and Srole, Leo. *The Social Systems of American Ethnic Groups*. New Haven: Yale University Press, 1945.

Weber, Max. "Science as a Vocation." In *From Max Weber*, edited by Hans Gerth and C. Wright Mills. New York: Oxford University Press, 1969, pp. 129–56.

Weinfeld, Moshe. "Deuteronomy: The Present State of Inquiry." *Journal of Biblical Literature* 86 (1967): 256–61.

Wilson, John. *Public Religion in American Culture*. Philadelphia: Temple University Press, 1979.

Index